The Victimization of Women

The Victimization of Women

Law, Policies, and Politics

Michelle L. Meloy

Susan L. Miller

OXFORD
UNIVERSITY PRESS
2011

OXFORD
UNIVERSITY PRESS

Oxford University Press, Inc., publishes works that further
Oxford University's objective of excellence
in research, scholarship, and education.

Oxford   New York
Auckland   Cape Town   Dar es Salaam   Hong Kong   Karachi
Kuala Lumpur   Madrid   Melbourne   Mexico City   Nairobi
New Delhi   Shanghai   Taipei   Toronto

With offices in
Argentina   Austria   Brazil   Chile   Czech Republic   France   Greece
Guatemala   Hungary   Italy   Japan   Poland   Portugal   Singapore
South Korea   Switzerland   Thailand   Turkey   Ukraine   Vietnam

Copyright © 2011 by Oxford University Press, Inc.

Published by Oxford University Press, Inc.
198 Madison Avenue, New York, New York 10016

www.oup.com

Oxford is a registered trademark of Oxford University Press

Library of Congress Cataloging-in-Publication Data

Meloy, Michelle L.
The victimization of women : law, policies,
and politics / Michelle L. Meloy, Susan L. Miller.
        p.   cm.
Includes bibliographical references and index.
ISBN 978-0-19-976510-2; 978-0-19-976511-9 (pbk.)
1. Women—Crimes against. 2. Women—Violence against.
3. Victims of crimes. 4. Victims of violent crimes.
I. Miller, Susan L. II. Title.
HV6250.4.W65M425 2011
362.88082—dc22   2010030672

Printed in the United States of America
on acid-free paper

For my daughter, Morgan. You are my sunshine day and night. —MLM

In memory of my father, Arthur Meloy. —MLM

For my son, Connor, my joy and fellow adventurer. —SLM

Acknowledgments

We have many people to thank. First, our students, who raise important questions, some of which we hope we address within this book. Some students in particular contributed with tracking down material in the library: Tiffany Foster, Michael Gallagher, John Kellenberger, Stephanie Manzi, Beth McConnell, Jaime McGovern, and Shannon Paradise, and we thank them very much for their enthusiastic assistance. Kristin Curtis was an invaluable research assistant. After this project the Rutgers-Camden librarians recognize her on sight and know her by name. Colleagues and confidantes Kay B. Forest, Ronet Bachman, Gail Caputo, Drew Humphries, and Jane Siegel engaged in lively conversations about the subject material and stimulated our own thinking. In many ways, each supported our efforts and encouraged us to forge ahead. We also appreciate our universities, Rutgers University and the University of Delaware, for providing environments conducive to scholarly work and debate. Our invited contributor, LeeAnn Iovanni, Aalborg University, offered incisive comments and generously gave of her time, reading and commenting on every chapter; it is a better book for her efforts. We appreciate her friendship and good humor. We thank our editors at Oxford: Peter M. Labella, for his patience and belief in this project, and Joe Jackson, for getting us to the finish line. And last, but never least, we thank our family and friends for their ongoing support and interest: Georgia and Julian Scott, Marilyn and Ken Miller, Arthur Meloy, Dee Phillips, Anthony Meloy, Nancy Getchell, Estralita "Cleo" Jones-Roach, Mellina Rykowski, Tara Woolfolk, Lisa Bartran, Patricia Tate Stewart, Lisa DeRosa, Daniel Atkins, Claire M. Renzetti, Carol Post, Sherry Pisacano, Nancy Quillen, and especially to Morgan Meloy and Connor Miller for making us laugh. Any mistakes are our own and cannot be attributed to the cast of characters above or to the authors and researchers that we name.

Contents

1 Introduction   3

2 Drawing the Contours of Victim Dilemmas   15

3 The Violent Victimization of Women: An Overview of Legal, Empirical, and Measurement Issues (Written by LeeAnn Iovanni)   37

4 Media, Gender, and Crime Victims   69

5 Sexual Victimization: Offenders Speak Out about Their Victims   87

6 How Battered Women Lose: Unintended Consequences of Well-Intentioned Legal and Criminal Justice Policies   117

7 Assessing Where We Are, Where We Should Go, and How Best to Get There   149

Notes   177

References   203

Index   237

The Victimization of Women

Introduction **1**

> What would we say about a movement that apparently forgot to invite most of its professed beneficiaries? What if we discovered, for example, in the victims' "movement," that victims were, politically, all dressed up but had no place to go? What kind of movement would it be? Would it really be a movement at all? (Elias 1993: 26)

Despite cultural training teaching that female victims should not be blamed for what happens to them, some of the most telling questions about crimes of personal violence committed against women continue: of a rape victim, "Did she know him? What was she wearing?" or of a battering victim, "What did she do to get him so mad? Why didn't she just *leave*?" This knee-jerk reaction reflects a deep-seated ambivalence in how we think about fault and responsibility. Surely it is the perpetrator who justly deserves our scorn and blame. But if this is so, then why do victims' behaviors and/or appearances remain under scrutiny? Are the lines between victim and offender more complicated than this suggests?

In recent years much academic literature exists to educate people about crime victims' experiences and the obstacles that limit their choices and abilities to prevent or handle their victimization. Blatant victim blaming has fallen out of vogue. Laws were enacted to reflect a movement away from victim precipitation or provocation theories. Protocols used by police and prosecutors to respond to crime victims were revamped, reflecting a change from traditional beliefs about shared victim responsibility to a new awareness of the support a victim needs when navigating the criminal justice system. Yet despite these best efforts, victim blaming and myths about victims persist.

We write this book to present in a readable, coherent manner the major debates, controversies, quagmires, unintended consequences, and unanswered questions about victims, victims' rights, and victim-centered policies. We not only summarize the range of positions held by scholars, social commentators, policy makers, and the public but also offer readers the tools to critically assess these arguments by providing statistical information, legal arguments, policy evaluations, and examples that inform and challenge the general beliefs people hold about victims.

The criminal justice system's focus is on legal guilt: did this person commit this particular act or not? Looking at the underlying context of the situation is often beyond the interest or scope of an investigation by a criminal justice system that favors efficiency and frowns on ambiguity. But victimization issues are far more nuanced and complicated than the incident-driven criminal justice system leads us to believe. In everyday conversations, entertainment shows about victimization, and media depictions of victims' circumstances resemble a sport, of sorts, for the producers of news, for lay authors of volumes written for the general public, and, yes, also for some academics. As the proliferation of television crime shows suggests (e.g., *America's Most Wanted, Cold Case, COPS, Criminal Minds, CSI: Crime Scene Investigations, Law & Order, SVU: Special Victims Unit*), dissecting the acts of victims and offenders is astoundingly popular. Creating dichotomies of victims as "innocent" and "good" and offenders as "guilty" and "evil" is the typical way that the general public, the agents of popular culture (TV, newspapers, bloggers, news Web sites), and the criminal justice system frame the players. These judgments are guided by decisions about who is worthy of our sympathies and financial support or government funding, and about who is undeserving and should be punished.

But this either/or scenario mischaracterizes most victimizations. Painting a picture of crime victims as passive, helpless, and incompetent, while casting offenders as strong and powerful, is flawed. While some victims have no control over their experiences, other victims are resilient and make reasonable choices and take reasonable actions despite being limited by their position in the social structure and the resources available to them.

Although we have selected certain victim issues for exploration in this book, we do not ignore, diminish, or trivialize the wide range of victims and victim issues that are not examined herein. Indeed, whole books could be and are written about victimization topics not included here, such as physical child abuse, elder abuse, victimizations against disabled persons, prison rape, human trafficking, same-sex intimate partner battering, or male victims of crime and violence. Rather, we provide a unique overview of the emergence of victimology as a distinctive area of study and its current status within sociology and criminology traditions, the victims' rights movement and discourse, research and policy issues, and the puzzling and contested aspects of victimization, especially as it affects female victims. Tackling the difficult issues, the messy ones, is a necessary part of the story of how our society characterizes crime victims and how these characterizations shape our responses to them personally, politically, and formally.

Researching Victimization

For female victims of male violence, assessments of victim culpability often turn on the individual circumstances of the crime, such as whether or not the victim knew her offender, what she was doing or wearing that may have enticed him, or what steps she could have taken to prevent her victimization. Yet we do not hold burglary or robbery victims to the same standards: imagine asking a robbery victim whether she fought back, or what she was wearing. How does this kind of victim blaming come about? Part of this stems from the early research conducted by victimologists, which focused on victim contribution as an integral part of crime. And part of this reaction is shaped by women's vulnerability to crimes of intimate physical and sexual violence committed by men and the fears that they raise. Violations against women are often devalued as a function of gender stratification itself, since the victimizers of women are frequently men.

In discussing research on victimization, Andrew Karmen distinguishes between objective and subjective methods of studying victims.[1] A subjective method interprets victimization from a moral, religious, emotional, or philosophical orientation and thus is vulnerable to the whims and interests of those with the power to confer labels. This method is viewed as less scientific, more based on visceral and descriptive musings than a rigorous examination of the issues.[2] Moreover, it is often the subjective studies that inflame people's passionate opinions about a victim's blameworthiness, regardless of the lack of supporting evidence.[3] Nonetheless, subjective methods remain common in some contemporary commentators' writings on victimization. During the 1940s and 1950s, a more objective method of studying victims of crime emerged, one that employed the methods of social science to examine the dynamics, patterns, prevalence, and distribution of victimization.[4] Following this tradition, early victimologists sought credibility with their academic peers by bringing scientific objectivity into their work.

Original Victimologists: The Beginnings of Blame

In the 1930s and 1940s the writings of the "pioneer" victimologists harbored an anti-victim sentiment that was reflected in their language, theories, and research agendas. In fact, an underlying belief in the culpability of some victims was behind the initial academic inquiries into the study of victim-offender relationships.[5] The initial victimologists were originally interested in the victim-offender dyad because of an underlying presumption that victims were responsible for causing their own harm.[6] Thus, victim blaming was born. The most popular theories of this era were shared responsibility, victim precipitation, victim provocation, victim resistance, and victim vulnerability (based on age, sex, race, and immigrant status).[7] The main hypothesis guiding these theories was that reciprocity exists between victims and offenders, often called the victim-offender "duet."

Hans Von Hentig (1941: 303), who was among the first to study victims, believed that "a real mutuality frequently can be observed in the connection between the perpetrator and the victim, the killer and the killed, the duper and the duped. The victim in many instances leads the evildoer into temptation. The predator is, by varying means, prevailed upon to advance against the prey."[8] Benjamin Mendelsohn (1940), another of the first "victimologists," was a criminal defense attorney in Romania.[9] He routinely investigated the behavior of his clients' victims before and during the crime. He contended that victims unintentionally invite their victimization, and he developed typologies based on victim-offender relationship to address degrees of victim culpability including innocent victims, crime-precipitating victims, victims with minor guilt, victims as guilty as the offender, victims as more guilty than the offender, and most guilty victims.[10] Menachem Amir (1971: 99), the researcher of the most frequently cited study on rape victim precipitation, stated that "the offender should not be viewed as the sole 'cause' and reason for the offense, and the 'virtuous' rape victim is not always the innocent and passive party." University of Pennsylvania researchers Thorsten Sellin and Marvin Wolfgang (1964) produced another victim-precipitation perspective of inner-city murders. These scholars introduced typologies differentiated by situations rather than by relationships. For example, their situational typologies included primary victimization (where someone is specifically targeted, such as a victim of a hate crime or domestic violence), secondary victimization, tertiary victimization, mutual victimization, and no victimization (i.e., victimless crimes). By at least one account[11] Sellin and Wolfgang continued to look at victim-precipitation theory to analyze victimizations that resulted from factors related to the victim's behavior and lifestyle.[12] In addition to victimization theories of victim precipitation, historically, the weight of that responsibility was placed on women, which served to protect men's power and privilege and offer greater impunity for their infractions.

Legacy of Victim Blaming and Its Implications

These early theories, focusing on victims' contribution to the crime, lay the foundation for the continued reliance on victim blaming.[13] However, nowhere is victim blaming as pronounced as in considerations of crimes of violence committed by men against women, such as sexual assault or battering.[14] Why is it that we tend to sympathize with someone who is mugged, burglarized, or injured by a drunk driver, yet victims of male-on-female violence often experience victim blaming and self-blame? Questions like these are probed in the forthcoming chapters.

It is also part of human nature to desire reassurance that we will not be hurt if we follow "the rules." If a victim is blamed for her actions or appearance, and we do not engage in the same behaviors or look the same, then it is easy to see why she was the target and we are not as vulnerable. This notion, the "just world hypothesis," assumes that bad things happen only to bad people.[15] Additionally, the greater one's social distance (i.e., socioeconomic class, educational attainment, prestige level) from a "typical" victim (i.e., poor, undereducated persons with limited social capital), the more protected one perceives herself to be and vice versa. Even victims themselves think about what they did to assist the crime. Social psychologist Ronnie Janoff-Bulman discusses two kinds of self-blame that victims employ. In the first, *behavioral self-blame*, victims seek meaning behind their attack and try to reestablish an equilibrium by focusing on the choices that allowed them to be vulnerable (i.e., choosing to walk in a certain neighborhood or accepting a ride). If they make different choices in the future, their likelihood of victimization will decrease. This process restores a feeling of control over the event because crime is seen not as something random but rather as something preventable. It reflects a need "to minimize the threatening, meaningless nature of the event," which is better than living in a world perceived as unsafe, unpredictable, and malevolent.[16] This response contrasts with the second kind of self-blame, *characterological self-blame*, in which victims feel they are bad people who deserve to be hurt, attributing their victimization experiences to something internally flawed within them (i.e., feeling that they are flirtatious or a bad person).

Sympathy and understanding for victims often turn on issues other than the facts of the crime. If a victim has a stellar background, a good job, and good family values, is well-educated and white, and was attacked by a stranger, preferably from a different race and armed with a weapon that caused injury, support overflows. But that description does not fit most victims of sexual assault, rape, stalking, or battering. In these cases, it is unlikely that the victim and offender are strangers to one another. Then, it follows that assessing a victim's worth rests on assumptions made about her character and background. If she lacks social capital in terms of education, socioeconomic status, race, or sexual orientation, she is held to a higher standard of credibility. While it is possible that victims' options may be blocked due to obstacles such as poverty, low self-esteem, fear, and limited access to needed supports such as help from family, friends, the criminal justice system, or religious and medical institutions, it should not follow that these limits further wound victims by facilitating poor treatment, limiting resources, or denying their pain.

The case of killer Jeffrey Dahmer raises questions about how the criminal justice system projects blame onto victims of lower status.[17] In 1991, Dahmer, a 31-year-old, employed white man, was on probation for sexually abusing a boy. He lured a 14-year-old Laotian male into his apartment with the promise of cash in exchange for posing for photographs. Dahmer then drugged, tortured, and sexually assaulted the teenager, but the boy escaped, running drugged and naked in the street, bleeding from his rectum. Two young African American women called 911 and waited with him for the police and emergency medical team to arrive. Meanwhile, Dahmer returned and tried to recapture the boy, but the two women thwarted his efforts. Despite the boy's visible fear, the lingering effects of the drugs, and his nakedness and bleeding, the police dismissed the paramedics. They performed a superficial investigation of the incident, believing Dahmer's story that the boy was an adult and that the two were lovers just having a quarrel. If the police had investigated further, they would have discovered the boy's age and found that Dahmer was on probation for molesting his brother. Shortly after the police left the scene, Dahmer strangled, sexually assaulted, photographed, and dismembered the boy.

The two witnesses to the street incident were outraged at the Milwaukee police response and followed up, demanding answers. A civil rights lawsuit filed by the victims' families stated that the police did not fully investigate the situation because the victim was Laotian, the witnesses were women of color, and it seemed that Dahmer and the victim were homosexual. Sadly, at least four other men were murdered by Dahmer after this incident. Dahmer's higher status, that of being employed and white and having English as a first language, diminished the credibility of the victim—despite his young age and obvious injuries—and of the African American witnesses. The Dahmer case shows how individual traits affect how the criminal justice system responds to both victims and offenders.

A (Brief) Respite from Victim Blaming

By the 1960s and 1970s, there was a movement away from a victim-blaming emphasis and toward a critique that was more system-oriented. During this era, more people questioned how the state allocated resources, and public concern about victims and social inequalities deepened, exerting an impact on the next wave of victimologists. Scholars were more concerned about crime victims' financial and emotional recovery through government assistance, and how the criminal justice and legal systems perpetuated and reinforced victim blaming.[18] Grassroots activists and victim advocates worked to expose criminal justice practices that failed to protect victims of rape and battering and to hold offenders accountable. In essence, the victims' rights movement gained momentum during this time. Chapter 3 contains more in-depth discussions on the victims' rights movement.

Political scientist William Ryan, in his groundbreaking 1971 book, criticized victim blamers, arguing that victims are not intrinsically or pathologically bad but that attitudes toward them are shaped by labeling people who are different as problematic. Once people are seen as problematic, the label sticks and is disseminated, and differences are exaggerated, and these differences may be used to justify mistreatment. Ryan was particularly focused on marginal or disenfranchised people. This perspective echoed the rise in the 1960s of concern for the rights of juveniles, women, victims, gays and lesbians, and prisoners. Ryan argued that one cannot hold powerless people responsible for their own victimization, especially if this "underclass" of people were products of a racist, sexist, or oppressive society. Sociologists contend that this "catchy expression, 'blaming the victim,' quickly took on a life of its own; Ryan's original focus on the underclass was soon lost as the phrase became applied to a broad range of victims."[19] Essentially, the reemergence of victim blaming effectively shut down the system-blaming conversation, discrediting any alterative argument.

Although the victims' rights movement is credited with facilitating changes in legal practice, creating greater understanding of victims' suffering, impacting the ideology of victimologists, and improving victim participation in criminal procedures, blaming of women for their own rape and battering did not disappear. Rather, as the study of victimization made its way into pop culture, horrific crime headlines became standard fare in newspapers. Journalists used lurid tales of victimization to sensationalize the news, commercial enterprises started selling personal protection devices and security systems that pandered to fear, and politicians manipulated the victims' rights platform and public fear of crime to garner votes and endorsements. People continued to distinguish between "real" victims, such as a victim raped by a stranger wielding a knife or gun, and less credible victims, such as someone who claims rape when the situation seems more like a "date gone bad." Thus, attention paid to victims by scholars and the social commentary about victim blaming and system blaming resulted in a cacophony of voices trying to establish themselves as "the expert" on victimization. Victim blaming was once again on the rise, after a temporary dormancy during the focus on system blaming.

Resurgence of Victim Blaming

The macro-level approach to understanding criminal victimization was quickly abandoned and replaced, once again, with a less controversial one: victim blaming. Ironically, this refocusing on victims' role and culpability as the key to understanding criminal victimizations resulted from the successes of the victims' rights movement. A pushback or backlash, aimed predominantly at feminists concerned with victims' issues, is evident in the popularity of many books, such as Christina Hoff-Sommers's *Who Stole Feminism*, Charles Sykes's *A Nation of Victims*, Alan Dershowitz's *The Abuse Excuse: And Other Cop-Outs, Sob Stories, and Evasions of Responsibility*, Robert Hughes's *Culture of Complaint: The Fraying of America*, Paula Pearson's *When She Was Bad*, Katie Roiphe's *The Morning After*, and Shelby Steele's *The Content of Our Character: A New Vision of Race in America*, sold in neighborhood bookstores across the country. The books born out of this backlash pushed back against what Cole says was perceived as the " 'nation of victims,' 'the victims' revolution,' the 'politics of victimization,' 'victicrats,' 'victimists,' and 'victimism.' "[20] Writings such as these, which often appeal to nonacademic audiences, criticize American culture for suggesting that victimization is omnipresent, that our society is overly litigious, and that everyone but the victim is responsible. These cultural writers warned the public that "nearly everyone has a chance to be a victim now."[21] According to Dershowitz, the high-profile cases of the Menendez brothers' trials for killing their parents, Lorena Bobbitt's trial for cutting off her husband's penis, and O. J. Simpson's criminal trial for murdering his ex-wife and her male friend all illustrate how today's criminals present themselves as yesterday's victims.[22] The judicial system's tolerance for the offenders-as-true-victims defense began with battered women's syndrome (BWS), according to Dershowitz.[23] BWS is discussed again in chapter 3. In brief, it is a psychological condition that is used as a legal defense to explain why a battered woman remains in an abusive relationship or kills her abusive partner.

Alyson Cole (2007: 22) assessed the cultural writers' perspective this way: "The most salient common element shared by these writers, by contrast with most previous uses of the term 'victim,' is that they employ it pejoratively. 'Victim' is deployed to dismiss, ridicule, and condemn rather than to evoke sympathy, empathy, or even pity. Individuals and groups who claim to have been victimized are portrayed as weak, manipulative, self-indulgent, helpless, hopeless dependents." These perspectives feed powerfully into falsehoods and stereotypes about crime and victimization. We debunk many of these myths in the coming chapters.

This Book's Goals and Content

Within these pages we demonstrate where visceral opinions about victimization are flawed, and we strive to make sense of the conflicting emotions and debates raised by such incendiary topics. As such, the personal becomes political: beyond our academic positions, one of the authors was a crisis hot-line worker at several battered women's shelters in different states; the second author was a member of an elite probation team that supervised sexual offenders. Collectively we conducted research with victims of battering, incest, marital rape, and stranger rape; interviewed family members who lost a loved one to homicide or had a child or family member who had been sexually molested; and talked with women temporarily housed in shelters, as well as women who have been arrested as "perpetrators" in their ongoing or former intimate relationships. These experiences shape our understandings of the ambivalence felt by some victims about their situations and provide us with opportunities to observe first-hand how well-intentioned policies can—and often do—collide with victims' issues and needs.

In the chapters that follow we made two deliberate decisions. First, instead of taking a more gender-neutral approach, we focus on crimes of personal violence committed by (mostly) men against (mostly) women and girls, such as sexual assault and rape, battering, and, to a lesser extent, stalking. This choice is deliberate: while we acknowledge the existence of male victims of such crimes (and the existence of female offenders), these crimes are disproportionately ones in which men victimize women. Although victimization within lesbian relationships involves female victims, that category is also beyond the scope of this book.[24] Battering and rape, whether heterosexual or homosexual, share similar roots in violence, power, and control.[25] To better understand woman-to-woman sexual violence, further investigation of the concepts of homophobia, heterosexism, biphobia, and misogyny are important since they exist within a broader framework of violence where men and women create and condone a culture of violence.[26]

As Pam Elliott contends, "the routine and intentional use of intimidation tactics in relationships is not a gender issue but a power one."[27]

Further, as "sexism creates an opportunity for heterosexual men to batter women, homophobia creates an opportunity for people in same-gender relationships to batter their partners."[28] Issues related to "coming out" to oneself and the related disclosure risks in families, workplaces, and other social situations make it more difficult for lesbian victims to seek help. The source of power in lesbian relationships differs from that found in hetero-sexual relationships: as one author states, "whereas in heterosexual relation-ships gender is overwhelmingly the defining factor, power in same-gender couples may be a function of one or more variables interacting with one another, such as education, class, work status, ethnicity, earning potential, immigration status, and age."[29] Once the context of battering is examined—whether heterosexual or same-gender—it becomes clear that a host of factors, both personal and societal, help us understand the use, motivation, and consequence of violence. Given space limitations and a dearth of research, while acknowledging that some of the issues we raise are relevant to any woman, straight or gay, we deliberately focus this book on male violence committed against women.[30]

Second, we choose primarily to use the terms "battering" and/or "intimate-partner violence" rather than the more sanitized euphemistic terms of "domestic violence" or "spouse abuse" or "family violence." To min-imize confusion about the original authors' intent in works we cite, there are times we use these euphemistic terms when referring to certain policies or when discussing certain source material. Still, we avoid language that obfus-cates responsibility or hides the fact that this phenomenon primarily consists of men's violence toward their female partners or former partners. This distinction is important, given our forthcoming discussion about the power of language and the ongoing debate concerning the gender sym-metry of intimate-partner violence. In a similar vein, rather than follow feminist nomenclature that uses the term "rape" rather than "sexual assault" or "sexual violence," we choose to use all three terms since the victimiza-tions and policies we discuss encompass a range of sexually violent acts, not solely penile vaginal penetration, and since these terms refer to specific legal and policy-related definitions.

We trust this book accomplishes our goals of introducing students and other readers to the general debates and confusion about victims, victims' rights, and victim policies and provides the tools needed to critically analyze and assess the arguments, the effects of policies, and the empirical evidence. We hope that this material stimulates critical thought and ideas for future efforts to respond to victimization debates. Finally, we are optimistic that it inspires further research for ultimately enriching our understandings of victims and improving the quality of our responses to victims' needs.

Organization of Chapters

We consider a number of different social constructions of "the victim." The chapters examine complexities in measuring, understanding, and responding to victimization and explore the social and legal structures that support such images. A common thread that weaves through the book is *whether* and *how* changes (whether historical, legal, or policy-related) advance victim support or knowledge about victimization. In examining such developments, the chapters focus on whether legislative reforms, popular cultural treatment of female victims, and empirical research have moved beyond rhetoric to create helpful programs and to enrich our understanding of victimization. To highlight the best practices for victims and their families, we end each chapter with scientifically grounded policy recommendations.

Chapter 2 traces the different images of victims and discusses how these images relate to our understandings of victimization and victim blaming. It explores in greater depth the competing ideological positions about the status and reality of victims and victims' issues and the ensuing victim backlash that occurred after the "successes" of the contemporary victims' rights movement.

Chapter 3, by an invited contributor, LeeAnn Iovanni, provides an historical overview and critique of the research on crimes of sexual and interpersonal violence committed against women: sexual assault, battering, and stalking. The findings from empirical studies presented in this chapter assist with the debunking of claims and myths about victimization. Chapter 4 describes the media's fascination with and representation of some crimes of violence committed against women and children. Also addressed are victim myths, as disseminated by mainstream media, and how language plays a powerful role in inflaming passions about victimization events.

Chapters 5 and 6 move away from macro-level victimization issues and introduce micro-level analyses using a case study approach. Chapter 5 focuses on sexual victimization and social reaction to it. We examine policies designed to protect victims, and next, using data collected from convicted sexual offenders, we explore how these men talk about their victims, what effect victim-oriented policies have on their behavior, and how this research helps in our understanding of nationwide victim-centered sex-offense laws such as sex-offender registration and community notification, proximity restrictions, GPS surveillance, and civil commitment. Chapter 6 further investigates consequences of policies for victims using examples drawn from the larger political arena. As the state becomes more involved in regulating citizens' lives, there is a potential for new policies to cause unintended harm to victims. The chapter explores dilemmas faced by battered women as a result of new crime-control policies and legal protections related to public housing, welfare reform, and civil forfeiture cases. Further, using data gathered from women arrested on domestic violence charges, the chapter questions the appropriateness of relying on an incident-driven criminal justice system to determine appropriate responses to the use of force, especially when women's use of force in intimate relationships may be more self-defensive than aggressive.

Chapter 7 examines several complex victim related issues that were not extensively addressed elsewhere in the book, such as the politics of victimization and topics germane to the social and legal labeling of crime victims and victimizations. We also examine what is known about the outcomes and efficacy of funded programs responding to violence against women. We offer suggestions for future research and policy directions. Finally, we explore alternatives to traditional criminal justice processing of cases and examine the potential advantages to victims of restorative justice programs and other dispute resolution options.

Drawing the Contours of Victim Dilemmas   **2**

> If we take the justice out of the criminal justice system we leave be-
> hind a system that serves only the criminal. (President's Task Force
> on Victims of Crime 1982: vi)

As you will see in chapter 3, victims were the forgotten piece of the criminal
act, largely ignored by the police and prosecutors unless they were viewed as
valuable tools in the apprehension or prosecution of offenders. This trivialization led victims to become more reluctant to seek help from the criminal
justice system or participate in criminal proceedings. Victim dissatisfaction
stoked perceptions that the decisions reached by the Supreme Court in the
1960s (such as establishing Miranda rights, creating limits on search and
seizure, and extending the right to counsel), while constitutionally sound,
further strengthened offenders' due process rights at the expense of the
needs of victims. As noted briefly in chapter 1, the 1960s and especially the
1970s experienced a growing recognition that victims were erased or deni-
grated by representatives of the criminal justice system, which ignited a national victims' rights movement to create more balance between victims'
needs and offenders' rights. This movement led to official government recognition that the criminal justice system must address the needs of victims
and their families.

Emergence of Victim Prominence

In 1982, the nation's first Presidential Task Force on Victims of Crime was
charged with the mission to remedy the situation for victims. In the

subsequent two and a half decades, victims' rights laws were enacted in every state. Within the first 10 years following the initial task force more than 10,000 victim assistance programs were established, and federal crime victims funds provided more than $2.3 billion from fines paid by federal criminal offenders to support many of these victim services.[1]

In addition to the efforts to increase victim involvement and participation in the criminal justice system as a whole, during this time, the country significantly shifted its approach to handling crimes of violence that disproportionately affect female victims. Several factors converged to facilitate this change. First, feminists and victim advocates forced society to recognize the extent of crimes, such as battering and sexual assault/rape and child sexual abuse. Second, with the support of the victims' rights movement, victims publicly identified the multiple reasons they did not seek help from the criminal justice system (such as their fear or shame or disapproval from relatives or communities) or, if they did seek help, explained how their needs were unmet. Their stories demonstrated why legal involvement was often a disincentive, since the system created a "second victimization" in which either the victims were blamed for their injuries or their needs were trivialized. Finally, laws and statutes were overhauled, reflecting the unfair treatment battered or raped women received by using different standards of proof than those required for other crimes. For instance, as mentioned in chapter 3, judges routinely dismissed cases of marital rape as complaints from unhappy wives about "bad sex." Rape in general required more stringent standards of legal proof than other crimes, such as the corroboration requirement or proof of victim resistance. Crimes involving nonstrangers as offenders, such as current or former intimate partners or acquaintances, were not viewed as "real" crimes, which greatly compromised the successful prosecution of offenders. Grassroots activists and feminist scholars exposed and dismissed these sexist practices, resulting in changes in laws, policies, and protocols used to respond to battering and sexual assault.

As a result of this visibility, victims' stories about their experiences were disseminated through open forums, word of mouth, and the media, resulting in the retraining of criminal justice and social service personnel. Hearing a victim's story is a powerful way to wake up a nation's consciousness and stimulate debate and change. Victims who told about their experiences of the crime itself and of the subsequent handling by the criminal justice system inspired many listeners to support a large-scale transformation in how the legal system responds to victimization, particularly in regard to violence against women. One important way that legislators responded to public concerns about violence against women is the Violence Against Women Act of 1994 (reauthorized in 2005 for fiscal years 2007 through

2011). This effort was bipartisan, with the intent of protecting the rights and lives of women in their homes, on the streets, and in the courtroom. The legislation is far-reaching, and according to the latest figures available from the federal Office on Violence against Women, over $2 billion has been earmarked or spent on efforts increasing penalties for offenders and improving resources for police, prosecutors, and victims' services providers, as well as implementing national stalker and domestic violence reduction programs, improving legal protections for battered immigrant and Native American women and children, providing legal protection of battered, stalked, and sexually violated women who move across state lines or live on college campuses, and barring the possession of firearms for batterers.[2]

Clearly, today victims are more highly prioritized, more visible, and more influential than they once were. Victims are also now better positioned to garner resources and have a louder voice in how their case is handled by the criminal justice system. Yet 25 years after the first Presidential Task Force on Victims of Crime demanded action, our nation continues to struggle with how best to address and serve victims' needs. Responding to victimization remains complicated both emotionally and politically, and policies sometimes work at cross-purposes. Furthermore, in important ways, being a victim has transcended its earlier deviant image. Where once victims were portrayed as passive, damaged, or helpless, deserving of their victimization or blamed in some way for provoking or precipitating the event, many recent images of victims not only evoke sympathy but also recognize victims as survivors capable of using a variety of skills to negotiate their situation. For example, after keeping her identity secret for over a decade, in 2003 Trisha Meili revealed that she was the infamous Central Park jogger. On April 19, 1989, she was beaten and raped while jogging in the park. She was 28 years old at the time of the attack, which left her in a coma, with brain damage and near-fatal injuries.[3] As a nation, we rallied behind the Ivy League graduate, cheered her recovery, and applauded the criminal justice system for finding, arresting, and convicting five men for beating and raping her.[4] She released a book, entitled *I Am the Central Park Jogger: A Story of Hope and Possibility*, as a way to further empower herself and help others recovery from trauma. The book sold tens of thousands of copies, and Meili was interviewed on national television countless times.

However, sociologist Joel Best argues that while having the status of victim may be advantageous in garnering resources for advocacy groups or other reasons, on a more individual level the label itself still remains undesirable because it carries negative connotations.[5] This is contested terrain, however: varying ideological positions vie for control over what it means to be a victim and over the appropriate responses to victimization. We explore many of these competing perspectives in this chapter.

Current Issues, Misinformation, and Unintended Consequences

Several events highlight the victim issues we address here, with more detail in subsequent chapters. One such issue is the media's influence in "educating" members of society about victims and victimizations through crime coverage on television and in newspapers. Sensationalized stories, depictions of injury or violence, descriptions of the character or appearance of victims—all carry tremendous weight in shaping how we think about crime and victims.[6] In some cases, the melodrama of crime- and law-related TV shows contributes to ways real-life cases are handled. Most readers remember that in 2002, a jury determined that Andrea Yates, the mother who drowned her five young children in her bathtub, could distinguish between right and wrong, sending her to a state psychiatric prison instead of a psychiatric hospital. No one contested the finding that she suffered from psychosis and postpartum depression. But some of the news coverage and related anecdotes about people's conversations showed a prurient fascination for her use of violence and depicted Yates as an evil woman and bad mother. An opportunity was lost to use media coverage as a forum to educate the public about the dangers of untreated severe postpartum depression. The leading expert witness, a psychiatrist who testified for the prosecution, claimed that Yates was sane and that she patterned the drownings after an episode of the popular TV crime show *Law & Order*, where a woman with postpartum depression drowned her children and, interestingly enough, was found by the courts to be insane. The implication was that Yates was sane enough to plot the murders, thus showing premeditation. However, in January 2005, her conviction was overturned when it was revealed that no such TV episode was ever produced. A Texas appeals court ruled that Yates should get a new trial since the false testimony may have significantly affected jury deliberations. While maternal homicide cases are rare, the media's sensationalization and putative woman blaming, regardless of the context of the situation, is common.

Another current issue involves the side effects of a general policy affecting an unintended group of victims. During the 2004 presidential campaign, George W. Bush promised to pursue a federal constitutional amendment defining marriage as a union between a man and a woman, thus banning gay men and lesbians from marriage. Buoyed by election results that supported a conservative agenda on marriage, President Bush strengthened his commitment to ban gay marriage. In late 2008 this issue exploded again. California's passage of Proposition 8 amended the state constitution to restrict marital unions to heterosexual persons, overturning an earlier California State Supreme Court ruling legalizing same-sex marriage within the state. Within several weeks of its passage, protests against Proposition 8 were held in major metropolitan areas across the country. In the summer of 2009, the California Supreme Court upheld Proposition 8, citing the right of the state's voting public to amend its state's constitution.

While on its surface this political hot potato does not seem related to the issues of violence against women that we address in our book, a number of states that passed similar constitutional amendments are discovering that such bans have consequences that extend far beyond the definition of marriage. Most of these unanticipated consequences involve the denial of "domestic violence" safeguards for unmarried couples, gay or straight. For instance, in Utah, a man claims that the state's similarly worded constitutional amendment invalidates a restraining order taken out against him by his ex-girlfriend.[7] Similarly, in Wisconsin, a constitutional amendment that bans civil unions would effectively deny protections for unmarried heterosexual couples as well as all gay and lesbian couples (since their unions would become unrecognized as "domestic").[8] And in Cuyahoga County (Cleveland, Ohio), the public defender's office asked a judge to dismiss domestic violence charges against unmarried defendants. As one Ohio public defender says, "You can only get a domestic violence charge now if you are a wife beater, not a girlfriend beater."[9] These examples illustrate how policies introduced in one sphere, even if they seem benign or controversial, can generate unintended consequences in another sphere. Under gay marriage bans, unmarried victims (gay or straight) of domestic violence are harmed.[10]

Our final current-event example demonstrates the danger of using scare tactics rather than relying on empirical research to inform the public about victimization. This example relies on an Internet-based email dissemination, dubbed "The Ponytail," which began circulating around 2000–2001 and continues to make the rounds today. The email shows how technology can increase fear and misinformation about violence against women. This is the beginning of the email:

> Hi, girls! I just finished taking the most amazing self-defense class, sponsored by Shandwick, and I wanted to share some really valuable info with you before it goes out of my head. The guy who taught the class has a female friend who was attacked last year in the parking garage at Westport Plaza in St. Louis. He started a

women's group and began teaching these classes soon after. This guy is a black belt in karate and trains twice a year with Steven Seagal. He and the others in this group interviewed a bunch of rapists and date rapists in prison on what they look for and here's some interesting facts. The #1 thing men look for in a potential victim is hairstyle. They are most likely to go after a woman with a ponytail, bun, braid or other hairstyle that can easily be grabbed. They will look for women whose clothing is easy to remove quickly. The #1 outfit they look for is overalls because they carry scissors around to cut clothing and on overalls the straps can be easily cut. The time of day men are most likely to attack and rape a woman is in the early morning, between 5 and 8:30 a.m. The number one place women are abducted from/attacked is at grocery store parking lots.[11]

The message continues with a number of other information points. All of the points are incorrect and misleading, yet many people latch onto "tips" from unknown sources because of their fear of rape. This misinformation feeds into the conventional practice of providing women with risk-avoidance measures to ensure their safety, which can backfire and be used to blame a victim if she does not heed such advice (in this case, if she wears overalls or a ponytail while grocery shopping). In addition, providing risk-avoidance advice to women fails to address the full range of measures needed to prevent rape, fails to target the offenders as well as the culture that supports their behavior. Once the empirical research about rape is contrasted with the misinformation contained in this email—or spread by word of mouth in other contexts—it is clear that the facts do not match the warnings that feed off fear. Although these "tips" may sound plausible, there is no evidence to support such assertions.

These examples demonstrate that victims and victimization are hot topics. Today, victims receive more attention and garner more resources than ever before. After having ignored them for years, politicians now embrace victims as symbols to persuade voters that they are tough on crime and sympathetic to victims' plight; in other words, in the name of victims, politicians manipulate the emotional reaction to their suffering by embracing harsher sentencing and decreasing due process rights for offenders. It should not be surprising, then, that victims have become big business—used as bait to attract government and state-funded programs and grants, used to sway elections, and used to capitalize on people's fear of victimization by home security systems installers and other anti-crime businesses. What has not changed, however, is the deep-seated ambivalence many people feel when hearing crime stories and discerning blame and responsibility.

Victims and Victimizations: Navigating Murky Waters

The public tends to feel a sense of satisfaction when things are unambiguous and can be neatly categorized and sorted into one box or the other. In fact, our legal system determines issues of either guilt or innocence, and some religious belief systems characterize people as good or evil. This same urge to classify people holds true when listening to crime stories, with offenders cast as bad or evil and victims as good or pure. While painting the picture of victims as pure and innocent has been an invaluable shield against accusations of blame in many respects, there are problems with this simplistic evaluation of victims and offenders. For instance, if a victim's purity can be assailed, sympathy for her—and perhaps justice—could diminish. In the "preppie murder" case, involving two upper-middle-class whites named Robert Chambers and Jennifer Levin, her alleged interest in kinky sex affected her murder trial. Chambers's punishment for fatally strangling Levin during sexual intercourse was mitigated due to the defense's argument that she liked "rough sex." Media scholar Helen Benedict argued that tagging Levin with this label was successful in downplaying Chambers's lethal violence while casting doubt on her credibility as a "pure" victim.[12] Rigid boundaries that define what makes a victim "bonafide" are harmful to all women seeking justice, particularly in the arena of battering and sexual assault, since these crimes involve some degree of intimacy and/or sexuality.

Identifying offenders pejoratively raises other concerns as well. There are cases where "offenders" might initially be victims who fought back. This issue is apparent in the debate over the "abuse excuse," or the suggestion that offenders' responsibility should be mitigated if they were previously abused. The infamous 1994 case of the Menendez brothers, who, as adults, killed their parents to avenge what they allege were years of extreme verbal and physical abuse endured at their parents' hands, illustrates this concept.[13] Where does individual responsibility fit? Even the initial juries in this case were unable to choose between manslaughter or first- or second-degree murder, resulting in mistrials; the Menendez brothers are now in prison after receiving life sentences. Similarly, in the same year, Lorena Bobbitt cut off her husband's penis following years of physical and sexual abuse by him, including earlier on the night she attacked him; like the Menendez brothers, she used her status as an abuse victim to argue against her responsibility, and was acquitted based on a finding of temporary insanity.[14] And in recent years, a number of governors commuted the sentences of battered women who killed their partners after suffering years of abuse with few options or support and were unable to present evidence of battering at their trials. All of these situations share the same defense: "The defendants were not criminals—murderers or assailants—but innocent victims whose victimization shaped, even caused, their eventual actions, innocent victims who should not be held responsible for actions that were not their fault."[15] Though legal scholars are divided about the legitimacy of using these defense strategies and worry about endorsing vigilante justice, many members of the public support "popular justice" actions and see these as rare, desperate measures.[16]

It is understandable to want to present victims as blameless. A "pure" victim makes the practice of victim blaming more difficult. Overpurifying victims so that perpetrators are held unquestionably accountable for their offenses is common.[17] However, victims are not one-dimensional or without agency. Without detracting from victims' real injuries, we recognize that most victims are not passive, weak, compliant individuals. Rather, victims hold a repertoire of emotions, actions, and reactions, whether this entails possessing the will (or wits) to survive, or having the resiliency of spirit to empower themselves to seek support (personally and/or institutionally), or resorting to violence when all other remedies fail. Individuals' experiences of their victimizations and their responses to their situations vary. Responsibility and blame for one's actions are often blurred. As the meaning and understanding of victims change, the ambiguity generates confusion over what role the criminal justice system should play in addressing victimization.

The social construction of "the victim" has multiple meanings, depending on who is doing the defining and why, as well as depending on the social status of victims and offenders. These variables greatly influence the way that victims are judged and treated by others. For instance, Ted Bundy, the "boy next door" serial killer of girls and women, evaded capture for years because he did not fit the public's profile of a serial killer due to his enhanced social status (well-educated, white, attractive, upper-middle-class), and his status trumped his victims' statuses (at least initially, when he targeted prostitutes, drifters, and victims of color).[18] The infamous case of the New Bedford, Rhode Island, woman who was gang-raped in a bar while onlookers cheered is a case in point. Initially, the public was outraged, and within the community, the rapists were demonized and the victim was supported. Over time, however, her character, her actions that night (drinking in the bar, flirting, dancing) and her reputation as a good mother were assailed, once the rapists and other community members felt that they were being unfairly targeted in the national spotlight because they were Portuguese (never mind that the victim was also Portuguese). The case was the basis for Jodie Foster's highly praised portrayal of a rape victim in the movie *The Accused.*

Sensationalized, familiar examples such as those above illustrate the elusiveness of justice that exists for some victims, underscoring the suffering of untold millions of victims whose stories do not make the front pages of newspapers or grace prime-time television.

Commodification of Victimhood

We use the term "commodification" because there are so many social commentators and scholars in competition to identify and define precisely who a victim is. Discussions about victimization take place within a cultural backdrop. Many groups are invested in gaining a stake in the victimization debate, exploiting the definition of "victim" for their particular purposes. These multiple perspectives may directly influence public understanding, even when the positions presented do not have the support of empirical data or any practical application to victim assistance.

Much of the dialogue and resources of social commentators targets women who are harmed by male rapists, batterers, stalkers, or sexual harassers. This social problem, male violence committed against women, is typically framed by two opposing ways of thinking about how much victimization exists. A "maximalist" ideology is one that takes the position that suffering is widespread and reaching epidemic proportions, believing that unless people and resources are mobilized, a crisis will ensue.[19] In contrast, the "minimalist" position is more skeptical about claims that victimization is omnipresent, believing that such alarmist exaggerations are used for self-serving purposes and that the massive financial and energy commitments they call for are not warranted.[20] This ideological clash influences the ways that victims' needs are evaluated and featured in commentaries about victim culture and victim empowerment.

Victim Culture

In what is called a backlash to the recognition of victims' rights, numerous books, book chapters, and articles emerged in the mid-1990s that addressed, in journalistic fashion, the rise of the "victim culture." Many of these works, often aimed at a lay audience, do not ground their arguments with factual data or empirical research. Their basic argument is that it is too easy to claim a victim status, a belief that strikes a chord with many members of the public. Americans have an astonishing appetite for crime stories, and enjoy evaluating whether a victim's claims are legitimate or exaggerated. Reflecting this phenomenon, a number of conservative social critics suggest that society embraces a "victim culture," such that being a victim has become fashionable or that victims are oversensitive and cry wolf or make mountains out of nuances or innuendoes, particularly in the areas of date rape and sexual harassment. Conservative writers often blame "radical" feminism for promoting victimhood and for exaggerating the incidence of victimization. Feminists are easy targets, since many were activists working at the vanguard of the rape or battered women's movements to expose the prevalence of such crimes and sought cultural and legal changes they believed would decrease victimization.

When one examines the mainstream writings that follow a victim culturalist perspective, some common ways of characterizing victims emerge. For instance, victims are seen as people who seek attention and revel in their identity as powerless, who are eager to claim victim status with its ensuing attention, who are happy in misery, and who fail to take the requisite responsibility for their victimizations. In particular, female victims are aggressively targeted by victim culturalists as partially responsible for their victimization. Responsibility is a key theme; victim culturalists believe that most victims share some responsibility over what happened to them. Furthermore, victim culturalists assert that victims are conditioned to abandon personal responsibility or avoid acknowledging that their actions might have contributed to their victimization.

Victim culturalist proponents view female victims of male violence in particular as beleaguered, fragile, and hysterical, and as fabricating or exaggerating their harms. However, some conservative "feminists" such as Katie Roiphe (1993) embrace the victim culturalist idea that feminism has perpetuated victimhood. She argues that when the pervasiveness and frequency of rape are exposed, women are constructed as easy prey rather than as sexually autonomous beings. Feminist social commentator Naomi Wolfe critiques female victimization and the connection victim culturalists make to feminism, saying that "victim feminism" operates "when a woman seeks power through an identity of powerlessness" and manipulates concepts of feminism by suggesting that suffering is a virtue, which produces "exactly the wrong images . . . helplessness, silence, pain, defeat."[21] This position is in contrast to the vast majority of empirical studies of the past 25 years documenting the high prevalence of violence that women sustain by current or former intimate partners or by other nonstrangers in their lives, suggesting that violence against women is pervasive and injurious.

Despite the empirical challenges to the victim culture position, it is thriving, particularly in books geared to an audience outside of academia. While some academics also embrace victim blaming, what is telling about the "academic" writings of victim culture advocates is the lack of scientific data upon which to support their suppositions. Within this genre of writing, characterizations of female victims of violence tend to be hostile, and writers use caricatures to denigrate both the "alleged" victim as well as any feminist scholar who advocates for them. The victim culturalists' efforts—and the examples they use to promote such images—trivializes women's victimization and engages in undisguised victim blaming. These diatribes are often splashy and aimed at a mass audience, with the messengers rewarded with media appearances on TV and radio talk shows. In fact, self-described feminists who support victim cultural arguments, such as Katie Roiphe and Camille Paglia, see forthcoming discussions, were popular on the media circuit because they were touted by victim culturalists as brave feminists who are "honest" in acknowledging women's shared role in victimization.

One of the earliest victim culture books for a mainstream audience is Charles Sykes's 1992 book, *A Nation of Victims: The Decay of the American Character*. Here, Sykes resurrects the earlier notions of victim blaming that were popular among victimologists of the 1940s and 1950s, arguing that victims evade personal responsibility with their battle cry, "It's not my fault." Sykes attributes the rise in "victimism" to the increase in social acceptance of seeking therapy when faced with emotional turmoil. Thus, he sees a link between the therapeutic culture, where (he feels) victims are excused for any improper actions, and the decline of self-reliance and strength of character. As part of the more general "culture wars" that attack political correctness, Sykes believes that it is impossible to engage in intelligent discussions about victims' contribution to their victimizations because too many people are afraid of offending someone.[22]

Victim culturalists assert that this position sets a dangerous precedent because if people refuse to critique victims for not taking responsibility for their choices and behaviors, it allows victims to receive attention, sympathy, money, and legal or government protection that is undeserved. The danger of having "a society of resentful, competing, and self-centered individuals who have dressed their private annoyances in the garb of victimism" is that the legitimacy of "real" victims and a heartfelt response to them is threatened because of the skepticism and gridlock that result from the excesses of "victim politics."[23] The victim culturalist suggestion to rid society of the victim mindset emphasizes individual-level approaches, such as rebuilding one's character as a way to solve social problems. This personal change would result in stronger moral restraint and a greater emphasis on personal

responsibility rather than perceived rights. Another popular victim culturalist recommendation to limit victimism is to decrease litigation and cap
awards so that victims have less incentive to file frivolous lawsuits. According to this train of thought, the emphasis on developing moral character
takes place within the education system wherein educators teach moral
values to children.[24] There is a connection here to more general culture wars
in which people with different perspectives attempt to shape educational,
social, and political issues with their own agenda.

Most victim cultural arguments dismiss the idea of holding social/legal
institutions responsible (or even partially responsible) for contributing
to acts of crime. Victim culturalists ridicule the "blame the social system"
position covered in our introductory chapter. In other words, they reject the
argument that an understanding of victimization requires one to take into
account the social-structural variables that increase the risks of being a victim as well as understanding how the criminal justice interface with victims
and its consequences. Victim culture advocates use examples to emphasize
"false" victims and to argue we are now a nation of victims. For instance,
they sensationalize single cases (like the McDonald's "burning coffee" civil
suit in which the coffee scalded the lap of a customer and she filed a multi-
million-dollar lawsuit;[25] or the case where a man deliberately leapt in front
of a moving subway in New York City and was awarded over half a million
dollars because the train failed to stop in time to avoid hitting and hurting
him; or the example of a family vacationing in Hawaii suing an overbooked
hotel that moved them to less desirable lodgings and were subsequently
compensated by the court for their economic losses and awarded cash for
their emotional distress and disappointment), and posits them as the norm.
This presentation trivializes and dismisses claims of victims and the desire
to explore valid issues of all victims.

Victim Culturists/Social Commentators Take Aim at "Radical" Feminists

It is no small task to sort through the competing voices for defining who a
victim is. Many of the victim culture writers, such as Charles Sykes, Katie
Roiphe, Christina Hoff Sommers, Paula Pearson, and Philip Cook, openly
express hostility and disdain for scholars who defend victims of sexual
assault and battering, scholars whom they label and dismiss as "radical feminists." This is most apparent among victim culturalists when exploring wom-
en's victimization by men. Their almost categorical dismissal of rape and
battering victims as hypersensitive or exaggerating is particularly chilling.

For instance, rather than using empirical data that suggests the contrary, Sykes argues that increases in the number of entertainment venues displaying women being brutalized have led to women's overidentification as potential victims, especially of sexism and harassment.[26] In other words, women internalize the image of a victim and then assess their experiences through this lens, magnifying trivial gender slurs into large-scale claims of harm and abuse. Empirically unsupported statements that are presented as "facts" by "authorities" strike a chord with the lay public, who may be suffering from compassion fatigue.

Victim culturalists (embracing minimalist positions) use the crime of rape as an example of how feminists "hype" its prevalence by expanding the traditional definition of rape to include other types of sexual assault. Sykes argues that this redefinition is problematic, since it now includes an "entire range of nuance, complexity, tentativeness, and confusion that surrounds the relations between men and women."[27] Camille Paglia (1990) is similarly dismissive of the "No Means No" anti-rape slogan, part of a sexual assault education campaign that is particularly popular on college campuses. She contends that "'No' has always been, and always will be part of the dangerous, alluring courtship ritual of sex and seduction, observable even in the animal kingdom." Another writer in this tradition, Katie Roiphe (1993), constructs two ways to evaluate claims of date rape. First, she dismisses most date rape allegations as "bad sex." She bases her dismissal on the fact that not a single one of her friends experienced rape, which she interprets to mean that there is no evidence of widespread sexual violence. Instead, Roiphe believes that the alleged "victim" was initially willing but changed her mind in the morning because she was embarrassed or had regrets. Second, Roiphe believes that women relish their victim status and the attention it generates, which prevents them from acknowledging any of their own responsibility in the incident. Despite these strong assertions, however, Roiphe contradicts herself by acknowledging later in her book that it is possible the date rape problem *is* real; but even then she argues that it could be controlled if only women were more assertive and feisty. Her prescription is for women to be more in command of their sexual desires and more honest.

As with many of the arguments made by victim culturalists there is a kernel of truth: women should play more active roles in their sexual and intimate lives. However, a belief in women's assertiveness does not negate the real occurrence of date and acquaintance rape. Moreover, the change in women's open acknowledgement of such crimes (e.g., sexual harassment, date/acquaintance rape) is welcome, since it indicates a significant social shift in recognizing acts of violence against women as unacceptable and no longer easily dismissed as "boys being boys." Thus, Katha Pollitt (1994: 165) argues, "cultural attitudes toward rape, harassment, coercion, and consent are slowly shifting. It is certainly true that many women today, most of whom would not describe themselves as feminists, feel outraged by male behavior that previous generations—or even those women themselves not so long ago—quietly accepted as 'everyday experience.'" Despite some movement away from victim blaming as evidenced by a greater openness in debating the issues of blame and responsibility, acts by offenders of certain statuses remain immune. For instance, it was possible for Arnold Schwarzenegger to be elected as California's governor in 2003 (and reelected in 2006) even though 16 female victims reported acts of sexual harassment and groping incidents that occurred in his past.

To recap, the victim culture perspective accomplishes two goals: first, it attacks the credibility of victims and their suffering by suggesting that victims evade responsibility for their own actions and perhaps even exaggerate their harmful experiences. This position moves away from scientific understanding of victimization and condemns scholarly efforts to study crime victims. By highlighting sensational cases that appear newsworthy because of their extremity, victim culturalists push their critique on the strength of its visceral appeal without using empirical data or statistics to prove their arguments. Second, in regard to female victims of male violence, particularly rape and battering, the portrait of women presented by victim culturalists is one of a hysterical, confused woman who overreacts to the situation. She is characterized as infantile and at fault; victim blamers are often condescending in their discussion of the harm she experiences. Furthermore, since violence against women seems to rest on an analysis of women's individual frailties and faults and not offenders' responsibilities, victim culturalists blame women and ignore the larger social forces and conditions that influence the attitudes and actions of victims and offenders. Despite the significant limitations of the culture perspective, the biases it introduces have entered mainstream culture and play a powerful role in shaping contemporary understanding of female victimization and reinforcing victim blaming.

Victim Empowerment Perspective

In contrast to those who see a "victim culture" that blames victims, another group of scholars and other writers recognize victims' survival skills and their ability to make choices in the face of often dangerous and damaging circumstances. This alternative characterization of victims is often referred to as a "victim empowerment" perspective. These writers concentrate on examining the context of the victims' situations and incorporating empirical research outcomes to better understand the dynamics of victim-offender relationships and other influential factors associated with criminal victimizations.[28] While this body of work does not designate victims of crime as morally superior, proponents of the victim empowerment perspective view victims as people who suffer harm but nonetheless remain self-assertive, capable, and independent. This perspective does not simply construct victims as completely innocent pawns, nor does it accept the simplistic depiction of victims as responsible for their own victimization. The primary distinction between the opposing arguments is that the assertions made by victim empowerment proponents are grounded in science.

In so doing, many advocates of the victim empowerment ideology acknowledge that there is danger in exposing the pervasiveness of women's victimization because of the social reaction to such a large-scale social problem. Yet the bottom line is clear: it is vitally important to expose the private injuries women experience within relationships or with acquaintances. Academic research is less likely to be courted as splashy topics for TV, radio talk shows, or Twitter posts, so the research findings are not as widely disseminated as victim culturalist positions. Perhaps these researchers—like most academics—need to do a better job of marketing their findings to mass audiences and the media.

One example of the comprehensive and contextualized fashion in which victim empowerment advocates assess victims and their situations is illustrated through their assessment of the pros and cons associated with the use of the "battered women's syndrome" (BWS) defense.[29] BWS is a psychological condition that is used as a legal defense to explain to judges and juries why a battered woman might remain in an abusive relationship or kill an abusive partner. If her lethal act occurred in a moment of violent confrontation, which is the most common scenario, the legal question surrounds the "reasonableness" of her actions. In instances of nonconfrontational homicides, which are far less common, the primary focus of the court is whether the victim's history of abuse diminished her ability to act as a reasonable person otherwise would have.[30] In other words, BWS is used to show that the battered woman had a reasonable fear, based on the man's past behavior, that she faced imminent danger, and that the use of force was justified in self-defense even if it occurred in an atypical fashion, like when the abuser was sleeping or passed out from intoxication.

BWS works hand-in-hand with the concept of "learned helplessness," which, simply put, describes how victims of repeated battering "learn" through the lack of response from the police or family or friends or religious leaders (and retaliatory beatings if these avenues are tried) that escape is impossible, so they do not attempt escape even if opportunities emerge.[31] BWS expands the legal focus of simply examining the instantaneous actions of the defendant (i.e., in this case the woman killing her intimate partner) by allowing judges and juries to understand the context (i.e., long-term abuse from the male partner who was subsequently killed) of the lethal act.

However, a victim empowerment perspective recognizes that there is danger in presenting victims as impaired because of their abuse, rather than viewing their acts as rational responses to life-threatening conditions.[32] If female victims of battering or rape are portrayed as passive or helpless in the face of male violence, women who respond with force against male attacks are stigmatized. These images could be used to reinforce stereotypes of women's dependency and helplessness in later parts of case processing, such as in divorce and custody proceedings where women are portrayed as incapable of protecting their children[33] or in the trial and sentencing phases where women used nonlethal or lethal force against their abusive partners or ex-partners.[34] Moreover, while it was vitally important to educate jurors, judges, and the public about the psychological aspects of the power dynamics associated with battering that enmesh women in abusive relationships, it hides not only that there are social factors that erect obstacles to leaving but also that the most dangerous time for a battered woman is when she actually separates from her abusive partner. Therefore, a critical assessment of all of these issues results in victim empowerment advocates voicing concerns over the construction of battered women as suffering from "learned helplessness" and its superficial analysis of the role of social-structural variables in explaining women's battering.

Furthermore, writers in the victim empowerment tradition, particularly feminist and legal scholars, document women's victimizations without suggesting that women are innately victims because of their sex. In doing so, these scholars highlight victims' resiliency in surviving and moving beyond the criminal incident and celebrate victims' strengths and coping skills. This perspective argues that focusing on a person's strengths and abilities moves us away from victim blaming and toward a more empowered and complete portrait of a victim. As feminist legal scholar and attorney Elizabeth Schneider contends, "Women do not identify with the term 'battered woman,' even if they arrive bleeding at a shelter, because no one feels that her totality is being a victim."[35] Viewing such a woman as a victim fails to take into account the range of women's experiences in relationships and what actions and resistance she did take.[36] Faced with violence in intimate relationships, battered women respond with great variation, and although remaining in the relationships may appear to outsiders as paralysis or stagnation, relationship continuation may actually be part of a pattern of resistance. In fact, many battered women respond to abuse with strong survivor tactics, only to find that their help-seeking efforts are largely unsuccessful.[37] Still, data suggest that women resist giving up and are assertive in protecting their children even in the face of injury, isolation, depression, guilt, danger, or poverty.[38]

Despite victim culturalists' belief that victims clamor for recognition of their status, many victims of male violence are loath to seek help because this entails acknowledgment of their victimization. For many women in our society, being labeled a victim of rape or battering is so pejorative and stigmatizing that it often prevents a woman from identifying or even being aware of agency in herself or in others, despite the healing offered by therapy.[39] This kind of denial is particularly cogent for battered women, given the social stigma associated with them: "Women who know their own strength therefore do not recognize their experience as battering, and some are deterred from seeking assistance."[40] This refusal to identify as a battered woman may be exacerbated for women of color: "bell hooks tells of giving Lenore Walker's first book, *The Battered Woman*, to a young black woman severely beaten by her [male] partner. The woman's family threw the book out—they did not want her to feel less self-esteem, and they perceived the label 'battered woman' as inevitably implying victimization."[41] The same holds true for rape victims. This reluctance to identify as a battered woman or a rape survivor is often present as women seek help from shelters and crisis hotlines because the victim does not self-identify as a victim.[42]

We do not suggest that the victim empowerment perspective is partisan or passionless; scholars who hold the victim empowerment position are often as contemptuous of those arguing from a "victim culture" perspective as those victim culturalists are about them. The difference is that these legal scholars and victimology researchers utilize empirical data to support their contentions, which is not a common practice among social commentators making assertions about the "culture of victimization." Since victim empowerment discourses are more likely to be published in academic journals and rely on statistical studies, the debunking of victim culture arguments with empirical data is less likely to be widely circulated to mass audiences. Moreover, as noted earlier, victim empowerment scholars face a powerful backlash in which (generally) conservative critics accuse "feminists" of either male-bashing or exaggerating and distorting statistics to make an ideological point, particularly those concerning violence committed against women.

Contrasting Victim Culture and Victim Empowerment Perspectives

Date Rape as an Example

The competing realities of date rape are characterized as the clash between maximalists, who believe there is a date rape crisis of epidemic proportions on college campuses, and minimalists, who argue that since few women report rape to campus or criminal justice authorities, it is a rare and isolated event.[43] The research statistics noted in chapter 3 contradict the latter position.

Proponents of the victim culture suggest that date rape rates are grossly inflated because of the researchers' overgeneralization of the term "rape" to include sexual encounters that are regrettable or coercive but fall into a gray area between sexual assault and consensual sex.[44] For example, one victim culturalist attacked a national date rape study for creating a "phantom epidemic of sexual assault."[45] However, date rape studies use definitions consistent with legal definitions of rape, even if the victims themselves did not define what happened to them as felony rapes.[46]

Moreover, it is not just antifeminist men who question the legitimacy of rape and battering victims or who attack "feminist" research. Christina Hoff Sommers, a self-described "equality" feminist (one who believes that men and women should have equal rights), uses her 1994 book to attack women's studies programs on college campuses as well as to question the veracity of statistics and research findings on rape and battering. Her position is that the goal of "gender feminists" (believing that women should get "special rights") is to "underscore the plight of women in the oppressive gender system and to recruit adherents to the gender feminist cause." One way that recruitment becomes possible, she argues, is through the use of exaggerated rape and battering statistics that terrify women. Hoff Sommers, like the other victim culturalists mentioned earlier (Sykes, Paglia, and Roiphe), believes that women are raised to think like victims and to interpret everyday vulgarity as intolerable acts of sexual harassment.[47] Hoff Sommers argues that since most of the "raped" women do not *call* it rape, it must not *be* rape.

However, in a study conducted at UCLA, researchers asked male students two versions of the same question: first "Would you rape a woman if you knew you would never get caught?" and then "Would you use force with a woman if you knew you would never get caught?" When "rape" was changed to "use force with," the number of university men who said yes jumped from 30 percent to over 50 percent.[48] Hoff Sommers dismisses the notion that forcible penetration by a finger or other object should count as sexual assault. Furthermore, Hoff Sommers agrees with Roiphe's belief that campus rape crisis movements are movements of privilege, reflecting the outrage that arises when women who "have it all" (i.e., white, educated, upper-middle-class women) discover that the world can be dangerous.[49] Despite her "analysis" of rape and battering, Hoff Sommers neither adds any suggestions for better assisting victims nor offers any solutions for how to address these enduring social problems.

Although not identified with the victim culture perspective, psychologist Sharon Lamb raises the important point that Katie Roiphe was at least courageous enough to discuss: date rape hype.[50] She believes that there is some merit to Roiphe's suggestion that "the constant portrayal of women as helpless victims merely reinforces old images of feminine frailty."[51] Roiphe (1991: 27) proposes, "Let's not chase the same stereotypes our mothers have spent so much energy running away from. Let's not reinforce the images that oppress us, that label us victims, and deny our own agency and intelligence, as strong and sensual, as autonomous, pleasure-seeking, sexual beings." While it is laudable to promote women's empowerment to seek pleasure without guilt, Roiphe perverts this goal when she questions the legitimacy of women's claims of rape. Roiphe also dismisses victims who share their stories of victimization in campus outreach programs because the narratives told by the victims sound stilted or rehearsed. Roiphe's dismissal of these victim speak-outs discounts one of their important features: the healing that often occurs when victims publicly share very private stories. Finally, Lamb's position argues that women have been silenced about their rape experiences: it is typical for victims to overestimate their participation and over-blame themselves.[52] Victims often do not report the crime and seek prosecution partly because they blame themselves; thus, victims are likely dissuaded from facing brutal cross-examinations by defense attorneys that insinuate victim culpability. In addition, Lamb says that women's silence is related to the fact they are traumatized and confused about the complexity of intimacy and assault issues.

Despite Roiphe's lack of empirical evidence, she became a sought-after talk show guest because of her controversial statements and the salacious content of her topic, a notoriety perpetuated by media who did not check out the other side of the story (e.g., statistics, research on healing processes). Other participants in the date rape "hype" also received national publicity for their victim-blaming stances. As victim empowerment proponents show, it is easy for victim culturalists to get public attention by claiming that "if these women are so confused about what happened to them, perhaps what happened to them wasn't all that bad after all."[53] What the victim culturalist viewpoints demonstrate is a trivialization of the extent to which violence committed by men against women is an ordinary occurrence, not a rare event.

Battered Husbands as an Example

Another battle between victim culture and victim empowerment perspectives involves intimate-partner violence. The minimalist argument (embraced by the victim culturalists) suggests that statistics are exaggerated and only tell part of the story of battering. They highlight a "newly discovered" victim group: battered husbands. Although much of women's violence against men in intimate relationships reflects a self-defensive response to men's use of physical force, a number of men's rights groups (men who are often joined by their second wives) have organized to address battered husbands' needs.[54] They are concerned about the invisibility surrounding this crime, which is created by men's reluctance to report their victimizations given the ridicule men might receive for not being masculine enough to control their wives, which in turn could create stigma, emotional stress, silence, and isolation for them. Their analysis fails to note that "battered" men typically have a crucial advantage over battered wives: they remain financially stable and thus able to leave a bad relationship, and men are rarely stalked, beaten, or killed upon separation.[55] In a 1997 book, *Abused Men: The Hidden Side of Domestic Violence*, journalist and men's rights leader Philip Cook claims that women's use of violence against men is a well-kept secret. He documents his evidence using verbatim text from interviews with 30 men connected to men's rights organizations that dealt with the effects of parental separation on children.

Cook based his arguments on the findings of two studies conducted by family sociologists Murray Straus and Richard Gelles in the 1970s, in which they reported that rates of spousal violence were nearly equal (see discussions on the Conflict Tactic Scale [CTS] in chapter 3). However, the extant empirical evidence reveals that this interpretation is not accurate, especially once context, motives, and consequences are taken into account.[56] According to Peter Lehmann (2000: 443), Cook's claims are questionable: "In what only can be seen as biased and unbalanced, . . . Cook's report of the data and his conceptual arguments are contradictory, out of context, and stretched to make a point." However, to the untrained reader's eye, Cook's engaging journalistic accounts of personal stories sound convincing, particularly for readers susceptible to arguments of a feminist conspiracy to emasculate men and blame them for all social problems.

A chapter of Hoff Sommers's book covers the topic of battering. In it, she dismisses statistics that show that women are disproportionately the victims of battering within relationships, basing her dismissal on the same Straus and Gelles survey results that reveal "gender symmetry," or that women are as likely to hit their male partners as men do women. What Hoff Sommers neglects to tell the readers is that most women fight back in self-defense, or engage in lower-level acts of aggression, and that once the context is uncovered, the pattern of "man as primary aggressor" is clearer and accounts for much of the "mutual combat" argument.[57] Hoff Sommers says abusive men are an anomaly. In fact, Hoff Sommers expresses disbelief that battering still occurs, given that it was outlawed in the United States dating back to the late 1800s. This position seems naive given the extensive research documenting police and prosecutorial non-enforcement and selective enforcement of battering, despite laws against domestic violence. This issue is covered more fully in chapter 3.

In another victim-culture-type book, journalist Patricia Pearson examines "how and why women get away with murder" in her 1997 book *When She Was Bad*. One chapter focuses on women who assault their spouses or lovers, and in these pages she argues that women can be as violent toward their intimate partners as men are. Pearson presents her case about women's propensity for violence by citing research on violence occurring within lesbian relationships. While lesbian batterers follow similar patterns of power and control as heterosexual male batterers, this is not evidence of women's symmetry in their use of violence. Like Hoff Sommers and Cook, Pearson castigates feminists and activists for their dismissal of lesbian battering, since it challenges the belief that woman battering is an extension of male political, economic, social, and ideological dominance over women.[58] Pearson also uses the 1970s Straus and Gelles research to claim that women use equal force in relationships, citing Hoff Sommers's arguments rather than addressing published research.

In the academic literature, the "mutual combat hypothesis" has long been debated and, by many accounts, discarded.[59] Refinements in prevalence measures augmented by findings from qualitative research reveal that once contextual factors (such as motivation, injury) are taken into account, it is men who commit the disproportionate amount of serious battering. Gender or sexual symmetry, as it is sometimes called, in domestic battering is most likely to occur among teen or dating couples or with less severe forms of violence like spitting, pushing, or pulling hair.[60] Battering that results in serious physical injury is overwhelmingly committed by males against their female partners or ex-partners.

Conclusions and Policy Recommendations

Defining victims raises questions of blame, responsibility, and credibility. While many citizens agree with the argument that being a victim should not erase or excuse all responsibility, a full accounting of victimization deserves exploration into the reality of the situation, one that is not based on a distortion of either empirical facts or victim perceptions. As discussed in our introductory chapter, blaming the victim features prominently in the theoretical writings of early victimologists who suggested that victims share some, if not most, responsibility for the crime. Although this belief is challenged by later researchers, vestiges of blame continue to affect our evaluation of victims, particularly for female victims of male violence. Scholars favoring a more victim-centered approach acknowledge the different resources and strengths that victims bring to their situations.

What the victim cultural scholars have in common is their minimalist disbelief in the pervasiveness of sexual violence and battering committed by men against women. They believe that the estimates of rape and battering of women are inflated, exaggerated, and incorrect. However, according to empirical research and government studies, the numbers of victims of these crimes are staggering. These are not studies commissioned or executed by amateur researchers or polemic feminists drawing on anecdotal data. Clearly, the importance of reconciling empirical facts with the emotional issues raised when examining victimization is necessary to develop a fuller understanding of violence against women. In this way, both the maximalist and minimalist positions can be challenged in our quest to better achieve social justice.

The Violent Victimization of Women: An Overview of Legal, Empirical, and Measurement Issues

For years a woman had been the subject of domestic violence. When the violence escalated, she called 911; the police responded but did not arrest the batterer. When the batterer began to threaten her children, the victim obtained an order of protection that required the batterer to leave the household. The issuance of the order seemed to incense the batterer, who began a campaign of harassment against the victim, including following her for four weeks. At trial, he was quoted as saying to her by telephone, "I am across the street watching you, and I'm going to kill you." No calls to the police were ever made. One day, while she was driving home from work, a car tried to run her off the road in the mountains. She stopped and began talking to witnesses of the incident. The batterer approached her in disguise and attacked and killed her. A copy of the protection order was found in his car. The batterer was convicted of first degree murder and sentenced by the jury to death, partly on the basis that he had been lying in wait, a statutory aggravating factor. (*People v. Poynton*, Cal. Supr. Ct. L.A. County [2001])

The case above occurred in 2001 in California and, unfortunately, is not an anomaly.[1] Media coverage of such lethal incidents has raised public awareness about violence in the private sphere, and in recent decades, the professional study of the violent victimization of women has flourished.[2] Legal remedies in addition to efforts at education, prevention, and direct intervention have painstakingly become a reality in a society slow to acknowledge violence against women. Yet intimate-partner violence (IPV) remains a fact of life for far too many women. Not all violent relationships escalate to the murderous situation described above, but approximately 33 percent of all murdered women are killed by their husband or partner.[3] In comparison, only 3 percent of all murdered men are killed by an intimate partner.[4] Furthermore, of all the cases identified as intimate-partner homicide, three out of every four victims was a female.[5] This tragic incident perhaps could have been averted with earlier and more rigorous intervention. But our policies and practices addressing violence against women are far from ideal, and our knowledge base about women's victimization is far from perfect.

In this chapter, we first examine society's treatment of violence against women through laws that serve to criminalize the behavior and legal policies meant to ensure that the criminal justice system functions to serve victims as well as hold offenders accountable. Next, we review some of the most significant research on female violent victimization. What is revealed in these studies is that most violence against women is committed by men who are former or current intimate partners, a victim-offender dyad where underreporting is pervasive. Therefore we also discuss some of the difficulties faced by researchers and mention ways in which they might be overcome.

The Criminal Justice Response to Men's Violence Against Women: A Historical Overview

Intimate-Partner Violence

Battering in intimate relationships is not new. In fact it is centuries old, contemporaneous with the subjugation of women in marriage. Sociologists and anthropologists suggest that the development of paired marriages, which replaced group marriages and extended family groupings, served to officially relegate women to second-class status.[6] Monogamous marriage gave women a protective mate and gave men a way to guarantee their identities and rights as fathers. Women were bought and sold as the property of men and were unable to own their own property and thus became socially, legally, and economically dependent on their husbands or fathers.[7] This sociohistorical view locates the root cause of intimate violence in patriarchy, a social system in which men are vested with power and authority and men's activities are vested with prestige regardless of men's actual capabilities. This system of social relations is still present, albeit to a lesser extent.[8] Of course, there are other competing theoretical ideals on the causes of IPV, including social learning theories which purport that behavior is learned by modeling the actions of others and through a system of rewards and reinforcements, or "subculture of violence" rationales that attempt to explain why family violence is overrepresented among poor households and impoverished neighborhoods, or the "intergenerational transmission of violence" concept, which suggests that domestic battery victims and offenders learn their roles from their family of origin's dispute resolution tactics.

Despite the fact that battering has been part of women's experience for centuries, society's definition of it as a social problem, historically speaking, is recent. Throughout the greater part of modern civilization, founded on patriarchy, it was considered normal when men exercised their right to discipline their wives or children.[9] From Europe and Asia, through ancient Greece and the Middle Ages, history is filled with examples of laws and customs of women subjected to various forms of cruelty, including being beaten, tortured, and killed by spouses whose actions were ignored if not commended.[10] As recently as a few decades ago, behaviors that today are defined as battering were considered acceptable actions by male heads of households.[11]

In the United States, the seeds of legal condemnation were planted early. American settlers based their laws on English common law,[12] which itself was beginning to question the old privilege that allowed a husband the right to "moderate correction" and "domestic chastisement." In 1641 the Puritans of the Massachusetts Bay Colony passed the first law in the Western world against wife beating, and a few years later husband beating was prohibited as well; a second law in Plymouth Colony in 1672 punished wife beating with "a five-pound fine or a whipping, and husband beating with a sentence to be determined in court."[13] Puritan laws did not take a gendered view of intimate-partner violence. Instead their laws reflected religious principles, which viewed family violence as a sin, and all sinful behavior was subject to community watchfulness. Laws against family violence primarily served a symbolic function, separating saints from sinners, but they were rarely enforced, as Puritans also respected the sovereign authority of husbands.[14]

Legal remedies occurred in waves and reflected the fact that violence in the private sphere was viewed more as a threat to social order than as injury to individual victims.[15] After those symbolic initial laws, legal prohibitions against wife beating did not appear again until a Tennessee statute in 1850 and a Georgia statute in 1857. There is other evidence of the criminalization of wife beating in various U.S. jurisdictions from 1830 to 1874.[16] These new responses reflected concerns about social order associated with immigration, industrialization, and urbanization and represented an effort to keep the behavior of the "dangerous classes" in check. The criminalization of wife-beating cases at this time fell more generally within violations of public order or breach of the peace, and formal complaints were rare.[17] Women victims bringing complaints faced reluctance on the part of police and prosecutors to mete out justice in the belief that action taken against a husband would be detrimental to a family's economic situation. Thus, although wife beating could be dealt with criminally as a public order problem, this period itself was not an era of great social concern about violence in the private sphere, and it is unclear to what extent these laws were actually enforced. If criminally charged, batterers might be fined but generally escaped with impunity, and battered wives who opted not to stay in the violent relationship could be charged with desertion if they left children behind.[18] In essence, the law offered no real protection for women, and the issue of wife beating was primarily a tool to control unruly and "dangerous" immigrants or to shore up the power of the criminal justice system.

Official disapproval against battering was more characteristic of the late 1800s and early 1900s.[19] Three states passed laws punishing wife beating with the whipping post: Maryland (1882), Delaware (1901), and Oregon (1906). Although by this time most states outlawed the whipping post as barbaric and actual use of flogging was rare, these laws sent a symbolic message that wife beating would not be tolerated and that offenders should be held accountable. This wave of legislation represented the converging interests of law-and-order Republican males, feminist groups concerned about crimes against women, and the efforts of women's temperance groups—"moral entrepreneurs" who did not espouse feminist ideas but rather were attempting to protect vulnerable women, preserve the family, and enforce their views of morality and social order.[20]

It was not until the 1970s that feminist activists and other social forces were successful in reviving an interest in battering and other acts of male violence committed against women.[21] The activities of the women's movement and the victims' rights movement and growing popularity of law-and-order ideals have generally succeeded in achieving society's condemnation of woman battering. Gradually, battering was lifted out of the private sphere and defined as a significant social problem, an issue of public concern requiring action. Today, battering is criminalized, and there are efforts to increase the certainty and severity of the legal response. Legislative reforms reflect the recognition of battered women as crime victims, but legal remedies do not always translate smoothly into practice. Law enforcement practices still reflect a degree of ambivalence about the notion that assaults perpetrated against intimate partners or former partners deserve legal action, as evidenced by the fact that violent crimes between strangers continue to be treated more punitively by the criminal justice system.

Contemporary Reforms in Response to Intimate-Partner Assault

Reform initially focused on the police as the gatekeepers of the criminal justice system, the first point of contact for victims. Traditionally, police operated with an explicit policy of non-arrest. Up through the 1970s and early 1980s, the prevailing view was that a man's beating his wife or child was a private matter. Trained to act as mediators and to keep the peace, police officers encouraged the parties to "work it out" or removed the batterer temporarily to allow him time to cool off. Police trivialized these calls, often taking the man's side and engaging in victim blaming.[22] Police received little or no special training in handling spouse assault and were generally loath to respond to "domestic disturbances," as these were not considered "real" police work. They believed these calls were dangerous to the officers themselves, although there is no evidence to support these findings.[23] Frustrated with the ineffectual-police response, women's groups brought class action suits against police departments who failed to protect victims from their abusive partners. Two legal settlements in the 1970s in favor of battered women, one in Oakland, California,[24] and one in New York City,[25] included agreements on improving police practices and let police departments throughout the country know they were vulnerable to being sued.[26] In the high-profile 1984 decision *Thurman v. City of Torrington, Conn.*, citing a violation to the Fourteenth Amendment's equal protection clause, a federal jury awarded Tracey Thurman $2.3 million in compensatory damages because negligent police failed to protect her from her abusive husband.[27] In this particular case, Tracey Thurman called the police numerous times to report his violence and stalking, but the police responded slowly if at all. In the final incident, the police stood by, watching her ex-husband kicking and stomping on her head and body, causing serious injuries. The threat of such enormous liability brought the message home to police departments that they needed to develop effective methods to deal with battering.[28]

By the mid-1980s, most states were strengthening laws dealing with "domestic violence." However, most police department's officers could not make an arrest in misdemeanor assaults unless it was committed in the officer's presence.[29] Stronger arrest policies took the form of pro-arrest statutes for misdemeanor assault in many states. A pro-arrest policy limits or guides police discretion to make a warrantless arrest in misdemeanor assaults even if officers have not witnessed the violence. Police must (mandatory) or should (presumptive) arrest batterers when probable cause exists, even when the victim does not desire it. This policy received support from the Minneapolis Domestic Violence Experiment,[30] which demonstrated that arrest deterred spouse assault better than mediation or separating the couple temporarily.[31] In addition to deterrence, a pro-arrest policy also aims to empower victims who may be too afraid to have their partners arrested, although some critics actually interpret these policies as removing victims' decision-making power.[32] Many jurisdictions require officers to employ crime scene investigation and evidence-gathering techniques so that prosecutors can effectively move forward without the victim's testimony. Under these new practices, victims must also be given information about legal options and services or be transported to shelters or hospitals if necessary. These mandates result in time-intensive paperwork for officers and extended periods of time on a domestic battery call.

Pro-arrest policies are meant to remove or significantly curb police discretion, yet in practice, much of it remains. Assessments of probable cause are often colored by ideological factors such as background beliefs about the "stupidity" of battered women who either stay with or return to their abusive partners, or beliefs about the violent culture of families in lower socioeconomic strata and in ethnic/racial minority groups.[33] Additionally, research examining police discretion to battering incidents points toward many different factors—legal and otherwise—related to decision making when the police arrive on the scene.[34] More serious injuries, the presence of a weapon, victim preference that an arrest occurs, and calls to the police made by a third party all increase the likelihood that an arrest will occur. Victims with socially acceptable lifestyles and exhibiting behavior deemed appropriate by law enforcement garner more sympathy from officers and elicit more formal criminal justice involvement than their otherwise "deviant" peers. Similarly, offender traits and offending characteristics can also play a role. For instance, disrespectful or aggressive behavior toward officers increases the chances of an offender arrest. Previous calls for help to the residence, an offender's history of violence, and being poor or a person of color also increase the likelihood of arrest. In addition, the couple's marital status, whether there are children or witnesses present, the involvement of a weapon, whether someone other than the victim called the police, and whether the incident occurs near the end of a shift can also affect police decisions.[35]

Police discretion is also influenced by their view of battered women as uncooperative and the concern that this lack of cooperation may undermine the prosecution. That concern is not entirely unwarranted, but it must be understood that battered women are operating within complex circumstances. Victims are frequently uncomfortable making their abuse public. Once the violence stops women often forgive the abuser, hoping their partner will change. Poor women may be reluctant to follow through on legal action because they are especially economically dependent on their abusive partners. Retaliation from abusers is a real concern and takes many forms beyond further physical abuse, such as the kidnapping of children or other forms of sabotage against the victim. This situation gets even more complicated if battered women are living in public housing or receiving welfare, as discussed in chapter 6.

Victims who engage the services of the criminal justice system to accomplish important goals such as protection from the violence, getting treatment for their abuser, enforcing collection of child support, or recovering property may withdraw from the prosecution process once these objectives are achieved.[36] This behavior can be interpreted by prosecutors as ambivalence and unreliability, as these goals represent something other than the system's primary goal of conviction.[37] One solution is the "no-drop policy," which allows prosecutors to move forward without the cooperation of the victim. Many prosecutors, however, still assign a lower priority to cases of battering in part because the lack of witnesses and concrete physical evidence make these cases difficult to prosecute and the least likely to result in a conviction. Research suggests that prosecution of IPV cases is most likely when physical evidence of the violence is present, the victim has serious injuries, the offender has a prior criminal record, and the victim's behavior and lifestyle are beyond reproach.[38] While no-drop policies are criticized for depriving victims of control over their own lives, they are credited with sending a strong criminal justice message that domestic battery is not tolerated and serve as a symbolic tool for victims to gain control in a relationship through the threat of prosecution.[39] Additionally, in at least one study, "soft" no-drop prosecution strategies that allowed victim-initiated criminal charges to be dropped at the victim's request were associated with a significant reduction in subsequent violence during the court process and for six months after that process began.[40] A promising alternative to the traditional prosecution for domestic battery is special courts that coordinate the services of police, prosecutors, judges, probation officers, and treatment counselors and can handle related civil issues such as child custody or protection orders.[41] These programs are characterized by open communication among all actors in the system, thorough documentation and consolidation of case information, and a high degree of victim support throughout the process. Another development is the use of court-ordered mandatory counseling for abusive men either as a condition of probation or after conviction.[42]

Another prosecution strategy is the use of victim advocates. Domestic-violence advocates can provide an array of support measures to victims, such as keeping them informed about the case's progress as well as addressing emotional and immediate safety needs. However, domestic battery advocates employed through the prosecutor's office are ultimately tasked with increasing victim participation in the prosecution of the case. Sometimes this goal is at odds with a victim's wishes.

Given that direct criminal intervention may not be the optimal solution for all battered women, today they may employ another hard-won remedy: the civil protection order. A protection order can provide various types of relief, such as limiting abusers' access to victims at home as well as at their place of employment, limiting access to children and their schools, and providing for financial and custody arrangements. Violation of a protection order is a criminal offense, so the effectiveness of the remedy ultimately rests on the response of law enforcement and the courts to arrest and punish violators. This fact notwithstanding, civil protection orders are valuable for the role they play in empowering victims. An order of protection requires contact with attorneys and judges, whose support to victims and reprimands to offenders reinforce the message that battering is unacceptable.[43] Civil protection orders also serve as a means of documenting the occurrence of abuse should a case ultimately reach prosecution and adjudication.[44] Furthermore, well-designed and case-specific permanent civil protection orders, when accompanied by aggressive prosecution, can reduce recidivism by offenders.[45]

In sum, the reactive nature of the system means that many victims of intimate-partner violence do not ever come to the attention of legal authorities because they are reluctant to report the abuse. An incident-driven criminal justice system, interested in physical evidence and successful conviction, is at odds with the reality of intimate-partner assault, which is often a series of incidents that may reflect increasing seriousness, with little physical evidence and no witnesses. Furthermore, most incidents are charged as misdemeanors, so offenders do not build up criminal histories that might influence officials' assessments of future dangerousness,[46] nor are they prioritized by the court system in the same way that felony cases are.[47] In addition, the adversarial nature of the system assumes that victims are interested in public conviction and punishment, when many are more interested in their own and their children's immediate safety and mental health counseling for the batterer. Victims and offenders in these cases are not adversaries in the traditional sense, but instead are often financially as well as personally interdependent; courts must also deal with child custody and contact issues. But the use of special integrated courts and treatment programs, as mentioned above, and trends toward community and problem-oriented policing represent adaptation and innovation in the criminal justice system's response to partner violence.[48]

Sexual Assault and Rape

The view of women and girls as the property of men means that for centuries the plight of rape victims was ignored. Rape was considered an offense that harmed the interests of a father or a husband, and the rape victim was considered "damaged goods" rather than someone who had suffered emotional and physical injury. In the days of *lex talionis* ("an eye for an eye"), the father of a raped daughter was permitted to rape the rapist's wife, "a rape for a rape."[49] Throughout history, the primary purpose of rape laws was to protect virginal daughters in wealthy families.[50] In eighteenth-century England, a rape victim had little credibility, as her own culpability was always in question; conviction of the offender was more likely in the event of an attempted rape where the woman's chastity was preserved or in cases where a husband or father was contesting his loss of property value.[51] Traditionally, a husband legally could not be accused of raping his wife. The first statement of the "marital-rape exemption" dates back to English common law and reflected the idea that a wife had "given herself" in this way to her husband in the matrimonial contract and that this consent could not be revoked.[52] Blackstone's eighteenth-century writings on English common law gave further support to the marital-rape exemption with the view that upon marriage a husband and wife become one, whereby a woman loses her own civil identity and becomes the property of her husband.[53] The U.S. legal system formally adopted the marital-rape exemption in an 1857 court decision.[54] Although the Married Women's Property Acts, which existed in every jurisdiction by 1889, gave women the right to manage and control their own property, work outside the home, and keep their own wages, this progress did little to change the realities of the oppression of women in the domestic sphere.[55]

Prosecution of offenders for rape was frequently based on the social status of the victim and the offender. In biblical times, a man could be executed for raping a virgin; on the other hand, a married woman who was raped could be considered blameworthy and executed too. In feudal times, rape of a peasant woman was acceptable, but rape of a woman of nobility was punishable, and as recently as the early twentieth century in the American Old South, a black man merely accused of raping a white woman risked lynching.[56]

It is necessary to address society's ignorance and confusion over "real" rape.[57] The "real" rape is the aggravated case, where the scenario[58] looks like this: The offender and victim are complete strangers and the offender is armed and surprises the victim. The victim is young or inexperienced and engaged in some innocent activity at the time of the attack and cannot be criticized for enticing her attacker. She fights back and sustains injuries.

Eyewitnesses hear her cries for help or perhaps witness part of the struggle. Finally, she runs immediately to the police, who find forensic evidence to confirm her story, and the offender is determined to be mentally disturbed and confesses.

Most rapes do not fit this strict characterization. The offender is usually not the disturbed psychopath lurking in the bushes; more often he is someone the victim knows and perhaps even dated or flirted with. There was no weapon, no apparent struggle or physical injuries, and there were no eyewitnesses. The victim waited days or weeks to report the incident, a fact that makes forensic evidence unlikely. To the frustration of victims and their advocates, when the crucial defining features of "real" rape are lacking, the victim's story is less likely to be believed and the offender less likely to be charged, prosecuted, and convicted; the victim is viewed as a contributor to the incident, which is written off as an unfortunate "misunderstanding."[59] The result is that rape victims remain reluctant to come forward if their experience falls short of the standard of "real" rape. Rape victims are often further deterred from reporting an assault because of the second victimization they face in the criminal justice system.[60] Because most rapes do not meet the ideal evidentiary requirements for a criminal case, police, prosecutors, and judges are not immune to victim-blaming attitudes and the acceptance of rape myths (see below). Rape victims must prepare themselves for an uphill battle defending their credibility and convincing the criminal justice system that a rape actually occurred.

Sadly, rape is still misunderstood and fraught with sexist stereotypes. Rape myths that amount to victim blaming include the notions that women cannot be raped against their will (they can successfully resist if they really want to); women secretly wish to be raped (they find forced sex ultimately pleasurable and satisfying); and a belief that most accusations of rape are false (a belief that serves to protect men and allay their fears of false accusations).[61] Feminists and others have worked to dispel these myths as well as the widely accepted idea that rape is an act of sexual lust. Rather, overwhelmingly rape is learned and rewarded behavior in a patriarchal society that teaches the superiority and sexual entitlement of men and the corresponding inferiority and sexual accessibility of women.[62] The American legal system also views "real" rape as interracial, with black males as perpetrators and white females as victims. However, the majority of reported rapes are intraracial, where the offender and the victim are of the same race.[63]

These rape myths and sexist stereotypes served to create a unique situation in the processing of rape cases where it was the victim, not the defendant, who was on trial and legally irrelevant information took center stage, rather than the degree of force or the extent of the victim's physical and emotional injuries.[64] Traditional rape law focused on the character and behavior of the victim—what she was doing or wearing at the time of the assault—rather than on the behavior of the offender. Rules of evidence required that the victim physically resist her attacker "to the utmost" and that there be corroborating testimony; the victim's past sexual conduct could also be admitted at trial.[65] The resistance requirement was particularly important in demonstrating the key element of nonconsent, and judges' opinions in the early 1900s served to strengthen this idea. In *Brown v. State* (1906), the Wisconsin Supreme Court reversed a rape conviction on the grounds that struggling and screaming was not enough resistance; the court wanted to see "the most vehement exercise of every physical means or faculty within the woman's power to resist the penetration of her person."[66] Similarly, in *People v. Murphy* (1906), the Michigan Supreme Court ruled that nonconsent required that a woman "did everything she could under the circumstances to prevent the defendant from accomplishing his purpose" and that "resistance must have continued from the inception of the case to the close, because if she yielded at any time it would not be rape."[67] The victim's past sexual conduct also figured into nonconsent, the assumption being that sexually experienced women would be more likely to consent to intercourse.[68]

Since the time of slavery, the rape of white women by black men has been treated more harshly than other types of rape.[69] Historically, a black female slave could not be legally raped by her white master, and even today the rape of a black woman is not treated as seriously as the rape of a white woman, regardless of the race of the rapist.[70] The operation of the legal system reflects societal attitudes regarding rape victims and offenders where gender and racial stereotypes operate in complex ways. The racial stereotype of the excessive sexuality among blacks compared to whites has endured. This means that black women are portrayed as more permissive and promiscuous than white women and thus "unrapeable," and black men have been viewed as being not only oversexed but also desirous of white women.[71] Alternatively, the stereotype of the disreputable white woman who involves herself with a black man can also result in victim blaming.[72] But the prevailing social view of rape as taking place between a black offender and a white victim has served to deny all sexual victimization experienced by black women as well as the experiences of white women victimized by white men.[73]

Contemporary Reforms in Response to Sexual Assault and Rape

Feminist activists of the 1970s succeeded in raising public awareness about the dynamics of rape and about the trauma to victims. Over the last 35 years, the efforts of women's groups and victims' rights advocates converged to bring about legislative reforms for rape victims. Rape law reforms were meant to put the focus squarely on the behavior of the offender so that the victim would no longer be required to prove her own innocence. The comprehensiveness and strength of legal reforms vary from state to state, but the most common features aimed at reflecting the reality of rape include: (1) an expanded and gender-neutral definition of rape to include a range of sexual assaults beyond intercourse; (2) the elimination of the requirement that the victim "resist to the utmost" to demonstrate lack of consent; (3) the elimination of the corroborating witness requirement, since this type of act usually occurs in a private setting; and (4) the enactment of rape shield laws that restrict the introduction of evidence related to the victim's past sexual conduct.[74] The overall goal of these reforms was to render the treatment of rape more similar to that of other crimes, lightening the burden on victims; the hope was that arrest, prosecution, and conviction rates would increase.[75] The Spohn and Horney study that spanned six large jurisdictions showed, however, that while there was some increase in rape reporting (perhaps due to the publicity surrounding the new legislation), reforms had only a negligible effect on key outcomes such as the number of indictments, convictions, and incarcerations, a situation that may be due in part to the fact that prosecutors and judges still retain a great deal of discretion.[76] These conclusions are echoed in other research that examined national trends over a longer time period. In 1993 Ronet Bachman and Raymond Paternoster found only small post-reform increases in rape reporting and in the likelihood of convicted rapists going to prison, as well as the likelihood that the criminal justice system would treat acquaintance rapes similar to stranger rape.[77] Susan Caringella's 2009 review of rape reform legislation studies concluded that reform efforts did not bring about the change or increases in police reporting that advocates and reformers hoped for.[78] Although her overall assessment of the impact of rape reform legislation is mixed at best, Caringella finds some positive outcomes.[79] "One kind of success has been that rapes other than the stereotypical stranger-out-of-the-bushes rape have been brought to court and resulted in judicial and juror determinations of guilt and sentences of imprisonment."[80]

The notion that a married woman does not have the right to refuse sex with her husband went largely unchallenged until the 1970s, when the women's movement argued that the spousal exemption should be abandoned on the grounds that it failed to provide all women with equal protection from rape.[81] Marital rape was first recognized as a crime in 1975, when legislators in South Dakota rejected the common-law exception that granted husbands virtually unlimited sexual access to their wives.[82] But it was not until 1993 that marital rape had become a crime in the sexual offense codes of all 50 states. By 1996, 17 states and the District of Columbia completely repealed their exemptions from rape prosecution granted to husbands. However, 30 states still allow husbands some exemption from rape prosecution. Remarkably, in many of these 30 states, when a wife is legally unable to consent—for example, when she is mentally or physically impaired, unconscious, or asleep—a husband is exempt from prosecution.[83] The weakness of marital-rape laws—the fact that a majority of states still allow these spousal exemptions—indicates that rape within the context of marriage is perceived as a less egregious act and treated by the criminal justice system as a less serious crime than if committed by anyone else.[84] Indeed, wives are still to a significant degree the property of their husbands.[85]

To recap, despite the legal reforms over the past two or three decades, sexist and racist stereotypes regarding rape and marital rape remain, and victims' credibility is still under suspicion. The notion of "real" rape still serves to invalidate cases of acquaintance/date rape and marital rape, where the relationship between the victim and offender relationship retains legal relevance. It appears that "as the victim-offender relationship becomes more intimate, the likelihood that the incident is defined as rape decreases, attribution of blame to the victim increases, and the level of perceived harm decreases."[86] Rape reforms have not resulted in broad changes in how rape crimes and rape victims experience the criminal justice system. While some researchers have found evidence of somewhat more sensitive treatment of victims and evidence of more enlightened attitudes in case processing,[87] it remains to be seen whether attitude changes or other symbolic victim-centered gestures will lead to actual improvements in convicting and punishing offenders who rape and in the treatment their victims experience.[88]

Stalking

The recognition of stalking as a social problem first came about when the cases of celebrity victims made headlines, particularly the 1989 shooting death of actress Rebecca Schaeffer, who was stalked by an obsessed fan. But today we are more aware of the general public's experience, where stalking all too often is part of the scenario of intimate-partner abuse. It is women who are most frequently stalked and terrorized by obsessive current and former husbands or boyfriends, although stalking also occurs to men and within same-sex relationships. In a 2009 BJS report, data indicated that during a 12-month period, 3.4 million adults were stalking victims.[89] The National Center for Victims of Crime (NCVC) defines stalking as "a pattern of repeated, unwanted attention, harassment, and contact." The NCVS defines stalking as "a course of conduct directed at a specific person that would cause a reasonable person to feel fear."[90] The Supplemental Victimization Survey (SVS), which was the basis for the 2009 BJS report on stalking, operationalized the behavior as consisting of unwanted phone calls, unwanted/unsolicited letters or emails, following or spying on the victim, showing up at a place without good cause, lying in wait for the victim, leaving unwanted gifts, and posting information or spreading rumors about the victim on the Internet or other public place or by word of mouth. The SVS considered a person a stalking victim if he or she had encountered at least one of the events on two or more occasions.[91]

Yet other definitions of the crime of stalking include acts such as following victims without permission; damaging the victim's property; threatening the victim, family members, or others to whom she is close; harassment through the Internet, often referred to as cyberstalking; and securing personal information without permission through public sources, private investigators, or other means. Consistent with other forms of violence against women, stalking is intraracial, and intimates or former intimates of the stalking victim were the most common perpetrator category.[92] Additionally, a closer look at the National Crime Victimization Survey's Supplemental Victimization Survey (SVS) data reveal that during a 12-month period about 14 in every 1,000 adults (18 years or older) were victimized by stalkers. Nearly half of these victims experienced unwanted contact from their stalker on a weekly basis, and divorced or separated persons are at greatest risk of being stalked (34 out of every 1,000 individuals). Women were more likely to be stalked than men, and 25 percent of stalking victims reported at least one form of cyberstalking within the last year.[93]

Contemporary Reforms in Response to Stalking

The high-profile cases of celebrities stalked or killed by obsessed fans prompted the first legislative action in California in 1990. The federal government, all 50 states, and the District of Columbia have anti-stalking legislation.[94] Still, the content of stalking laws varies across states. The differences relate to: (1) the type of repeated behavior prohibited and the description of that behavior, such as harassing or communicating, or contact by phone or mail, or appearing within sight of the individual; (2) whether an actual threat is required (most states assume that threat is implied in the repeated behavior); (3) the kind of reaction required by the victim, such as "substantial emotional distress," or whether the behavior "alarms," "torments," or "terrorizes" the individual; and (4) the stalker's intent: for example, whether there was "specific intent" to cause the individual to fear death or personal injury.[95]

Stalking victims can also obtain restraining orders against their assailants, but most states require that the actual offending behavior has occurred.[96] Stalkers can be obsessed with their victims for years, and reapplying for a new restraining order every few years can be overly burdensome, so at least one state, New Jersey, has allowed a conviction for stalking to serve as an application for a permanent restraining order.[97] The advantages of restraining orders generally are that they provide victims with legal recourse if an order is violated, and they help document victims' fear, which is a necessary requirement for most state statutes.[98] Still, even after two decades of experience with these issues, misunderstandings persist. Indeed, "policymakers need to understand that stalking cases: are more common than they think, are more dangerous than they appreciate, and require specialized staff skills for investigation and prosecution."[99] Perhaps this explains why stalking perpetrators were arrested in only 8 percent of victim initiated reports. Police were twice as likely to give the victim self-protection advice (17 percent). In addition, of the victims who reported the crime to authorities, only about half said they were satisfied with their criminal justice experience.[100] Some good news from a system's perspective, however, is that victims of stalking perceived police intervention as the primary reason the stalking desisted.[101]

The Extent and Nature of Violence Against Women: Sources of Knowledge

The legal remedies that exist today to help female victims of violence are the result of hard-won struggles owed in part to the substantial body of research that now informs of us about the extent of female violent victimization. Initially, grassroots efforts brought violence against women out from "behind closed doors" and dispelled many myths of domestic battery and rape. Interviews of battered women and rape victims brought the traumatic experiences of these victims to light. It was social scientists and, more recently, public health researchers who brought qualitative and quantitative scientific methods to bear on these issues, further documenting the extent and nature of battering, rape, and stalking. This section reviews what we know about the occurrence of female violent victimization, as well as some of the problems and challenges faced by researchers.

Criminologists and victimologists have long known that official crime statistics such as the police-based FBI Uniform Crime Reports (UCR) underestimate the extent of crime because many victims do not report their incidents to the police. This is particularly true of violent acts committed against women. There are many barriers to reporting domestic battery or rape to authorities, not the least of which is that victims often do not consider these acts to be crimes when the perpetrator is someone they know. Furthermore, women from racial and ethnic minorities may be reluctant to call the police out of distrust or fear. African American women in particular may fear racist treatment and police brutality against black men or view calling the police as a betrayal of the African American community.[102] Moreover, the UCR data is not detailed enough to allow identification of violence between intimates and acquaintances, which is the nature of most violence against women.

Two additional components of the FBI data, the National Incident Based Reporting System (NIBRS) and the Supplementary Homicide Reports (SHR), provide information on the victim-offender relationship, but these are relatively new creations. The NIBRS has the potential to greatly increase our knowledge of victim-offender relationships. since its core elements are standardized across states and localities so that large data sets can be obtained. Additionally, the NIBRS expanded the UCR definition of forcible rape beyond "carnal knowledge of a female forcibly and against her will" to include male and female victims, incidents where a victim was not violated by force but was unable to give consent, assaults with objects, and forcible fondling; additionally, sexual assaults between persons of the same sex are included under forcible sodomy.[103] The use of NIBRS has been gradually increasing since it was first introduced in 1985. According to at least one source, as of September 2007, 31 states have been certified to use NIBRS in official reporting to the FBI.[104] Currently, 25 percent of the population is covered by NIBRS reporting, which represents 26 percent of reported crime nationally. Another 12 states or agencies are in the testing phase, and 7 states or territories are still in the developmental phase; only 5 states currently have no plan to report incident-based crime data.[105]

Victimization surveys are the most widely used method for supplementing the limitations of official data based on police reports. They serve as a primary source of knowledge about the types of violence committed against women, how many women are victims of violence (prevalence), how often they have been victimized (incidence), and by whom (victim-offender relationship). This knowledge is necessary to understand the causes of violence against women, to develop legislative policy that takes into account the realities of women's lives, and to obtain funding for direct intervention and prevention. We turn now to an examination of some of the most significant sources of knowledge. These include national-level surveys such as the national family violence surveys, the National Crime Victimization Survey, the National Violence Against Women Survey, and the National College Women Sexual Victimization study. We also examine examples of community surveys, as well as studies that employ qualitative interviews, as these can provide more detailed information. Major findings are reviewed, limitations are noted, and the challenges for research are discussed.

The National Family Violence Surveys

Murray Straus and Richard Gelles and their colleagues at the University of New Hampshire's Family Research Laboratory are leaders in the study of family violence. They conducted three nationally representative surveys of households of married or cohabitating couples, asking them about violence in the general context of conflict resolution. While the term "family violence" confuses the issue sometimes—these studies also asked couples about violence occurring between parents and children and violence between siblings—the findings on couples' violence fit our interest here. The findings from these surveys are widely cited. In the family violence surveys, violence was generally defined as "an act carried out with the intention, or perceived intention of causing physical pain or injury to another person" (54–55).[106] Abuse was defined as those acts of violence that had a high probability of causing injury to the person; an injury did not actually have to occur.[107]

The first survey was conducted through in-person interviews with a sample of 2,143 respondents.[108] The latter two surveys were telephone interviews with samples of 6,002 and 1,970.[109] The first survey revealed the oft-cited and alarming prevalence finding that just over 16 percent of all the wives or girlfriends interviewed had been struck by a husband at some point during their marriage; furthermore, 3.8 percent had been victims of "physically abusive" violence in the previous year.[110] Remarkably, although findings regarding overall violence against wives or girlfriends did not change from the first to the second survey, incidence rates for severe battering declined somewhat, from 38 to 30 incidents per 1,000 women.[111] In the third survey, a further decline in severe acts of violence, to 19 acts per 1,000 women, was noted.[112] The researchers speculated that factors such as later marriage and childbearing ages, a decrease in the number of unwanted children being born, and improved economic times during the later survey periods could account for this decline.[113] However, the researchers themselves admit to the criticism that the decline could be due to the fact that the second survey missed a segment of people without phones. Homes without phones tend to be poorer than homes with phones. This is potentially important to the survey outcomes because violence is overrepresented in lower socioeconomic homes. These surveys also represent one of the first attempts to address family violence in the African American community, examining differences in victimization for black versus white women. In the first survey, African American women were four times more likely than white women to report experiencing severe violence. The second survey evidenced a decline in this difference: the rate of severe violent victimization for African American women was twice that for white women.[114]

In their efforts to measure violence in the home, Straus and his colleagues are credited with developing the Conflict Tactics Scale (CTS). The first version of this scale consisted of 14 questions about how people resolve disputes in both nonviolent and violent ways on a scale of increasing severity, from threats of violence to using a weapon.[115] The revised version, the CTS2,[116] contains 39 questions about violent and nonviolent behaviors with finer distinctions about minor and serious violence than the original CTS. It also includes items about unwanted sex, verbal (psychological) abuse, and items that attempt to measure the consequences of events such as differentiating between only a slap versus a slap that results in injury.

While the CTS2 attempted to improve on its predecessor, much criticism remains, primarily because these scales merely counts violent events. It does not reflect the situational context, meaning, and motivation of the event. More specifically, it does not separate violence that is aggressive or instigating from violence that is self-defensive or retaliatory.[117] The CTS also does not measure the cause of the violence, such as the intent to dominate, or the consequences of the assault, such as the type and extent of injury, be it physical or emotional.[118] These distinctions are important because when violent events are simply counted, devoid of context, it gives the impression that men and women are equally violent in intimate relationships, an issue that has been referred to in the literature as "the myth of sexual symmetry."[119] Context, then, is crucial, and some researchers attempted to incorporate refined questions that ask about self-defense, fighting back, or initiating an attack.[120] Still, the CTS violence items or variations on them are among the most widely used quantitative techniques for gathering data on violence committed by intimate partners in large surveys. The difference in men's and women's violence in relationships is covered in chapter 6.

U.S. Federal Agency National Surveys and Other National Studies

Another primary source of this knowledge about violence against women is the National Crime Victimization Survey (NCVS) conducted by the U.S. Department of Justice, Bureau of Justice Statistics. Respondents are asked about many types of criminal victimization, including battering. The NCVS covers a nationally representative sample of 45,000 households. All members of the sample households age 12 and over are interviewed every six months for three years, where some of the interview cycles are in person and others are by telephone. Recent NCVS data for 1992–1993[121] featured improved question methods and formats compared to earlier versions. This improved survey provides evidence that much of the violence experienced by females (measured as rape/sexual assault, robbery, aggravated assault, simple assault) is committed by assailants who are not strangers. Indeed, 75 percent of all single-offender violence against women and 45 percent of multiple-offender violence was perpetrated by offenders known to the victim (intimate partner, friend, acquaintance, or relative), and 29 percent of all single-offender violence against women was committed by an intimate partner (husband, ex-husband, boyfriend, ex-boyfriend). An examination of the most recent NCVS figures on intimate-partner violence, like most other violent crimes, reveals that for the years 1993–2004 overall rates of violence have declined. However, between the years 2003–2004 rates of non-lethal intimate-partner violence actually increased for black females (from 3.8 to 6.6 victimizations per 1,000 persons) and for white males (from .5 to 1.1 victimizations per 1,000 males).[122]

Callie Marie Rennison and Sarah Welchans's research confirms that black females reported experiencing intimate-partner violence at a rate 35 percent higher than that for white females and about 2.5 times higher than of women of other races.[123] It is important to note that the data also revealed that race alone cannot account for the higher rates of intimate-partner violence among black females; in addition to being black, factors such as being young, divorced, or separated, an urban dweller, and of lower socioeconomic status were all associated with higher rates of violence.[124] The apparent increase of intimate-partner victimization against males noted in the NCVS findings, although accounting only for a fraction of the abuse females endure, is a disturbing and potentially complicated issue to disentangle. Chapter 6 addresses the notion of gender symmetry in intimate-partner victimization and offending in greater detail.

The revised NCVS was improved to ask respondents directly about rape and violence in the context of intimate and other relationships rather than depending on respondents themselves revealing the context as in earlier surveys.[125] Furthermore, forced or unwanted sexual acts are directly asked about, and the definition clarified upon a respondent's request as follows: "Rape is forced sexual intercourse and includes both psychological coercion as well as physical force. Forced sexual intercourse means vaginal, anal, or oral penetration by the offender(s). This category also includes incidents where penetration is from a foreign object such as a bottle."[126] As might be expected, these improvements resulted in higher estimates of battering and sexual assault than in the earlier national crime surveys.[127] Still, while the results of the NCVS are revealing, the intensely personal nature of these crimes and the shame, embarrassment, and denial of abuse associated with rape and domestic battery result in lower response rates for these types of crimes.

In an effort to address this problem, the National Violence Against Women survey (NVAW survey) was conducted in the context of "personal safety." Researchers from the Center for Policy Research with joint sponsorship from the National Institute of Justice and the Centers for Disease Control conducted telephone interviews with a national random sample of 8,000 women and 8,000 men (18 years and older).[128] Respondents were asked about experiences with physical assault as adults by any type of perpetrator, and experiences with forcible rape, as well as assaults when children by adult caretakers, and stalking at any time in their lives by any type of perpetrator. In the NVAW survey, physical assault was measured by a modified version of Conflict Tactics Scales that includes threats, attempts, and actual incidents of physical harm, with items that ranged from throwing something to actually using a weapon.[129] Among the findings, 22 percent of the women in the study (compared with 7.4 percent of surveyed men) reported being physically assaulted by a current or prior intimate partner at some point in their lives. Furthermore 1.9 percent of the women surveyed said they had been physically assaulted in the previous year.[130] Finally, these researchers suggest that roughly 1.3 million women are the victims of physical violence by an intimate partner each year.[131]

With respect to sexual assault, the NVAW survey found that roughly 18 percent of the adult women in the study (and 3 percent of men) experienced an attempted or completed rape at some time in their life. In general, the risk of being sexually victimized in the course of a lifetime does not seem to be affected by a victim's race/ethnicity. The prevalence rates were similar (17.9 percent for nonminority and 19 percent for minority women), and the differences were not statistically significant.[132] However, disaggregating race/ethnicity categories reveals that American Indian/Alaskan Native women are in fact more likely to experience a rape in their lifetime than are other women of color or white women.[133] Rape was defined as "an event that involved the use or threat of force to penetrate the victim's vagina or anus by penis, tongue, fingers or object, or the victim's mouth by penis. The definition included both attempted and completed rape."[134] The researchers caution, however, that these findings are based on very small numbers of American Indian/Alaskan Native and Asian/Pacific Island respondents. Moreover, the difference might be due to cultural differences in the willingness to report violence that is primarily intimate-partner violence. The survey also found that 0.3 percent of the women experienced an attempted or completed rape in the previous 12 months.[135]

Similar to the National Crime Victimization Survey, the NVAW data also showed that women's experiences with violence occur primarily in the context of intimate relationships, where 76 percent of the women who were raped and/or physically assaulted since age 18 were victimized by a current or former spouse, cohabitating partner (opposite or same-sex), or date, compared to 17 percent by a friend, neighbor, or coworker, 14 percent by a stranger, and 9 percent by a relative other than a husband.[136] The data also clearly show that women's violent victimization is most likely to occur at the hands of men. Ninety-three percent of the women who were raped and/or physically assaulted since age 18 were victimized by a male. With respect to injury, 41 percent of the women physically assaulted by an intimate partner since age 18 reported sustaining at least some minor physical injury during their most recent physical attack.

Both the NCVS and the NVAW survey also compare violent victimizations for women and men. The important conclusion of these studies is that although women are *less likely* than men to be the victims of violence overall, they are *more likely* than men to be victimized by a nonstranger and by an intimate partner.[137] For example, a report of the 1998 NCVS data showed that women were victims in about 876,340 violent incidents (rape/sexual assault, robbery, aggravated assault, simple assault) committed by an intimate partner, versus 157,330 for men.[138] Furthermore, for the period 1993–1998, intimate partner violence accounted for 22 percent of violent crime committed against women, versus 3 percent for men.[139] Similarly, the NVAW survey found that 25 percent of the women as opposed to 8 percent of the men said they were raped and/or physically assaulted by a current or former spouse, cohabitating partner, or date at some time in their life.[140]

Rape is also examined in research that focuses particularly on women on university and college campuses. Given the college social scene, dating practices, and the fraternity culture, women on college campuses can be especially vulnerable to the "forced or coerced sexual intimacy" known as date rape. This term describes the type of acquaintance rape where the offender and the victim experienced a romantic or dating relationship, even a brief one, but are not married or living together; the victimization can occur on the first date or years into the relationship.[141] In one national study across 32 representative campuses, a total of 6,159 college women and men were administered the Sexual Experiences Survey.[142] The study found that 15 percent of the women had been raped, and 12 percent had experienced an attempted rape, since age 14.[143] The vast majority of these cases (8 out of 10) involved known offenders, and slightly more than half occurred in a dating context.[144] In addition, 3 percent of the men reported having committed rape and 4 percent a completed rape. The researchers concluded that the male respondents do not admit to the amount of sexual aggression reported by women, but this may be due to the fact that women and men perceive sexual encounters differently,[145] although Mary Koss and Sarah Cook's research calls this conclusion into question. It was also found that in 84 percent of the cases the women knew their attacker, and of these nonstranger assaults, 57 percent of the attackers were a date.[146]

The U.S. Department of Justice conducted the National College Women Sexual Victimization (NCWSV) study with a randomly selected sample of 4,446 women attending two- or four-year colleges or universities.[147] The women were asked about their sexual victimization during a seven-month period with detailed questions about completed, attempted, and threatened rape (vaginal, oral, or anal penetration by penis, fingers, or foreign objects) as well as other types of unwanted or coerced sexual contact. The NCWSV data showed that almost 2.8 percent of the sample experienced either a completed or an attempted rape. When extended to a one-year period, this means that nearly 5 percent of college women are victimized in any given year on college campuses. This is a higher rate than that found in the NVAW survey conducted in the general population (0.3 percent for women ages 18 and over in the previous year). In addition, given that the average length of a college career is now five years, it is estimated that 20–25 percent of college women experience a completed or attempted rape before graduation. The study found a rate of 35.3 completed or attempted rape incidents per 1,000 women. Incidence rates indicate that for a campus of 10,000 women, one would expect 350 separate events of completed or attempted rapes in a given academic year.[148] Once again, most victims knew their attacker; in cases of completed and attempted rapes committed by single offenders, approximately 90 percent of the offenders were known to be a classmate, friend, boyfriend/ex-boyfriend, or acquaintance.[149]

The NVAW survey also provided the first-ever national evidence on the prevalence of stalking.[150] The results bolster the passage of anti-stalking legislation in the early 1990s and attest to the fact that although the definition of stalking is gender-neutral, women are more likely to be victims of stalking than men, and men are more likely to be the perpetrators. More specifically, 78 percent of stalking victims were women and 22 percent were men, and 87 percent of the stalkers identified by victims were male. The researchers measured stalking by asking: "Not including bill collectors, telephone solicitors, or other sales people, has anyone, male or female, ever: followed or spied on you, sent you unsolicited letters or written correspondence, made unsolicited phone calls to you, stood outside your home, school or workplace, showed up at places you were even though he or she had no business being there."[151] The NVAW survey found that 8.1 percent of all the female respondents, compared to 2.2 percent of the males, were stalked at some time. Results confirmed that unlike celebrity cases, most victims know their stalker; only 23 percent of the female victims and 36 percent of the male victims reported being stalked by a stranger.[152] Women are more likely than men to be stalked by an intimate partner; overall, 59 percent of the female victims, compared to 30 percent of the male victims, were stalked by a current or former husband, cohabitating partner (either sex), boyfriend/girlfriend, or date.

Because it is often presumed that stalking occurs when a women attempts to leave an abusive partner, the NVAW survey specifically examined the timing of stalking in a relationship. Interestingly, 21 percent of stalking begins prior to the termination of the relationship. The same survey also demonstrated that there is a link between stalking and violence.[153] Eighty-one percent of the women stalked by a current or former husband or partner were physically assaulted by that partner, and 31 percent of the women stalked by a current or former husband or partner were sexually assaulted by that same partner.[154] The NCWSV found that 13 percent of female college students were stalked within a seven-month period.[155] Again, most of the college women, 80 percent, knew their stalker. He was most likely a boyfriend or ex-boyfriend, but could also be a classmate, acquaintance, friend, or coworker. The most common consequence of stalking was psychological or emotional injury for nearly 3 in 10 women.[156]

Community Surveys and Qualitative Interview Studies

Surveys conducted on smaller, community samples supplement our knowledge of battering and rape. Moreover, we often learn more about the content and the process of intimate-partner violence from smaller, qualitative studies that draw their samples from women who have contact with battered women shelters or criminal justice agencies. In-depth interviews with victims reveals that "the *combination* of events in an abusive relationship is often as important as the events themselves" in understanding violence between intimates.[157] Quantitative and qualitative research supplement and inform each other, measuring the extent of the problem (prevalence and incidence) as well as describing its nature in terms of the dynamics of violent episodes and how women experience and interpret violence and other types of harm. We now turn to some examples.

Rebecca Emerson Dobash and Russell Dobash (1984) interviewed 109 battered women living in shelters who were married or living with a partner.[158] The women were asked about their first, last, and worst violent episodes, where violence was defined as acts of physical force (not including attempted assaults or threats) with and without the use of weapons. The researchers determined that although most physical attacks begin after some type of argument, violent episodes can generally be viewed as having no exact beginning or end point. Rather, violence is an integral part of the relationship; the sources of conflict that lead to violent events are ongoing. A man was most likely to become physically violent when a woman questioned his authority, challenged his argument or behavior, argued or refused to argue back, or asserted herself through name calling or hitting, or threatening or attempting to leave. In other words, "violent episodes should be understood as often constructed intentionally by the aggressor," and men who use violence "usually enter verbal confrontations with the intentions of punishing, regulating and controlling their wives through various means including physical force."[159] Furthermore, the seriousness of the violence and the resulting injuries increased over time.

In her oft-cited study of women who killed or attempted to kill their abusive husbands, Angela Browne (1987) interviewed 42 women from 15 states.[160] Physical abuse was defined as "any physically assaultive act by one person against another, with or without evident resultant physical injury."[161] The women in Browne's study related that during courtship and early marriage, a husband's jealousy, possessiveness, and control intermingled with and became confused with signs of romantic love. Physical violence usually started after marriage. Verbal disagreements escalated into physical attacks. Violent events consisted of a combination of physical assaults, verbal abuse, and threats. Isolated violent events gradually evolved into a pattern of sadistic, brutal beatings over time that resulted in serious injuries and were very often accompanied by rape. Alcohol and other substance abuse by husbands were typical. Children were also frequently the targets of a husband's violence. According to Browne, homicide was an extreme reaction by battered women to escape an extreme level of abuse and injury. It was the ultimate act of survival in a relationship characterized by what some have since referred to as "intimate terrorism."[162]

Browne's study of battered women supplements the findings from large surveys that *both* physical violence *and* sexual assault/rape can occur in the context of intimate relationships. Other studies of battered women generally find that marital rape is likely to occur among women who also experience physical abuse in their intimate relationships, but prevalence rates vary depending on how questions are asked.[163] In interviews with 137 battered women and an additional group of 89 nonbattered women, another researcher asked respondents if their husbands had raped them; 34 percent of the battered women were raped, compared to 1 percent of the nonbattered women.[164] Interestingly in this same study, the less threatening the phrasing of a statement, the more likely women were to agree with it. When asked to respond to the statement "Sex is unpleasant because he forces you to have sex," 43 percent of the battered women and 2 percent of the nonbattered women agreed. When presented with the statement "He pressures you

to have sex," 73 percent of the battered women and 37 percent of the nonbattered women agreed.[165] Mildred Pagelow's research conducted about the
same time also found high rates of rape in her interviews with battered
women; 37 percent of a sample of 325 battered women responded yes to the
question "Were you ever sexually assaulted by your husband? (Forcible rape
is an assault.)";[166] nearly three out of four of these women were raped more
than once, and 10 percent indicated that sex was always on demand.[167] Additional research reported a somewhat lower prevalence rate, where marital
rape occurred in 23 percent of 146 battering relationships using a volunteer
sample of mostly white, middle-class respondents.[168] But even higher prevalence rates are found elsewhere. For example, Nancy Shields and Christine
Hanneke's 1983 study of 92 wives of violent men found that nearly half of the
women were raped by their spouse. Similarly, Lenore Walker's study the
following year found that 51 percent of 435 battered women responded yes
when asked if they had ever been "forced to have sex" by their abusers.

In 1998 several researchers interviewed 252 couples in marital therapy
compared to 53 couples in the general community about experiences in the
past year.[169] Researchers measured the prevalence of physical and sexual
violence using modified versions of the CTS and of the Sexual Experiences
Survey. The results showed that 36 percent of the wives in the clinical therapy
group reported experiencing sexual coercion by their husbands, compared
to 13.5 percent of wives in the community group. In addition, 5 percent of
the clinic wives reported experiencing threatened/forced sex by their
husbands, and none of the community wives reported this experience.[170]
Furthermore, in the clinic group, there was a link between physical and
sexual violence: wives who experienced serious violence were also more
likely to report experiencing sexual coercion and threatened/forced sex.[171]

Finally, research conducted on community samples finds disturbingly
high rates of marital rape in general. Diana Russell's groundbreaking study
based on a random sample of 930 San Francisco women asked respondents
about sexual abuse by strangers, family members, and husbands.[172] The
study found that 14 percent of the married sample experienced rape by a
husband or ex-husband; 10 percent reported both rape and other types of
assault, 4 percent reported only wife rape, and 12 percent reported assaults
without rape. Similarly, David Finkelhor and Kersti Yllo noted that 10 percent of their sample of 326 Boston women, who had been married or living
with a partner, had sex by "force or threat of force" at least once with that
partner.[173] These researchers also report that while some men both rape and
batter, there are also men who engage in only one of these behaviors.[174] Thus
marital rape is sometimes a distinct phenomenon but it is also frequently part
of the overall pattern of violence and control in abusive relationships. About

half of marital rape victims report being beaten immediately before or during sexual contact.[175]

Conclusions from National and Community-Level Surveys and Qualitative Studies

The national surveys discussed above show that women are more likely to be physically and sexually assaulted by intimate partners than they are by strangers or other known individuals. Women are also more likely than men to be stalked, and their assailants are usually intimates or ex-intimates. The studies further reveal that a large percentage of women experience physical injury, but most of the violence is minor. Moreover, while females are less likely than males to experience violent assaults overall, they are much more likely than males to be victimized by an intimate partner or another known assailant. The studies also provide some evidence that black and Native American women are at increased risk for intimate-partner victimization, in part because of poverty's overrepresentation in these populations. Differences in survey contexts and question formats can lead to different results. But despite somewhat discrepant findings, the overall results indicate that rates of rape and sexual assault, battering, and stalking are alarmingly high, and given that underreporting is a particular problem, all research findings should be looked at as underestimates. In-depth interviews supplement our understanding of the dynamics of battering and show that violence is part of an overall pattern of control. Again, despite some differences in the findings, battered women are also likely to be raped by their husbands or partners. Other community studies find high rates of marital rape in general, and while marital rape is sometimes a distinct phenomenon, it is often accompanied by other physical violence.

The Challenge for Research

The violence that women experience—battering, rape/sexual assault, and stalking—occurs in the context of intimate relationships, and this intimate context makes it difficult to study. The existing research and writing reflects a lack of consensus on how violence should be conceptualized, what behaviors should be asked about, and how findings should be interpreted and reported for policy makers.[176] It also reflects inattention to differences among ethnic minority subgroups. And given the vulnerability of this study population in general, researchers must always be conscious of victim safety and well-being. We turn now to these issues and their implications.

The Definition of Violence

One of the most basic issues researchers face is what to include in the definition of violence.[177] The debate centers on the question of a narrow versus a broad conceptualization—whether researchers should be measuring psychological and emotional violence as well as physical and sexual violence. From the victim's perspective, violence is a matter not only of physical injury, but also of the psychological harms that accompany physical violence, such as depression; symptoms of post-traumatic stress disorder; feelings of fearfulness and feelings of being trapped; and general functioning difficulties in going to work, parenting, and carrying on relationships with family and friends.[178] In the national family violence surveys, for example, severely abused women reported higher levels of stress and depression, psychosomatic symptoms, and poorer functioning than women who had not experienced abuse.[179] In a study by Diane Follingstad, Larry Rutledge, Barbara Berg, Elizabeth Hause, and Darlene Polek, of 234 battered women, more than half reported experiencing emotional abuse, in the form of ridicule, restriction, or jealousy, once a week or more, and ridicule was considered more severe than other forms.[180] In addition, 72 percent of the women rated the impact of emotional abuse in their lives as worse than that of physical abuse, and this was particularly so for women who had experienced ridicule.[181] Sexual assault also produces devastating psychological effects. Researchers have learned that rape survivors constitute the largest group of persons with post-traumatic stress disorder.[182]

Even with agreement on the definition of violence, the decision on which components to include—physical, sexual, verbal, or emotional abuse, threats, attempts, physical injury, and psychological consequences—differs across disciplines and individual researchers.[183] Differences also exist over which victim/offender relationship is specified—husbands only, any current or former intimate partner, same-sex partners, or any perpetrator outside the intimate context. Also, do we focus on the behavior of perpetrators or the experience of victims? Do we count the number of people or events, the number of perpetrators or victims? All these issues can affect research results and interpretations of findings. These in turn can have implications for how we develop theories to explain the occurrence of sexual assault and rape, battering, and stalking, and how we design, implement, and evaluate policies to address the problem.

Reporting Problems

Survey research on violence against women carries both the reporting problems of survey research in general, such as respondents simply not being able to remember events (recall bias) or being reluctant to answer stigmatizing questions (social desirability bias), and its own unique challenges, which can affect results. Underreporting of intimate violence is a particular problem in victimization surveys because many victims have difficulty viewing battering or forced sex in a marriage or cohabiting arrangement to be actual violence or, in the context of crime victimization, viewing it as a criminal event.[184] Similarly, some women are often reluctant to define a sexual victimization as a rape for reasons such as embarrassment, not fully understanding the legal definition of rape, or not wanting to view someone they know as a rapist.[185] Survey researchers have tried to overcome these problems. For example, the NCVS and the NCWSV study employed a two-stage question design consisting of a series of screening questions to first determine whether an event might possibly be a victimization, followed by an incident report that contained detailed questions about the events that actually occurred.

Other problems when surveying victims include the private nature of the violence, fear of retaliation from the assailant, and the belief that no purpose is served from the reporting.[186] Also, victims—particularly those who have been in long-term abusive relationships—have a tendency to play down the severity of violence as a way of coping with their situation.[187]

The circumstances of battering victims compound the problems of administering surveys and conducting interviews.[188] Self-administered surveys by mail generally suffer from low response rates even when followed up with reminders. Furthermore, a survey mailed to the home of a battering victim may jeopardize her safety if its discovery sets off a violent event; a setting other than the home may be preferable. Interviews conducted by phone with either victims or perpetrators, too, can jeopardize a woman's safety, and can also run the risk of excluding respondents of low socioeconomic status who may not own a telephone. Also, it is more and more common for many younger people to have only cell phones and not land lines. Results could be improved by conducting face-to-face interviews with both victims and perpetrators, as this is likely to yield more in-depth information and allow for the collection of qualitative data rather than responses to only closed-format survey questions. Face-to-face victim interviews conducted in a setting other than the home are less likely to pose a danger to victims and may also help to build rapport and a sense of trust between interviewer and interviewee.[189]

Women of Color

Sampling is a significant problem when investigating rape and battering and ethnic group differences. Studies using random, representative samples often combine ethnic subgroups whose cultural backgrounds are in fact very different, such as lumping all "Asians" together; either samples must be large enough to allow for meaningful study of racial and ethnic subgroups, or minority groups should be oversampled.[190] Culturally appropriate questions must also be asked, because what constitutes violence or harm may differ across groups. For example, Japanese women may perceive overturning a dining table as form of abuse, as it questions the woman's legitimate role and place in the family.[191]

The use of larger samples, however, is only a partial answer. Ethnic minority groups face unique cultural pressures and isolation that can prevent them from talking about their experiences to researchers, as well as calling the police or seeking help from social service providers. The reasons for underreporting vary across different groups. For example, in patriarchal, male-dominated cultures such as Mexican American, Latin American, and Italian American cultures, "family honor" is valued above all else.[192] Many Asian cultures emphasize women's subservience to men, as well as respect and subservience to elders and those in positions of authority. Behavior that amounts to resisting violence would be viewed as inappropriate, and seeking outside help or responding to researcher risks "loss of face" for oneself and for the family.[193] For Native American women, often isolated in rural areas or on reservations, it is culturally unacceptable to make problems known or seek help outside their own community.[194] As mentioned earlier, African American women may be reluctant to report violence by their male partners, fearing it will fuel racial stereotypes about violence in the black community.[195] Similarly, Lori Girshick's study of violence within lesbian relationships found that sexual minorities are reluctant to report domestic or sexual abuse for fear it will increase homophobia and reinforce stereotypes that GLBT persons are more deviant than heterosexuals.[196]

These problems are amplified for immigrant women, who may also experience increased vulnerability for battering and rape. Their isolation not only creates barriers to seeking help but also makes them a difficult population to study. As mentioned above, immigrant women are often dependent economically and otherwise on husbands or in-laws, who themselves may be economically insecure. Their lives are further complicated by fears of deportation if they are of illegal status or in arranged marriages, and they may also face a language barrier.[197] Most of our knowledge on diverse immigrant groups is limited to findings from smaller, qualitative studies, and more research on larger samples is needed to understand the problems within and across immigrant communities and create viable policies.[198] However, as with racial and ethnic minority groups in general, even if immigrant women can be reached, cultural contexts and practical problems require more sensitive research methods and measures.

Ethical Issues

Accurate reports of violent experiences are necessary in order to help victims, but researchers have learned that first and foremost they have an ethical obligation to victims' experience as research subjects.[199] In addition to concerns for victims' immediate safety, interviewers must be trained to handle the sensitive nature of the events they are asking about to ensure that victims do not relive the trauma of their abuse. The concern over trauma was taken up in the NVAW survey as well as the Canadian Violence Against Women Survey conducted in 1993.[200] Both of these telephone surveys used interviewers specially trained in dealing with sensitive issues, provided toll-free numbers for respondent call-backs in the event of problems, and had national lists of shelters and service providers on hand during interviews.

Women who are experiencing or have experienced battering, rape, and stalking are vulnerable in other ways too. Their victim status can carry with it a societal stigma, their physical and/or mental health status may be compromised, and they may have experienced the criminal justice system, which is often biased against them. For many victims, the cultural complexities of minority group status compound their vulnerability. Ethical researchers must take care that the good that comes from a study outweighs any harm or risk of harm to the study participants; be culturally sensitive in their research so that the measurement of violence, the conducting of interviews and data analysis, and the interpretation of results take into account race/ethnicity issues; ensure that potential participants feel free not to participate or to withdraw; offer not only confidentiality but also anonymity; and ensure that results not only make clear the complexities of women's victimization experiences—minimizing the risk of simplistic, victim-blaming interpretation—but also are used as a catalyst for change.[201]

Conclusions and Policy Recommendations

Combating violence against women remains an enormous challenge. In this chapter we discussed the strides made in the condemnation of intimate violence, but also noted that the policies and practices as well as the research still fall short in responding to the reality of women's experiences. The recognition of female victims of rape and battering by the criminal justice system is relatively recent, and the intimate context still presents the system with the "difficult case," particularly when it comes to cases of date or acquaintance rape. While there are signs of systemic change, the system's primarily incident-driven nature is incompatible with the complexity of battered and raped women's situations, and the discretionary power of its actors means that sexist and racist stereotypes, traditional attitudes, and ambivalence can still operate to the detriment of victims. Policy makers and criminal justice officials are urged to seek legislative and policy changes to more accurately reflect the incident-driven experiences of battered and raped women. Specific police and prosecutor recommendations for responding to sexual victimizations, stalking, and intimate-partner violence are presented in chapters 5 and 6.

We also see that just as it is difficult to develop and implement policies related to violence in intimate relationships, uncovering the extent and nature of that violence carries its own complications. Variations in the way violence is defined or measured across the various disciplines and types of studies make it difficult to determine its magnitude and scope and to accurately characterize it. In order to capture the complexities of women's experiences, survey research has been moving toward the use of multiple measures and broader conceptualizations of violence. As mentioned earlier, the NVAW survey[202] asked respondents about harm beyond physical violence, such as stalking and emotionally abusive and controlling behaviors. In addition, the Centers for Disease Control and Prevention (CDC) has developed "uniform definitions" and "recommended data elements" to improve the scientific quality of data in the surveillance of intimate-partner violence.[203]

The use of "hybrid strategies" that combine different types of methods such as in-depth qualitative interviews and self-administered surveys in order to obtain more detailed information and increase the validity of our evidence is also advocated.[204] Data sources such as telephone surveys and hospital and police records can be combined, allowing researchers to reach a larger population of victims, although this type of strategy requires eliminating duplicate counts of incidents. Research designs must take into account the many factors related to definitions of violence and measurement strategies. Efforts to reach racial and ethnic minorities must be increased through adequate attention to cultural contexts. Attention to these kinds of issues will help us obtain the most accurate, comprehensive, and sensitive results, which in turn will help us to monitor changes so that we can best inform those making decisions and policy. It is only through continued vigilance and study that activists and academics will inform the development and review of legislation, policy, and practice, with increased attention to education and prevention.

> "Murders of prominent citizens, children, and attractive women are all good stories. Murders of down-and-outers or those who dabbled in the vices are little or non-important [crime stories]. Murders of black people were not even [considered] news," says media commentator Russell Baker. (Krajicek 2003: 2)

Mainstream media sources are one of our most influential storytellers. Public sentiment regarding women, crime, and victimization is directly influenced by the media's linguistics, visual images, and case selection and by the gendered nature of the profession.[1] These factors express causality, establish or reestablish social norms, present ways of interpreting certain events, and affect how these variables exert an impact on women's daily lives. Television, newspapers, radio, and the Internet are the public's primary source of information on breaking stories and current events, which affords the media almost unparalleled authority to select, define, and construct our understanding of women, crime, and victimization.[2] Americans spend more than 40 percent of their leisure time interfacing with media sources,[3] and this does not include interface time on the World Wide Web. This figure represents more time than we spend reading, visiting with friends and family, or being outdoors. Not surprisingly, there is a direct correlation between the time individuals spend consuming media and their "buy-in" of its images and stereotypes.[4]

It is important to know whose story is told (and how), and whose story is not told (and why). The fewer cases covered or emphasized in the media, the more removed and invisible some victims become to the public.[5] This chapter highlights the media's use of language and female images, the social and personal implications of media-constructed victim-blaming presentations, the media's use of euphemistic language, and the consequences of the media's failure to analyze violence against women as a structural issue rather than a micro-level problem. We also examine the media's overreliance on crime stories in their broadcasts, and ways in which the industry's organizational priorities impact crime reporting. We conclude with examples of how accurate and responsible media reporting can legitimize the existence of social problems, increase public awareness and education, and empower victims of crime.

It's All in the Presentation

Evaluating how the media selects, reports, and presents crime and victimization begins with how it uses words and images. Stated alternatively, mainstream media's power to frame stories about women, crime, and victimizations is embedded in the language and visual depictions used to tell the story. Deliberate choices are made in presenting any victimization incident. Since media success is consumer-driven, presentation is everything. Media scholars contend that when journalists introduce a story about crime, they focus on the most salacious details in order to attract readership, even if these details are not germane to the events. These factors can create a victim-blaming tone: "neutral" presentations of facts or euphemisms deflect culpability or downgrade the seriousness. Americans live in a victim-blaming culture where the tendency to project culpability is most pronounced for female victims of violence, especially disenfranchised and marginalized women.[6] Assignment of blame serves the dual purpose of explaining the cause of the criminal event within individual terms on the part of the victim (i.e., something she did or failed to do caused the victimization) or the offender (i.e., the male perpetrator was not "normal," he was mentally ill) while simultaneously teaching women that any deviation from traditional gender norms places them at increased risk for harm.

Portrayals of women's innocence or culpability are often associated with assessments of personal traits.[7] Determining whether she is a "good girl" (angel) or a "bad girl" (whore) are dictated by the degree to which she conforms to social expectations.[8] In essence, when women step outside the expected boundaries of appropriate female behavior they are often constructed as rule-breakers and held responsible for any harm that comes their way.[9] Researcher Helen Benedict's analysis of how the press covers sex crimes demonstrates its preference for using words that titillate readers and deflect attention away from harm and the fact that a crime has occurred by using terms like "fondled" rather than "touched," or describing a woman as "naked from the waist down" rather than reporting "wearing only a jacket and a sock." If it is not readily apparent who is at fault in these situations, female victims will be saddled with the blame while male offenders are absolved of responsibility.[10]

Another common descriptive technique of the media is to foster the appearance of neutrality and a "nothing but the facts" approach to crime reporting when in reality even subtle references about the victim, the offender, the location of the crime, and so on, can have far-reaching implications for how the public perceives the victimization.[11] For instance, when a reporter notes that a woman was killed by her husband when he discovered she was having an extramarital affair, it implies that she bears some responsibility for what happened to her, and it reminds women of the potentially catastrophic consequences of being unfaithful to their spouse. Social psychologist Sharon Lamb argues that this passive-voice reporting technique of love-triangle-gone-bad muddies our understanding of the gendered aspects of crimes and who is ultimately responsible.[12] Similarly, reporting what a rape victim was wearing prior to being attacked is often justified by journalists as nothing more than "factual" or "neutral" news coverage. Yet the result is both a transfer of culpability onto the victim and a reinforcement of the commonly held rape myths that rape is about sex and that a rape victim somehow deserved what happened to her because of her violation of a socially acceptable dress code.[13] These examples demonstrate the power of language and how even nuanced or "neutral" references to the location of the crime ("urban setting"), the profession of the victim ("sex worker") or offender ("super-star athlete"), and activities leading up to the crime ("drinking at a local bar") set the tone for the story and how the women within it are depicted.

Euphemisms downplay men's violence, hiding their sexual and physical exploitation of women and children: "Men beat their wives, but the media talks of spouse abuse, battered spouses, and domestic violence. The last phrase, domestic, hides male agency and focuses our attention on the places where men beat their wives and children (dwellings), disguising violent acts as well as erasing the male agents. Men rape children but we talk about incest, sexual abuse, and molestation, making the men who commit crimes of violence against children invisible."[14] When we talk only about "victims" and "offenders" of battering, without assigning proper pronouns such as "he" or "she," we conceal the gendered victimization (female) and offending patterns (male) typically associated with violence within intimate relationships, so that it becomes a generic social or individual problem rather than a problem of systemic male violence.[15]

Concern about the words we use and their inherent power over victims is a major issue. For example, in their work with rape victims, researchers Kim Scheppele and Pauline Bart found that counselors avoid using the term "rape victim," preferring instead the term "raped women" so that the women will not internalize the word "victim" as part of their identity.[16] The word "survivor" has been suggested as an alternative to reduce the harm of being labeled a "victim." The term "survivor" sounds more positive and suggests that the harmed individual is now "on the road to recovery, overcoming hardships and adjusting successfully to his or her present circumstances."[17] Other writers suggest, however, that the term "survivor" is not an appropriate alternative for the word "victim" because "as a relational word that throws the mind constantly back into some dreaded, powerless past experience(s), the word 'survivor' perpetrates women's feelings of powerlessness and their perceptions of themselves as victims."[18] The problem is that either we do not know how victims perceive themselves or we are generating our own assumptions about how they feel. For example, in a media event televised in April 2003, for the first time in 14 years the Central Park jogger who was gang-raped, beaten, and left for dead revealed her name and identity as part of her healing process. She refused to call herself a victim; rather, she believes she is a survivor. Her example captures the discomfort and ambivalence frequently associated with the "victim" label.[19]

Excessive Coverage of (Violent) Crime

The second influential factor in understanding how the media creates its image of violence and victimization is its reliance on crime stories. A content analysis of television news reporting in 58 U.S. cities determined that crime coverage is the number-one news category for local news stations; local stations in some cities devote as much as 85 percent of their news to crime stories.[20] It is important to note, however, that "reports of crime don't match actual crime rates."[21] Thus, compared to their actual occurrence, the media disproportionately reports on crime, especially its most deadly forms.[22] To illustrate this bias toward reporting on violent crime, a content analysis of the *Chicago Tribune* revealed that 26 percent of the newspaper's crime stories were about murder, while only .02 percent of crimes reported to authorities involved a homicide.[23] Similarly, half of crime reporting in New Orleans involved murder cases, whereas only .4 percent of crimes reported to police involved acts of lethal violence.[24] In a more recent investigation, the *Los Angeles Times*'s crime reporting revealed a similar tendency to report on homicides at the expense of other types of crimes. Eight in 10 murders were covered in the paper, but only 2 percent of physical and sexual assaults were reported, skewing the reporting of the types and frequency of the crime and violence that actually occurred.[25] Furthermore, overreliance on crime as a source of news does not mean that all victimizations are considered equally "newsworthy." Many factors increase or decrease the likelihood that cases will get media attention. It is important to understand why this occurs so that consumers have tools to evaluate media content.

Crime is good for the news business. Beginning a newscast or news article with a violent act engages the media consumer.[26] As a result, crime stories often depict the most dramatic crime scenes: "graphic images of violence and abuse, journalists and TV reporters swarming the court house for a glimpse at the victim/offender or any opportunity to capture an emotional outburst from one of them."[27] Also, the more uncommon the violent crime, the more media coverage it garners.[28] The pressure to capture crime as a leading news story and preempt the competition leads to obsessive reporting that may result in an invasion of victim privacy, or, in the more extreme cases, initiate stalking and harassment-like behaviors. Thus, victims of crime may experience a second victimization by callous or insensitive media coverage. To illustrate, the alleged rape victim in the Kobe Bryant case was hospitalized to deal with the anxiety and emotional stress that she and her family firmly attributed to the media's efforts to discover novel facts about her dating history and report on her past sexual experiences.

The overreliance on crime and homicide as a news story sends the message that society is becoming more dangerous (especially, or only, for white women), even though official crime data indicate that violent crime is on the decline and has been for nearly every year of the past decade. Gender, age, socioeconomic status, and victim-offender relationship biases exist in homicide case selection and media reporting.[29] Why does this occur? At least a partial answer to this question is that some crimes, some victims, and some offenders are perceived as more interesting (i.e., "newsworthy") than others. When the media prioritizes the victimizations of "worthy" victims over others, and unusual crimes over more typical forms of violence, accurate and balanced reporting takes a back seat to sensational storytelling and high ratings. "The manner in which a story is told may greatly affect the way media consumers perceive events in the world. Every journalistic choice, from the types of sources used to the perspective taken (victim, perpetrator, or bystander), helps determine the prominent themes or meanings within or perceived from a news story as a whole."[30]

Case Selection

The third major factor influencing the media's presentation of crime and violence is related to how they determine which stories to cover and what victim images to portray. As just mentioned, the dynamics of a case affect its appeal to newsmakers. Some of the most consistent predictors of the news "value" of a case are the seriousness of the offense, its dramatic appeal (such as stranger-danger cases), the prestige associated with victims, the offenders' notoriety, the training and ideologies of reporters and their management team, and what media producers believe consumers want.[31] To illustrate, in at least one study 96 percent of news stories on child molestation involved an unknown assailant, even though child molestation is much more likely to occur between victims and offenders who know one another or are related. Unfortunately, only 4 percent of the child molestation news stories mentioned this fact.[32]

These criteria create an environment of competing extremes in the presentation of victims. On the one hand, women are overrepresented as victims, usually sexual in nature, even though men are more often the victims of nondomestic crime and violence.[33] Several studies examined how news sources from across the world depict women in the media and uniformly concluded that women-as-victims consistently top the list; however, images of female professionals are rarely seen.[34] On the other hand, the factors designating a case as newsworthy means that the most common types of crimes committed against women, as well as the victimizations targeting disenfranchised or marginalized females, are regularly ignored by media venues.

To illustrate, as much as 95 percent of all reported crimes against women do not make the news.[35] Because violence against women is most likely to involve an intimate, ex-partner, or family member, it is hardly viewed as "sensational." Also, male-on-female violence typically occurs at the victim's or offender's residence or in another private place, which is not perceived as being as "exciting" as attacks that take place in dark alleyways or other public locales.

The most dramatic example of women's victimization being "left out" of the media's storytelling is the failure to report on crimes of battering,[36] the single most common form of violence and injury to women.[37] When a case of intimate partner violence is reported, it is only the most extreme examples of abuse (i.e., domestic homicide) or the most sensational of characters that possess the prerequisite news value necessary for selection.[38] Media researcher Cathy Bullock's work noted that when battering was considered newsworthy, the coverage was often pro-defendant. In nearly half of the intimate-partner assault articles studied, a plausible motive or justifiable excuse was offered for the male batterer, and nearly 20 percent of articles directly blamed the victim for the violence.[39] For example, extensive media coverage of R&B singer Rihanna's February 2009 beating by her then boy-friend, R&B superstar Chris Brown, illustrates that domestic violence victim blaming is alive and well. Brown was charged in Los Angeles County with two felonies: assault and making criminal threats.[40] Raina Kelley, a reporter for *Newsweek*, documented numerous examples suggesting that Rihanna "provoked" Brown. A CNN anchor began a sentence the following way when reporting on the case: "The incident that sparked the fight . . ."[41] Furthermore, the AP coverage stated that "the 'argument' was 'provoked' by Rihanna's 'discovery of a text message from another woman.'"[42] CNN's online coverage of the assault quoted an anger-management counselor who explained the pattern of women returning to their abusers as a product of evolution, comparing a woman's leaving her abuser to that of the saber-tooth tiger's experience with breaking ties in an emotional relationship, which would inevitably result in the tiger's death by starvation. Kelley's *Newsweek* article reflected on the evolution comment this way: "This kind of argument . . . seems to naturalize the torture of women. . . . In most domestic-abuse cases, we're talking about a situation where one person is wielding power over an individual through, pain, fear, and domination. It's not about being scared to leave because of the dangers that await you in the world, it's about being too scared of what's at home to leave."[43] Finally, singer Kanye West is quoted as saying the following about Brown's arrest when appearing on the music video network VH1: "Can't we give Chris a break? . . . I know I make mistakes in life."[44]

The O. J. Simpson case illustrates that even stardom might not be enough to trump the limited news value possessed by nonlethal domestic violence crimes. Although the defendant was acquitted in criminal court, some argue that the Simpson murders and wrongful-death judgment for the killings of Nicole Simpson and her friend Ron Goldman illustrate the ingredients needed (i.e., domestic homicide) to make domestic violence newsworthy. In 1995 the defendant was tried in Los Angeles, California, for the death of his ex-wife (Nicole Brown Simpson) and her male friend (Ronald Goldman), in what the majority of news sources called the "Trial of the Century." The case involved the horrifically violent stabbings of two attractive white victims, both of whom had modeled professionally. O. J. Simpson, a good-looking former NFL star, is arguably the most famous black professional athlete of his time. Throughout the trial there were accusations of infidelity, drug addiction, and evidence that O. J. was frequently violent toward his wife throughout the course of their marriage. As history taught us, O. J.'s documented beatings of Nicole were not in and of themselves news. The double homicides, however, captivated the nation's attention for months, especially as it included elements of race and fame.

Thus, the more socially valuable the "players" in a crime story are, the more newsworthy the story is. The factors associated with finding a "good" crime story result in the devaluation and invisibility of many victims.[45] Media researchers Carolyn Byerly and Karen Ross point out, "As with other kinds of crime reporting, issues of gender are further complicated by issues of race."[46] Not only are marginalized and disenfranchised female victims deemed less interesting than white middle-class women (meaning that their victimizations receive less news coverage), but the media also depict them in stereotypically unflattering ways (i.e., black women as "Jezebels") and project blame and culpability onto them.[47] To further build upon the notion of selectivity in crime reporting and the media's influence on how issues are framed, communication scholars and public health analysts note the tendency for crime reporting to reinforce racial stereotypes where black males are repeatedly represented as the bad guys and where lethal violence between intimates and homicides occurring in poor neighborhoods continue to be underrepresented.[48] In part, the presentation of black males as the archetypal offender may be due to the overselection of cases involving black defendants. A multi-year content analysis of *Time* magazine revealed that over the observation period when an offender's race was noted in a crime story, it was overwhelmingly (74 percent) a black offender even though only 28 percent of arrested offenders during these years were black.[49]

There are exceptions to mainstream media's pattern of omission of large-scale news coverage involving victims of color, especially in incidents of black-on-black violence. In 1992, for example, the former heavyweight boxing champion Mike Tyson was indicted for the rape of Desiree Washington, a contestant in the Miss Black America Pageant. The victim stated that she visited Tyson in his Indianapolis, Indiana, hotel room, where he forcibly raped her. The next day she reported the sexual attack to law enforcement. On February 10, 1992, Tyson was found guilty of rape and sentenced to six years in prison. By most mainstream news accounts, the black female in this case was not demonized, nor was her accusation of rape dismissed or belittled by officials. Washington may have benefited from Tyson's own violent "bad boy" image and the more generalized stereotype of black men as savage, lust-crazed beasts.[50] For instance, some of the newspaper headlines and stories referred to "The 'Animal' in Mike Tyson," and one article said, "What Mike Tyson has never understood was that only until he stopped acting like an animal outside the [boxing] ring would he be fine."[51] Negative racial stereotypes about black men in general, and Tyson in particular, may have eclipsed the typical suspicion and disrespectful treatment that many victims of color experience from the media, the public, and the criminal justice system.

Another example of how race and class impact media case selection is illustrated in the 2002 disappearances of Evelyn Hernandez, a nine-months-pregnant woman, and her five-year-old son, Alex. The two were reported missing by Hernandez's boyfriend, Herman Aguilera, who was also the father of her unborn child. Hernandez was an immigrant from El Salvador living in a working-class neighborhood not far from San Francisco. A few days after the disappearance, Hernandez's wallet was located near her boyfriend's house. At the time of the disappearance of Hernandez and her son, Aguilera was married to another woman. About two and a half months after the two vanished, the torso of Hernandez was found floating in San Francisco Bay. Her body was eventually identified through DNA testing. Her son's body was never recovered. As of this writing, no arrests have been made. Very limited media attention was given to Hernandez's case until another woman's body (and that of her unborn son) also washed ashore in San Francisco Bay. The second woman was Laci Peterson, and her disappearance resulted in a large-scale media frenzy.

On December 24, 2002, Laci Peterson, a white middle-class homemaker who was eight months pregnant, was reported missing to the Modesto, California, Police Department. Her husband, Scott Peterson, told authorities that he had been on an all-day fishing trip and did not realize his wife was missing until he returned home later that evening. Weeks after Laci's disappearance, authorities learned that Scott was having an extramarital affair with another woman, Amber Frye, with whom he continued to have frequent contact even while a massive search was under way for his wife. Not long after learning of the affair, law enforcement officials confirmed that Peterson was considered a suspect in his wife's disappearance. Peterson denied having any involvement in the case. Laci Peterson's badly decomposed body and the body of their unborn son, Conner, was eventually discovered on the shoreline of San Francisco Bay, just a short distance from where Scott Peterson told authorities he was fishing on Christmas Eve, and very near where Evelyn Hernandez's body was found. On the discovery of Laci's and Conner's bodies, Scott Peterson was arrested on two counts of first-degree murder. Peterson was found guilty on both counts. He was sentenced to death and is awaiting execution at San Quentin Prison.

As long as victim and offender characteristics such as race, class, and social prominence continue to influence the "newsworthiness" of a crime, the choice of overemphasizing some victims and underemphasizing others has little to do with the real danger it presents to the public, and more to do with the social status of who was harmed and/or who did the harming.

Thus, the media's selection of cases skews images of victimization against women in two primary ways. First, it overrepresents certain sensational gendered crime types (e.g., intimate-partner homicide, stranger-assailant rapes, and interracial sexual assaults) and certain victim characteristics (e.g., white victims, famous victims, wealthy victims, victims with social capital and prominence). Second, it underrepresents specific gendered crimes (nonlethal battering, date or acquaintance rape, sexual harassment), and virtually ignores some groups of victims (women of color, poor women, and "prestige-less" women). These distorted narratives mean that some individuals are left with a false sense of safety that may place them at risk, while others may be so consumed by exaggerated levels of fear that they restrict their actions beyond what is necessary.[52] Furthermore, by erasing entire groups of women, we miss opportunities for generating public understanding, empathy, and tangible support for victims. Since the media are often perceived to be an objective and realistic mirror of society, the invisibility of some groups of women both denies the existence of an entire class of victims and curtails the emotional support, intervention, and resources they need.

The Male World of Crime Reporting

Gendered employment patterns within this industry are a fourth factor influencing representation of women and women's victimization. White males hold most of the high-level and high-visibility media positions, giving them the power to direct news agendas.[53] This presence can significantly shape which cases are selected for news coverage, which cases are screened out, and precisely how the stories and victimizations are presented. Carolyn Byerly and Karen Ross found that female journalists believed the industry to be highly sexist. "Newsroom culture that masquerades as a neutral 'professional journalism ethos' is, for all practical and ideological purposes, actually organized around a man-as-norm and women-as-interloper structure."[54] For instance, in 1991 the media reported that Sugar Ray Leonard, a former boxing champion and sports and advertising icon, admitted to battering his wife and to the prior use of illegal drugs. In a scheduled press conference Leonard admitted to reporters that he punched his wife with his fists, the same fists that made him a world-class fighter, and denied none of the testimony given by his ex-wife regarding the extreme physical and mental abuse she suffered during the course of their marriage. Although the sports journalists who covered the incident,[55] who were almost exclusively male,[56] initially placed the battering and violence against Juanita at the center of the unfolding events, the case was quickly reframed as a drug-abuse story.[57] Even in the earliest days of news coverage of Sugar Ray, when battering was still a focal point of the newspaper articles, there was often an accompanying picture of the couple kissing one another or sharing a happier moment. Within only a few days, none of the story headlines or lead paragraphs even referenced the battering, choosing to focus exclusively on Leonard's cocaine use. There is some evidence to suggest that female sports reporters embrace a more humanistic, "less technical" perspective,[58] and therefore female reporters may have been less likely to drop the intimate-violence conversation from the unfolding story, which Juanita Leonard and other battered women might have regarded as the most important part of the story and the one that most needed to be told.

The overwhelming male presence in the news-making business does not mean that "women's issues" are ignored by the press. They are in fact more likely to be covered today than prior to the 1970s. However, news stories featuring women as the pivotal characters continue to focus on wealthy, influential, white women while virtually ignoring poor women and women of color. The stories themselves tend to be relegated to human interest, entertainment, or "soft news" segments.[59] This disconnection from primary or "hard news" sends the message that issues of importance to women are not on par with the "real" or "serious" news of the day.[60] It is possible that the "maleness" of the news industry contributes to the failure of most mainstream media to recognize that gendered violence is a societal-structural problem and not solely an individual-level problem.[61] "The concept of male power is interwoven throughout all interpersonal male-female interactions, constituting a structural dimension of society in which violence against women and other demonstrations of male power act to reproduce and maintain male dominance and female subordination."[62] This interpretation suggests that when the media does report on male-on-female violence, it often does so with the agenda of denying the cultural normalcy of violence against women and therefore highlights only the most extreme acts of male-perpetrated violence.

Nearly all key administrative positions in news organizations are occupied by white men, as are the "go to" organizations that media turn to for information (i.e., police departments or other law enforcement entities).[63] It also appears that gender exerts a strong impact on both the employment positions available to women in the media and the type of assignments given to journalists. Male journalists and male reporters are more likely to be assigned crime stories than are female journalists and female reporters.[64] Similarly, male news anchors are more likely to be given the headline or lead stories, often involving criminal events, and are likely to speak for longer periods of time than their female counterparts.[65] Since males are more likely than females to accept rape myths as fact,[66] the gendered nature of crime reporting may be linked to the media's reliance on rape myths to explain crimes of sexual violence (for a discussion of rape myths see chapter 3).[67] Male-dominated crime reporting and the use of rape myths when reporting on sex crimes can explain why news stories about women tend to emphasize physical attributes and marital status, whereas stories having to do with men rarely mention such details.[68] "Women are frequently defined by appearance or by relationships with others, whereas men are more typically defined by activities, accomplishments, or positions."[69] When reports on crimes against women reference their appearance, hair color, or style of dress, it leads the public to focus on these irrelevant factors while ignoring the more germane issues and concerns.

Yet another facet of news reporting that is linked to "maleness" is the close relationship the media shares with the law enforcement community (approximately 90 percent male).[70] Newspapers and newsrooms often use police scanners to stay abreast of breaking stories, and they interview police officers to obtain more information about the crimes. Clearly, then, the media industry is characterized by a masculine hierarchy of decision making and (white) male perspectives. All of these factors impact how the media views and selects gendered violence and presents it to the public.

Biased reporting on violence against women can have dangerous consequences that threaten women's safety in exchange for sensational news coverage and higher TV ratings or increased print readership. Skewed coverage may result in women's unnecessary and misguided fears over stranger-rape, stranger-assault, or other unlikely events while ignoring the more realistic scenarios of women being battered or harmed in their own homes and/or at the hands of someone they know well.[71] The following section shifts the focus away from the social and political ramifications of news media reporting on violence against women, and toward the personal and emotional consequences of reporting for crime victims and their families.

The Relationship Between Crime Victims and the Media

Media reporting (or nonreporting) on violence against women has both macro-level (structural) and micro-level (individual) consequences for female victims. At the structural level, media reporting influences and shapes public understanding about the extent of male-on-female violence, the causes of violence against women, the most common victim-offender relationships associated with this type of crime, and the likely forms of violence committed against women. The overreliance on crime stories in news making, especially stories involving (white) female victims attacked by strangers, results in "a climate that keeps people imprisoned in their homes."[72] When the fear of victimization is linked to media images of violence, it has profound consequences on women's lives. First, it can unnecessarily restrict or control women's freedom in the public arena, as women elect to "pass" on employment or educational opportunities that require them to be out late at night and/or choose to decline social invitations that require their presence in public for fear that it significantly increases their risk of harm.[73] Second, it misdirects women's attention away from the most dangerous situations (e.g., apartments, homes, other private areas) and relationships (e.g., intimate partners, dates, acquaintances) because the violence they see in the media does not match this picture.

When media's coverage of rape consists disproportionately of individual attributes of a case (e.g., what the victim was wearing, where it occurred, or the mental status of the offender), without placing it in the sociological context of violence against women (e.g., prevalence rates, causes of male-on-female violence, risk factors, available resources), it is haphazard and irresponsible. Furthermore, looking for causal factors in individualistic terms negates the systemic nature of violence against women. Feminist theorists posit that unless/until society accepts the role that patriarchy plays in explaining women's victimization, intervention strategies have only a minimal impact.[74] A best-practices guide for responsible media reporting, published by the Dart Center (2005), suggests achieving these goals through a "social impact narrative" where a topic of social significance (i.e., a woman's rape) is contextualized from a broader perspective (i.e., the social problem of sexual violence). Thus, rather than focusing only on one woman's rape, her victimization experience is woven into a macro-level discussion of sexual violence, prevalence rates, risk factors, prevention strategies, and so forth. Thorough and responsible news media coverage, albeit more time-consuming and less sensational than traditional crime reporting, could perform an invaluable public service by providing accurate images of crime and violence. "Media have the power to dispel the myths about rape, heighten awareness, and mobilize men and women to take action."[75] Media should provide society with statistical and empirical data on the actual causes and risk factors associated with sexual assault, rape, battering, and other types of violence. Hopefully, more news agencies will adhere to these sorts of suggestions.

Media reporting on violent crime is associated with increased levels of stress and trauma for victims and their families.[76] Media researchers learned that the public believes journalists are insensitive to the emotional needs and situations of victims and that the public's approval of how media reports on crime and violence is declining.[77] There is evidence that small community newspapers achieve greater success with responsible reporting, and victim sensitivity, than national news sources do.[78] The alleged victim in the Kobe Bryant criminal case was reported to suffer from a severe case of national media–induced "emotional distress." This revictimization can result from multiple sources, such as confrontational and heavy-handed reporting tactics, questions and reports that blame the victim or excuse the accused, graphic or revealing images of the victim, and the release of a victim's name without consent.[79] When media revictimizes victims—for example, by reporting the names of rape survivors who want to maintain their privacy—the process can add to a victim's feeling of violation and disempowerment. Migael Scherer, a journalist and self-proclaimed rape survivor, describes her emotional roller coaster as a victim of sexual assault and how the media can either facilitate a victim's recovery or become an obstacle to it:

> After I was raped 15 years ago, my immediate need was for compassion and protection, not scrutiny and exposure. The aftershock—the numb fear, the nightmares and flashbacks—lasted for months. What I did not have to deal with additionally, thank god, was the publication of my name and all that represents. Instead, I could choose who to tell and who not to tell. And each time I made this decision, small as it may seem, I reclaimed a little bit of what the rapists had taken from me: a sense of control.[80]

Victims are reluctant to report rape, partly due to concerns that their identity will be revealed by the press, thus causing many victims additional emotional trauma (i.e., a second wound). Sensitivity to these concerns prompted the print media to adopt a policy whereby most editors (68 percent surveyed) decline to print the name of rape victims.[81] The sexual assault charges against NBA superstar Bryant ignited an intellectual debate as to the fundamental fairness of the media's policy of naming alleged accusers while protecting the names of alleged victims. Ultimately, some media forums did not honor the victim-identity protection tradition in the Bryant case, as the victim's name and photograph were released earlier in select national magazines and on national cable news networks. Opponents of the policy of protecting the anonymity of victims allege that the practice further stigmatizes and alienates rape victims by treating them differently than other victims of violence, thus fueling the stereotype that rape victims are responsible for their victimization in ways that victims of other crimes are not.

Arguments in favor of victim name disclosure include the community's right to know, the defendant's right to a fair trial, and the media's right to be free from censorship.[82] Most victim advocates dismiss these assertions and maintain that protecting the identity of raped women is critical to empowering victims by allowing them to decide if and when they choose to go public with their story.[83] Still, others believe that the practice of giving faceless victims a human identity might ultimately reduce the stigma surrounding being raped.[84] For example, in a personal essay printed in a popular women's magazine, a rape victim describes her decision to include her name in the newspaper article. Her father, the journalist who wrote the column, told her that the newspaper would mention only the shooting, not the rape. However, she thought, "Am I supposed to be ashamed of the rape? Why does society think it's more shameful to be a rape victim than a gunshot victim?"[85] This victim believed that if people were more open about rape, women would not be so hesitant to report it, but she also believed rape victims should be able to choose whether or not they want their name in the paper. Her father's column began with these sentences: "My daughter was raped. The stigma from this awful crime should be on the predator, not the prey. . . . We honor her courage in not only surviving the attack, but also in not being ashamed."[86] Clearly not all raped women will want to be named; being "outed" could be very traumatic for victims without emotional support from family and friends. However, for those victims who do go public, such disclosure might help them to regain feelings of empowerment and regain control over their lives.

Conclusions and Policy Recommendations

This chapter examined the power of language and how the media's use of words and visual depictions to describe violence against women contributes to the attribution of blame and culpability or generates empathy for "worthy" victims. The present criterion for media case selection skews the risks (or likelihood) of danger and renders many victims "invisible." We also discussed the media's failure to analyze violence against women as a structural problem inherent in societies characterized by gender inequality. Rather, the media prefer to examine individual attributes of offenders and victims as it searches for causation, a practice that often leads to victim blaming and the emotional aftermath of a second victimization. We viewed the news-making process and explored the personal and sociological implications of the media's overreliance on crime as a leading story and how the organizational priorities of the news industry contribute to an inaccurate picture of crime and victimization.

On a more promising note, we see that the media are uniquely positioned to facilitate positive change. The media's positive impact could be felt through public awareness and through strategies to empower victims by giving them a voice and forum to be heard. Media also helps confront crime through the rapid dissemination of critical information, such as AMBER alerts and notifications of bombings, natural disasters, or other national security concerns.

Research suggests that the media's greatest influence on victims is in large measure determined by how victimization is covered. Sensitive and informed media coverage can be therapeutic for victims and their families and educational for media consumers. A "hot off the presses" educational example is the 2009 *Newsweek* article that took advantage of the publicity surrounding Rihanna's assault by her boyfriend, Chris Brown, to offer serious coverage of the domestic violence issue. *Newsweek*'s Web site contained a piece dedicated to debunking the greatest myths about domestic violence. It urged readers to be informed about the issues and advised parents to educate their sons and daughters about dating violence.

> We've all heard that (this case) should be a "teachable moment," a chance to talk about domestic violence with our kids. But children and teens aren't just listening to your lectures; they're absorbing how the media describes it; they're reading the gossip Web sites. When you tune in to all the talk about Rihanna and Chris Brown, it's scary how the same persistent domestic violence myths continue to be perpetrated. Celebrity scandals have a short shelf life, but what we teach kids about domestic violence will last forever.[87]

One approach to achieving victim-sensitive and responsible crime reporting is to contextualize crime stories within a public health model. In practical terms, this means framing specific crime stories around statistical and empirical data. Reporting of this nature can make crime feel less scary or random because it focuses on base crime rates (which are much lower than the public tends to believe), risk predictors (which arms media consumers with knowledge), and public policy responses and resources such as reporting information on shelters and other resources.[88] In other words, a public health approach to crime reporting educates consumers about the realities of crime and violence and can advocate best practices of crime prevention.

The Dart Center for Journalism and Trauma, a global organization dedicated to responsible media coverage of victims and victims' issues, recommends that reporters be better informed about the emotional fallout often associated with victimizations and better understand and appreciate how media can be used to empower victims. One could argue that, at a minimum, journalists should take a proverbial oath to "do no harm" to victims and their families. Other approaches to victim-centered crime reporting include making victims and victims' experiences the focus of the story rather than the conventional model of highlighting offenders or law enforcement perspectives. For example, the Rhode Island Coalition Against Domestic Violence took a proactive approach to encouraging responsible domestic violence media coverage by creating an educational handbook for journalists suggesting how (and why) domestic homicides should be addressed in ways that convey their seriousness and provided guidelines for how journalists should interact and question witnesses and victims. Some of the included recommendations come directly from domestic violence victims themselves.[89]

The media occupy a unique position to better assist victims and communities. Their characterizations of subjects and the language used to cover stories, in addition to the stories they choose not to cover, reveal how easy it is to either exacerbate a problem with euphemistic, victim-blaming language or to achieve responsible, balanced reporting. An award-winning six-part series titled "Homicide in Detroit: Echoes of Violence," published in the *Free Press* in 2005, is a good example. Here the author contextualized killings as part of a larger social problem of urban decay, poverty, and youth violence, all of which "touch the lives of ordinary people who often exhibit extraordinary resilience in the face of the senseless violence around them."[90]

Thorough, balanced, and empirically sound crime-reporting media can serve as our mightiest and most effective educational tool. In fact, the responsible media coverage of the congressional hearings on violence against women is credited with garnering support for the most influential legislation ever passed on the issue, the 1994 Violence Against Women Act (VAWA).[91] Journalists covered the issues and hearings as told by victims themselves, which resulted in many nationwide editorials and articles. Media coverage focused on victims of violent attacks (such as a female model savagely slashed with a razor) as the primary story and established the need for the passage of the VAWA as the secondary part of the story.[92] "It is likely that this media attention did a great deal to raise public awareness," since much popular support for the legislation was generated by these media accounts.[93]

This media strategy is sometimes called the "social impact narrative," an approach to covering important safety issues by including victims' stories to bring larger social problems to the forefront of public discourse.[94] For instance, the *Houston Chronicle*'s "Legacy of Love and Pain" 2003 series on domestic violence begins its report with statistical data and then moves into a personal narrative by a domestic violence survivor.

> Every 15 seconds, a woman in America is beaten by her husband or boyfriend. Each year, a million-plus are left black and blue by men who claim to love them. They are the lucky ones. Every day, four of them die. Others live a lifetime with mental and physical scars. . . . On April 9, 2001, in Houston, a brutal attack forced three generations of women to face their family's legacy of violence.[95]

One of the most extensive mass media campaigns aimed at preventing violence against women was developed by the Family Violence Prevention Fund and called "There Is No Excuse for Domestic Violence." Nationwide public opinion polls conducted after the inception of the education campaign suggest that Americans now have a better understanding of intimate-partner violence and believe it to be a widespread social problem.[96] Thus, education remains an essential ingredient in creating a climate for change and zero tolerance for the violence that so many women and children are subjected to in their very own homes every day.

In closing, responsible media coverage gives a voice to victims by telling their stories honestly and compassionately. The goal for the journalist who covers stories about survivors of violence, especially violence committed by intimates and family members, is to describe the recovery process honestly, with all its pitfalls and perils.[97] It can show other victims that they are not alone, a critical acknowledgment that brings comfort to victims. Furthermore, conscientious media reporting both teaches the dynamics and causes of violence against women and provides victims with contact information for area resources and shelters. This measure alone can save lives. Without the media, the ability to disseminate this information to the public would be severely curtailed.

Citizens cannot understand a sex attack on a child, and this incomprehensibility fuels reactions of fear. . . . The attack and investigation become front-page news . . . describing the failure of the justice system to protect vulnerable persons, which fuels a strong public reaction. . . . Government officials then feel compelled to act. (Lieb, Quinsey, and Berliner 1998: 11)

As noted in chapter 4, there are several characteristics that designate a crime (i.e., being unusual), an offender (i.e., being famous), or a victim (i.e., being important) as "newsworthy." With child sexual victimizations, additional patterns emerge when examining the media's selection of cases, especially among the crimes with the highest profile. Consider the intense national media coverage of the kidnapping and victimizations of Polly Klass, Megan Kanka, Amber Hagerman, Danielle van Dam, Elizabeth Smart,[1] Jessica Lunsford, and Sarah Lunde, and most recently the August 2009 discovery of Jaycee Lee Dugard, who was 11 years old in 1991 when the paroled sex offender kidnapped her while she was waiting for her school bus. She and her two children, fathered by the rapist, were kept in the defendant's backyard for the next 18 years.[2] The victims in these super-high-profile cases were all young, white, female, and assaulted by strangers or non–family members, and each offender had a lengthy history of sexual abuse and violence against women or children. Policy makers and other officials responded to the public's fear over this type of sex offender, in part by singling out these criminals for differential treatment and legal sanctions. To illustrate, all 50 states now require sex offender registration and community notification, and as of this writing 46 states report using GPS monitoring to supervise sex offenders residing in the community; there are 35 state-level proximity laws restricting where sex offenders can reside or be physically present, and 19 states have civil-commitment procedures for (adult) sex criminals deemed too dangerous for release, even after serving their criminal sentence.[3] In addition, since 2005, every state has joined the national AMBER (America's Missing: Broadcast Emergency Response) Alert network to help locate kidnapped children.[4] In this chapter we discuss what features separate sex crimes from other forms of violence and how these differences manifest in unique legislative responses. In addition to covering the history and scientific information on sex offender laws, the chapter delves into the thought processes of convicted sex offenders and how they perceive their victims. Policy implications and best practices for responding to sexual violence are also covered.

How Sex Crimes Are Different

Several factors distinguish sex crimes from other violent offenses. First, sex crimes have distinctive gendered traits. Sex offenders are nearly always male (about 90 percent), and their victims are overwhelming female (roughly 85 percent).[5] This is different in that most nondomestic crimes of violence involve males harming male victims, not female victims. But in the case of sexual victimization, females are seven times more likely than their male counterparts to be sexually assaulted at some point in their lifetime.[6]

Also, the trauma and injury caused by a sexual victimization surpasses that of most other serious crimes.[7] There are a host of immediate and long-term effects of sexual victimization, such as physical pain, nausea, headaches, unwanted pregnancies, STDs, severe depression, suicide ideation, eating and panic disorders, self-mutilation, and engagement in numerous risky lifestyle behaviors.[8] Research indicates psychological distress associated with sexual victimization is most severe when the offender was someone well known to the victim, like a family member, intimate partner, or friend, because of the significant betrayal involved.[9] Given that most sex crimes mirror this pattern, severe psychological trauma is common. Furthermore, at some point after the attack, as many as one in three victims of sexual assault experience rape related post-traumatic stress disorder (PTSD).[10]

Finally, sex-offender profiles are atypical from those of other violent criminals. Sex offenders are more likely to be white (as are their victims); more likely to be older; more likely to have been molested as children; less likely to have prior criminal records; and less likely to victimize strangers than incarcerated offenders of other crimes of violence.[11] The issues discussed thus far, in tandem with the heightened public concern and fear following widespread media coverage of stranger attacks against children, have culminated in an aggressive social-policy campaign aimed at stopping sex offenders. Toward that end, the first half of the chapter examines the legal history of sex-offender laws and reviews the science associated with today's most popular forms of sex-offender legislation. The focus then shifts to examining what convicted sex offenders say about their crimes, their victims, and the policies designed to stop sexual victimizations.

Overview of Sex-Offender Laws

Socio-legal scholars identified three specific periods of sex-offender legislation. The first wave of sex-offender statutes appeared in the 1930s, when legislatures passed "sexual psychopath" laws as a response to violent and sexually charged attacks of children and young adults.[12] These early sexual-offender laws represented an attempt to cure "sick" sex offenders and divert them out of the prison system and into the mental health arena, where the emphasis was treatment and preventive detention. This rehabilitation-oriented social policy agenda remained in effect through the 1950s, in part because psychiatrists and psychologists were active participants in defining how sexual violence was viewed.[13] As a result, the medical or psychopathology perspective (e.g., that sex offenders were mentally ill) prevailed during this era. By 1960, when rehabilitation ideals were still very popular, 26 states and the District of Columbia routinely invoked involuntary commitment and psychiatric treatment for "sexual psychopaths."[14]

The 1970s marked the beginning of a second wave of sex-offender policies.[15] The impetus for this middle wave of sex-offender legislation is distinct from both the first wave and the third in that it was not initiated as the result of intense media reporting of a highly publicized child rape and murder but was instead directly related to the increased awareness of male-on-female violence against women.[16] Women's groups, often through grassroots efforts, raised awareness of the magnitude and pervasiveness of sexual violence in intimate relationships and family settings. Victim's advocates pushed for legislative changes on a national scale that would (1) encourage victims to report their sexual assaults to authorities; (2) enhance the support and responsiveness of the law enforcement community to issues of violence against women; and (3) help protect the interests and privacy of rape victims.[17] Rape reform legislation and congressional acts such as the Violence

Against Women Act of 1994 (reauthorized in 2005 for fiscal years 2007 through 2011) publicly acknowledged the seriousness of sexual assaults and crimes against women and children generally.

In the 1970s, criminal justice goals were shifting away from rehabilitation and toward a more punitive ideology. The civil rights movement was gaining momentum, and as it did, concerns about the practice of involuntary commitment increased. Skepticism was also on the rise regarding the efficacy of sex-offender treatment. As a result of these factors, by the mid-1970s nearly half of the states had repealed their sexual-psychopath laws, which meant that the individuals previously confined in state mental hospitals were now incarcerated in prisons.[18]

By 1990, the third and most recent wave of sex-offender legislation was under way. Once again, intense national media coverage of stranger abductions and victimizations against children were the impetus for most forms of contemporary sex-offender laws. Sex-offender registration with community notification was the first type of sex-offender law created in this wave. It was designed with the hope that community knowledge of the names and whereabouts of convicted sex offenders would help to allay the public's fears and empower parents by providing them with the information necessary to protect their children and to deter sex offenders through the added punishment and stigma of public notification.

Washington State originated the concept of community notification in 1990 after the sexual assault and mutilation of a young victim by a paroled sex offender who warned prison authorities of his continuing fantasies about raping and killing children. Just a few years later, another high-profile tragic crime against a child occurred, this time on the East Coast. On July 2, 1994, a 7-year-old Hamilton, New Jersey, girl named Megan Kanka was raped and asphyxiated by her 33-year-old neighbor, Jesse Timmendequas. He was a convicted child molester who lived with two other paroled sex offenders. According to police reports, Megan was lured into the home by Timmendequas under the pretense of meeting the neighbor's new puppy. The killer described what happened once Megan was inside the house:

> I grabbed her by the back of the pants to pull her back [into the bedroom] and her pants ripped. I grabbed a belt off the door and threw the belt around her. It ended up around her neck. I twisted my arms and she just fell to the floor. She was just lying on the floor and she was not moving. Blood was coming out of her mouth.

Many states and the federal government (see Jacob Wetterling Crimes Against Children and Sexually Violent Offender Registration Act) emulated

New Jersey's sex-offender registration and community notification act, commonly referred to as "Megan's Law."

During this same year (1994) the state of Kansas sought civil commitment of Leroy Hendricks as a sexually violent predator.[19] Broadly speaking, today civil commitment refers to the involuntary confinement of a "mentally disordered" sex offender after the completion of a prison term.[20] The idea of preventive detention through civilly committing offenders originated in the 1930s and reemerged in today's unique format in the 1990s (initially in Washington State).[21] Civil commitment statutes from this era are criticized on a many fronts: lack of clarity with respect to what constitutes a "mental disorder," due process concerns, the absence of treatment for individuals detained under these laws, fiscal inefficiency, and skepticism about whether they will increase public safety.[22]

Another type of stranger-danger child victimization that inspired new legislation in this third wave is the AMBER Alert System. The program is designed to quickly disseminate news regarding kidnapped children by publicizing the information over the radio and television and by posting electronic highway signs. The system itself was first used in 1996 after a 9-year-old girl, Amber Hagerman, was abducted from her Arlington, Texas, neighborhood while riding her bicycle on a sunny Saturday afternoon. Neighbors reported hearing Amber scream and witnessed a man drag Amber off her bike and pull her into his truck before speeding away. The kidnapping riveted the local community and generated a tremendous amount of media attention. Four days after her disappearance, Amber's body was recovered from a drainage ditch only a short distance from her home. Her throat had been slashed. Interviews with neighbors provided police and the FBI with a description of the suspect and his vehicle. Although authorities searched extensively for the killer, the crime was never solved. The community responded to this kidnapping and murder by forming a partnership between law enforcement officials and media broadcasters. The AMBER system was modeled after severe weather warning alert systems: it uses radio and television to broadcast news bulletins about the abducted child and any details pertaining to the kidnapper's description and the type of vehicle used, and requests help from listeners or viewers.

In 2003 a federal version of this Texas program was signed into law, and by 2005 all 50 states were part of the nationwide AMBER Alert Network. The U.S. Department of Justice originally allocated $10 million for the federal program and since that time has spent roughly $5 million each year to help local municipalities implement and adapt the program so that alerts can occur across state lines.[23] Also included in the federal version of the law is an "add-on" section of the bill, known as the Feeney Amendment, that allows federal judges to levy more punitive sanctions when sentencing sex criminals.[24] For instance, federal judges can order sex offenders (only) to serve lifetime terms of probation once they are released from prison and can impose mandatory life sentences for two-time sex offenders who victimized children.[25]

In 2005, there were two more high-profile rapes and killings of young girls that resulted in more sex-offender legislation: Jessica Lunsford (age 9) and Sarah Lunde (age 13), both in Florida, in unrelated events by two different convicted sex offenders. Several days after her abduction from her bedroom, Jessica's body was found buried behind a neighbor's house. The confessed killer, John Couey, was living there with his sister. According to one of the lead investigators in the case, Jessica was still holding a stuffed animal in the shape of dolphin when her body was discovered. Several weeks later the body of Sarah Lunde was found in a pond not far from her home. The defendant in the case, David Onstott, was an ex-boyfriend of Sarah's mother. Onstott told law enforcement that he strangled Sarah and dumped her body in the shallow pond. The intense publicity and public outcry over these crimes resulted in Florida's "Jessica's Law." The law's key provisions are a mandatory 25-year prison sentence and lifetime electronic monitoring for adults convicted of lewd or lascivious acts against a victim less than 12 years old. Florida's law was soon emulated in a federal version of legislation aimed at amending the Jacob Wetterling Crimes Against Children Act. The bill was not passed before the 2005 federal session ended, so it did not become law.

Still, "Jessica's Law" is believed to have resulted in the current nationwide popularity of state-level sex-offender residence restrictions and GPS monitoring of released sex offenders.[26] Although using electronic technology to monitor convicted offenders was not a new concept, Jessica and Sarah's victimization and this Florida law catapulted GPS legislation into high gear. Proximity restrictions are designed to limit where convicted sex offenders can live, and in some cases they also place restrictions on where these offenders can work, walk, or be physically present. These statutes are commonly referred to as child-safety or child-protection zones or exclusionary zones. The restrictions take many different forms but are typically designed to prohibit sex offenders from living within a certain number of feet from specified locations. Schools, parks, daycare centers, playgrounds, and other places where children are likely to congregate are the most commonly prohibited locations. Delaware (1995) and Florida (1995) were the first two states to enact state-level residence restrictions on their sex offenders, a legislative trend that has become much more common in recent years.[27] Presently, nearly every state has a sex-offender restriction law in existence, has one under consideration, or has local exclusionary ordinances.[28] According to the *Dallas Morning News* (2006), many states have developed and implemented their own versions of Jessica's Law, and the majority maintain a condition requiring GPS surveillance of offenders.

The most commonly cited goals of GPS monitoring of offenders are increased public safety, client compliance, and deterrence of additional crimes.[29] A "no victim contact" order or "no contact with minors" condition is common for sex offenders and domestic violence abusers on probation or parole,[30] and these mandates are easier to monitor with GPS tracking. Having precise map points for an offender's whereabouts at any given time can also assist law enforcement in criminal investigations, as these data can confirm an offender's presence near a crime scene at a critical time or exclude him or her from consideration.[31] Under certain circumstances, GPS software can be programmed to signal an alert if an offender is in range of his or her victim's residence or other excluded locations, such as parks or schools.

Efficacy Issues

Although the popularity of contemporary sex-offender legislation is well established, questions regarding its efficacy remain largely unconfirmed. The August 2009 discovery that a paroled sex offender kidnapped then 11-year-old Jaycee Lee Dugard, fathered two daughters with her during her 18-year captivity, and kept all three in his backyard ignited a public debate about the efficacy of sex-offender laws because the defendant was subject to every form of today's sex-offender supervision legislation. As stated in a September 2, 2009, CNN article by Elliot McLaughlin, "Phillip Garrido was registered as a sex offender, regularly visited by parole officers and fitted with an ankle bracelet to track his movements—but nothing prevented him from being around children, according to a victims' advocacy group." The article continues with a quote from Robert Coombs, spokesman for the California Coalition Against Sexual Assault: "Here we have a guy who is essentially under every kind of supervision we allow. Law enforcement had every tool available to them, and [the tools] failed."

In addition to anecdotal concerns, empirical science is unable to confirm the public safety guarantees promised by these laws. To date there are only a handful of investigations on the deterrent effect of sex-offender registration and community notification. A 1988 California study found that sex-offender registration was effective in helping identify, locate, and arrest suspected sex offenders. However, sex-offender registration did not result in meaningful reductions in recidivism rates.[32] In 1995, an initial community notification (impact) investigation was conducted in Washington State. Investigators followed 125 registered high-risk adult sex offenders for 54 months. These offenders were compared to a control group of similarly situated convicted sex offenders (i.e., in terms of victim selection and seriousness of offense) who were not subjected to community notification. Outcomes indicated that sex offenders subjected to community notification were almost as likely to be arrested for a new sex crime (19 percent compared to 22 percent) than those who did not have to register or be subjected to community notification were.[33] However, the timing of reoffense was significantly different for the notification and comparison group. Those who were subject to the notification laws were rearrested for new crimes more quickly than those in the comparison group: the median failure time for the notification group was 25.1 months, compared to 61.7 months for the comparison group.[34] Does this finding indicate that notification contributed to the accelerated pace of recidivism or that law enforcement simply caught their recidivistic behavior more quickly? At this point, we have no definitive answer.

A few years later, Anthony Petrosino and Carolyn Petrosino (1999) conducted a retroactive analysis of the deterrent effect of registration and community notification in Massachusetts by investigating the criminal histories of 136 designated sexual psychopaths. The investigators concluded that 36 of the 136 repeat sex offenders would have been mandated to register with law enforcement if the law had already been in place. Extensive investigations into the recidivistic cases led the researchers to conclude that registration and notification may have reached victims in six of the repeat (new) sex crimes. In the end, the authors were not convinced that Megan's Law was making Massachusetts's citizens safer. Findings on the effects of Iowa's sex-offender registration law compared the failure rates of 223 sex offenders convicted the year before the registration law was passed with that of 201 sex offenders on the registration list during the first year the law was in use.[35] Researchers found that sex offenders on the state's registration list failed (reoffended) only .5 percent less often than the comparison group of offenders not on the list.[36] Thus, the effects of registration seemed negligible.

A legislatively mandated 2005 study reevaluated the impact of sex-offender sentencing policies on recidivism in Washington State.[37] The study tracked 8,359 offenders released from Washington prisons before (1986–1989) and after (1990–1996) the passage of the 1990 sex-offender registration and community notification law. Findings suggest that while (nonsexual) felony recidivism rates remained constant before and after enactment of the sex-offender statutes, violent and felony sexual recidivism rates decreased by two and five percentage points, respectively. These statistically significant results suggest that registration and community notification may be reducing sexual violence in Washington State.[38] Still, the study could not confirm a causality effect of the notification laws because there was no comparison group of sex offenders who were not on community notification, and there were other confounding factors, such as the overall decrease in crime rates during the post-law-passage observation period and the use of longer prison sentences for convicted sex offenders.[39]

One of the largest investigations into the deterrence associated with sex-offender registration and community notification was conducted by Jeffrey Walker and colleagues (2006), in sponsorship with the Arkansas Crime Information Center. Specifically, using time-series analysis, this report examined the incidence of rapes before and after the implementation of these laws in a sample of 10 states. Findings indicate that in 6 of the 10 states there was no significant difference in the number of rapes committed before and after the sex-offender laws were in place; 3 of the 10 states experienced a decrease in the number of rapes committed in their jurisdiction after the implementation of these laws, and a fourth state experienced a sharp increase in the number of rapes within its geographic borders after mandatory registration and community notification were in place. Reasons offered for these mixed findings focus on legislation and research methods.[40]

Two of the most recent studies to investigate the impact of sex-offender registration and notification on recidivism reach different efficacy conclusions. In 2008, researchers from the Minnesota Department of Corrections conducted a retrospective quasi-experimental design comparing the three-year recidivism rates of 155 high-risk sex offenders subjected to broad-based community notification with two control groups that were not (one group was convicted prior to the law [$n = 125$], and the other control group comprised 155 registered lower-risk sex offender not subject to intense notification). Their results confirmed the deterrence efficacy of broad-based community notification. The 155 high-risk sex offenders subject to the most intense community notification were rearrested for a new sex crime in equal or lesser numbers (5.2 percent) than the control groups (5.2 percent and 7.5 percent), were reconvicted of a new sex crime less often (3.2 percent) than the control groups (3.9 percent and 6.0 percent), and reincarcerated for a new sex crime less often (2.6 percent) than the control groups (2.7 percent and 3.9 percent).[41]

However, another 2008 investigation into the relationship between sex-offender registration and rates of sex crimes and the effects of community notification on the frequency of sexual violence using NIBRS (arrest) data from 15 different states produced more equivocal findings.[42] More specifically, outcomes indicate that while sex-offender registration with law enforcement decreases the occurrence of sex crimes (especially for local residents), notification laws have only a general deterrent effect (i.e., dissuading potential offenders). No specific deterrent effect among known sex offenders was detected.[43] Therefore, given state-to-state variations in registration and notification laws themselves, variability in research designs, and inconclusive deterrence effects, there is no definitive conclusion on whether registration and notification strategies increase public safety.

Civil commitment of sex offenders is also an example of the third wave of sex-offender legislation and an area where the public safety effects are even less clear. Evaluations pertaining to civilly committed offenders are scarce. No study has definitely answered the question of whether civilly committing sex offenders reduces sexual violence in the community and improves public safety, partly because of the definitional issues surrounding who is considered a danger to the community or society, and partly because of the vague and ambiguous criteria for completing treatment.[44] In addition, since very few, if any, offenders are released from civil commitment, their recidivism rate once back in the community is nonexistent.[45] A small number of offenders have been released, but their rearrest and/or reconviction data has not been examined.

Even though civil commitment may produce a myriad of unintended consequences and is tremendously expensive, the actual process of civilly committing a sex offender has undergone little rigorous study.[46] In 2004, however, Jill Levenson conducted one of the few analyses of offenders selected for civil commitment and compared them to offenders who were released.[47] The findings suggested that those sex offenders who have the highest likelihood of reoffending were selected for commitment.[48] The results of this study are unable to be generalized to other states, as the evaluations are subjective and only cover a one-year span in Florida.[49]

Donna Schram and Cheryl Milloy (1998) tracked offenders in Washington State for whom a petition for civil commitment was recommended but was not filed due to a legal technicality. Nearly 30 percent of these offenders were arrested for a new sexual offense,[50] a rate more than twice as high as the 13.4 percent recidivism rate typically revealed in meta-analysis.[51] Two additional studies completed in 2003 and 2007 tracked 89 and 135 offenders, respectively, who were recommended for civil commitment but for whom no petition was filed. These offenders were tracked for six years and conviction data was collected. Here again, Milloy calculated that nearly 3 in 10 offenders were convicted of a new sexual offense.[52] However, the authors caution about the generalizability of these findings because the sample sizes were small in all of the studies.

To recap, the effectiveness of civil commitment laws is equivocal because offenders are rarely released.[53] Furthermore, civil commitment is extremely costly. The annual cost to house a civilly committed offender is four or five times more than the annual cost of incarceration. Washington State pays nearly $150,000 per civilly committed individual but only one-fifth that much to incarcerate an individual in a state prison.[54] Likewise, the state of Minnesota pays just under $142,000 per year to house one offender in civil commitment, but about $30,000 to imprison an individual.[55] In 2002 Minnesota paid approximately $20 million for its civil commitment program, and the annual cost is expected to quadruple by 2010.[56] The civil commitment program in Minnesota comprises almost 90 percent of the treatment budget for the corrections department while targeting only 8 percent of the sex-offender population under supervision.[57] Many states severely underestimate the number of offenders subject to civil commitment. For instance, when Wisconsin implemented its Sexually Violent Predator law, the state attorney general estimated that fewer than 10 individuals would be committed per year. A mere five years later, however, over 100 individuals had been committed, and another 100 were waiting disposition.[58] Not only does civil commitment cost corrections departments a relative fortune; these expensive programs rarely provide treatment.[59] In California, only 20 percent of civilly committed sex offenders are engaged in a treatment program.[60] Because sex-offender treatment produces measurable reductions in recidivism among sex offenders, individuals who assess the effectiveness of civil commitment policies must determine whether these laws are worth the high cost and the consumption of scarce resources.[61]

The outcome data on the public safety impact of AMBER Alerts is only slightly encouraging. To illustrate, a 2007 study finds that although the system seems to played a positive role in the rescue of children who have been abducted by family members, it almost never saves a child from the statistically rare but more dangerous stranger abductions. One notable exception is the successful recovery of two teenage girls who were abducted in California. Tamara Brooks and Jacqueline Maris were rescued after an armed kidnapper took the girls from a parklike area. The unknown kidnapper held Tamara and Jacqueline captive in a stolen vehicle for over 12 hours; they were rescued when a citizen tipped authorities off after learning of the case via the AMBER Alert.[62] The kidnapper was shot to death by police after he refused to surrender and turn over the girls. Thankfully, the teens were rescued unharmed. Newspaper accounts state that as many as 68 children nationwide have been saved as a direct result of AMBER Alerts, but few of these cases, if any, have involved stranger abductions.[63]

Undoubtedly, however, there will be complications and unanticipated consequences associated with this victim-oriented practice. Since the accuracy of the AMBER Alerts often rests on eyewitness testimony (which is often faulty), misinformation regarding suspect and/or vehicle characteristics is likely to be transmitted over the airwaves. There are already documented cases of full-blown AMBER Alerts that resulted from false abduction reports filed with police. False reports are dangerous in many regards. In May 2009 a full-blown AMBER alert was issued in Philadelphia and surrounding areas based on the words of a white suburban mother who called authorities to report she and her 9-year-old daughter, Julia Rakoczy, had been kidnapped. The mother, Bonnie Sweeten, made a frantic 911 call to Philadelphia authorities indicating she and Julia had been carjacked by two "black men" and held in the trunk of another vehicle. The following day the mother and daughter were spotted at the Grand Floridian Hotel in Orlando, Florida. Sweeten was extradited back to Pennsylvania and has pending criminal charges for false reports to law enforcement and for fabricating the story about the abduction. Authorities worry how these hoaxes might hinder the credibility of the emergency alert system. Furthermore, excessive alerts may engender a laissez-faire attitude among the public, to the point that they do not take the alerts seriously when they occur. They could potentially be used as a weapon between battling parents engaged in hostile child custody suits. They could also divert suspicion from the real assailant. For instance, the first AMBER Alert enacted in the state of Maryland (February 2003) was from a call for help from a young father who reported that his two-month-old daughter had been abducted by the driver of an unlicensed cab. It turned out that the 20-year-old father, Kenneth Jenkins, had murdered the infant and disposed of her body in a trash can. He was eventually charged with first-degree murder for killing the little girl. At one point, half of Maryland's AMBER Alerts were based on what was later determined to be false abduction reports, leaving policy makers concerned that "the tool for finding missing children will come to be regarded as car alarms are—more often ignored than heeded."[64] Finally, false abduction reports, and the ensuing alerts, result in the misuse and abuse of scarce law enforcement resources, which could potentially place other victims at greater risk of harm, since police may be unable to respond to actual distress calls as expeditiously as they otherwise could.

Proximity restrictions, which limit residential and employment geographical options for sex offenders, are among the newest and most popular forms of sex-offender laws. There is limited evidence that the proximity of a sex-offender's residence to places where children congregate is positively correlated to sexual reoffending. For instance, the Minnesota Department of Corrections (2003) followed 329 high-risk sex offenders for a two-year period. Four percent of these offenders reoffended, and the circumstances regarding these new crimes were examined. These sex-offender failure rates are consistent with those in the extant literature, and markedly lower than the recidivism rates for other kinds of released felons.[65]

Extrapolating from findings on the 4 percent of recidivists, the authors concluded that the proximity of offender residence to schools and parks was not significantly related to reoffending. Similarly, the state of Colorado (2004) tracked 130 convicted sex offenders sentenced to probation for 15 months to determine whether there was a relationship between where sex offenders lived and their recidivism patterns. Investigators examined the proximity of recidivists' homes to schools and daycare centers. Results indicate that the child molesters who recidivated ($n = 15$) lived no closer to schools and daycare centers than the probationers who did not.[66]

A few years later (2007) the state of Minnesota researched the issue again. The study examined the potential deterrent effect of residence restrictions on the reoffense patterns of 224 recidivists released from prison between 1990 and 2002.[67] Results indicate that the proximity of an offender's residence to places frequented by minors does not appear to influence sexual recidivism. More specifically, "not one of the 224 sex offenses would likely have been deterred by a residence restriction law."[68] In sum, the three research projects to date that specifically investigated the relationship between proximity and sexual reoffending do not support the proximity-recidivism thesis.[69] In July 2009 *Newsweek* published an article examining the creation and current status of Florida's residence restrictions. The residential displacement impact for sex offenders of the 2,500-feet restriction zones were immediate and severe. "Entire cities were suddenly off limits. . . . they became . . . confined to remote and shrinking slivers of land."[70] Therefore, the Association for the Treatment of Sexual Abusers (2007: 7) states that "there is no research to support the idea that residence restrictions prevent repeat sex crimes."

Despite the strength of these studies, a definitive conclusion regarding the failure of residence restrictions to achieve specific deterrence would be premature. Two separate investigations suggest that where a child molester lives *may* impact recidivism. Although not able to test this relationship directly, Walker and colleagues (2001) and Richard Tewksbury and Elizabeth Mustaine (2006) both found that child sex offenders were somewhat more likely to reside near children's places of congregation than were convicted sex offenders who offended against adults. One of the hypotheses about residence patterns is that child molesters make deliberate decisions to live near places where children congregate, to have easier and/or greater access to potential victims. However, there are other possibilities. For instance, affordable housing options are more likely to be located in urban areas near schools, parks, daycare centers, and other locations that are off-limits due to "child protection zones."[71] Clearly, more research is sorely needed if we are to resolve the question of public safety.

There have also been a handful of studies on the collateral consequences associated with these laws and how unanticipated outcomes might impact criminal desistance.[72] In brief, residence restrictions (as well as sex-offender registration and community notification laws) are believed to adversely affect many of the factors typically associated with the successful community reentry of offenders.[73] Some of these factors include stable housing, stable employment, strong informal social networks, and community reintegration.[74] Finally, housing options become limited as a result of residence restrictions. A study of the impact of residence restrictions on the housing options for sex offenders in one Florida County found that about 95 percent of the urban communities fall within the exclusion zones.[75] One of the most troubling results of this is the colony of over 70 homeless sex offenders who live under the Julia Tuttle Causeway, near Miami's Biscayne Bay. The men and women who live under the bridge say the sex-offender residence restriction policies make it impossible for them to secure suitable housing.[76] Furthermore, these laws appear to result in the relocation of many offenders who previously lived in urban settings into more rural communities, which typically offer fewer of the resources and supports they need to stay crime-free.[77] "If sex offenders are forced to live in areas that afford them little access to treatment facilities and programs, successful reentry may not be realized."[78] Susan Brown-McBride, chair of the California Sex Offender Management Board, says this about residence restrictions: "This very well-intentioned policy is making the public less safe. It destabilizes [offenders] by making them homeless."[79]

With respect to electronic monitoring of released offenders, we know more about its fiscal impact on offenders and states than about its direct consequences on public safety. The cost of GPS, for the state and for the offender, varies by jurisdiction. According to Tracy Brown and colleagues (2007), the average total cost per unit per day is about $15 for active GPS and $13 for passive tracking systems, while other research reflects a lower average daily rate of $8 for active real-time tracking systems and half that for passive GPS.[80] Some critics argue that the high costs of electronic monitoring are unwarranted, given that it can only reveal an offender's whereabouts, not prevent crime. However, even the highest estimates are considerably lower than incarceration costs, which exceed $80 daily or nearly $30,000 annually[81] and much lower than the roughly $100,000 to $150,000 per year for civil commitment. Others have noted that GPS use can alleviate jail and prison overcrowding by providing judges or criminal justice officials with a more intensive community-based supervision option, making probation or parole a reasonable, if not preferable, choice for more offenders.[82]

Despite the potential strengths of GPS monitoring, it cannot prevent crimes; it only serves as a warning of an offender's location and enhances community supervision by making it easier for officers to monitor offenders' whereabouts.[83] According to a *USA Today* (2006) article, empirical data do *not* support the notion that GPS technology prevents sexual assaults.[84] In reality, the only way the criminal justice system can ensure that offenders do not recidivate is through lifetime incarceration/commitment or the implementation of the death penalty. These options are problematic on fiscal, legal, and moral grounds.

There are several pragmatic limitations with today's use of GPS as a community supervision tool. Common problems include equipment failure, lack of tamper-proof bracelets, and loss of GPS signals. As a result of these factors and others, a survey of criminal justice agencies found that investigating the actual cause of a GPS "violation" (i.e., offender rule breaking or technical failure) can be difficult, if not impossible. Furthermore, some geographical areas and/or offender employment positions are not conducive to GPS tracking. The common perception that GPS tracking prevents crimes can lead to a false sense of security.[85] As one released sex offender pointed out, monitoring "tells you where the offender is, not what he's doing."[86] Furthermore, some sex offenders will recidivate even with GPS monitoring.

In sum, the first part of this chapter has placed sex-offender laws into a socio-legal context to examine many of the concerns, perspectives, and fears that affect public policies regarding sexual victimizations. In doing so, we asked tough questions about the likelihood of these legal initiatives to better protect victims from sex crimes and/or child abduction. Unfortunately, there is limited empirical support for the efficacy of most of these policies. The implications of this conclusion is addressed later. We now shift our focus. In the second half of this chapter, we reveal what a group of male sex-offender probationers say about the criminal justice system that punished them for their crimes, what led them to commit their criminal sex offense(s), and what they think about their victims. Similar to journalistic strategies reported in chapter 4, sex offenders often feed into common victim-blaming ideology by displacing responsibility for their crimes onto their victims and minimizing victim harm.

In Their Own Words

This section presents selected results from a larger study in which 29 convicted male sex offenders talked about their crimes, their victims, and their opinion on the criminal justice system's ability to deter future acts of sexual violence.[87] The offenders included in this analysis were selected specifically because they were serving a term of probation rather than being sent to prison. Their perceptions toward victims and criminal deterrence are particularly relevant because they are living in the community—the public's worst nightmare. Each offender was assigned to both a probation officer and a surveillance officer to monitor his activities and assess his compliance with court orders. Each participant also had a counselor and was part of a treatment group. These counseling sessions were held at least once per week.

Victim-Offender Characteristics

Roughly 85 percent of the probationers within this specialized caseload were friends or family members of their victims. Forty-one percent of the probation cases examined here involved child victims (90 percent of these victims were female children). Only about 20 percent of these sex offenders committed rape against adult women. An almost equal number of probationers (17 percent) were on probation for offenses similar to statutory rape. In other words, these men described their arrests as resulting from "sex" with dating partners or acquaintances, but these individuals were under the legal age of consent in the state where these data were collected. Finally, nearly one in four of the probationers who were interviewed were convicted of possession of child pornography, public indecency, or Internet solicitation of a minor.

Offender Traits

The mean age for this sample was 33 years old, and more than half of the sex offenders were nonwhite (predominantly Hispanic and black). By contrast, much of the extant literature finds that convicted sex offenders are overwhelmingly white. Perhaps the racial difference in our sample stems from the fact that it is a probation sample, whereas many of the investigations on convicted sex offenders were conducted on prison populations. Over half of the probationers were not married at the time of the offense, and most of these offenders had completed high school or attended some college. As a group, on average, these men were employed 9 of the 12 months in the year these data were collected. Manual labor (predominantly in the construction industry) was the most common job. Four out of 10 probationers indicated that they too were victims of sexual or physical abuse at some point, usually during childhood. Finally, less than two in ten men had previous felony convictions of any kind, and the average time served on probation was 31 months. Nearly all of the probationers were at least four years beyond the date of their arrest.

Sex-Offender Program

A "containment approach" to community-based sex-offender supervision has three main components.[88] One, intensive supervision of sex offenders is mandated and includes weekly or biweekly office visits to the probation officer, community surveillance of the offender, polygraph (or other objective testing) examinations, and verification of other important information. Two, the probation program's primary objectives are successful completion of a cognitive-behavioral and relapse-prevention group therapy, where empathy for victims and offender acceptance of responsibility are required for successful completion. Third, close working relationships between community partners—courts, police, probation officers, and clinicians—is crucial.[89] One of the distinguishing attributes of this form of community-based supervision is its sensitivity to victims. For example, victims have access to their offender's probation officer and an opportunity to request special sanctions during sentencing, such as "no contact" orders and restitution for related therapeutic or medical issues; traditional probation often does not consider these "extras." Furthermore, as noted above, victim empathy and offender accountability are prioritized features of the behavior-modification portion of the containment approach. The prominence of sex-crime victims and the policy of victim protection forces both probation officers and probation departments to consider the victims' risks and needs.

The Blame Game

When offenders were asked to discuss the actions that led to their arrest for a sex crime, approximately 60 percent of them attributed at least some degree of responsibility to their victim. It is interesting to see how the psychological distancing of wrongdoing plays itself out within the context of victim-offender relationships. Many of these offenders committed crimes similar to statutory rape. When this occurred, offenders projected all or partial blame for the sex act onto the victim. Kevin,[90] for example, was 18 years of age when arrested for attempted criminal sexual abuse of a minor three years younger than him. This is what he says when asked to describe the event: "I had no idea this girl was younger than me. She told me she was 18. She looked like she was 18. How was I to know she was lying to me and that she was only turning 15 [years old]? *She* came on to me. She seemed to know what she was doing. And she sure didn't look 15 [years old]." Because his victim "lied" about being of legal age to consent to sexual activity, Kevin felt he had not done anything wrong. Statutory rape is examined further in the final chapter, including victim perspectives on the issue.

Lawrence was also an 18-year-old man when he was arrested for his sex crime. His case is similar to the above situation in that he, too, asserts that his victim said she was older than she actually was. This is how Lawrence describes it:

> I got a call from a young lady and she wanted me to meet a friend of hers. I took them both out to dinner and we went back and we watched movies. My friend who called me and invited me out is my age [18]. I knew her for a couple of years. I asked her, "How old is she [the victim]?" And she says, "Well, she just turned 18." This girl I met, she was very attractive. She had on one of those little cut-off shirts, and then pounds of makeup so you really could not tell that she was 16 years old. One thing led to another; we had intercourse. I did not know she was only sixteen but the criminal justice system does not care about that. They don't care that she told me she was older. "You had sex with a minor, end of story."

This excerpt illustrates the offender's belief that because he was "duped" by these girls and lured in by the victim's appearance, this somehow negates his moral or criminal responsibility.

Although the tendency for offenders to project blame onto the victim and away from their own actions was most pronounced in cases involving sexual contact between a young adult and a teenager, and in cases where offenders were on probation for less than six months, victim blaming was not isolated to statutory rape instances. For instance, Marcus, a middle-aged man who is on probation for criminal sexual abuse against two boys (ages 13 and 11), states,

> These boys [the victim and his younger brother] needed someone to love them. They were lookin' for help and I was givin' them help because they asked me to and I got too close to them. They were lookin' at me, askin' me to adopt them, you know, and then *they* started huggin' on me and this caused this whole mixed-up emotional thing to happen in me.

Marcus blames the boys for what happened, declaring that *they* came to him and *they* started being physical and affectionate with him, which he says led to his confusion and the subsequent molestation. The "blame game" cases were similar in that offenders confessed to their crimes but simultaneously projected blame onto the victim. The actions of offenders in statutory rape cases involving victims only a few years their junior is generally viewed as less serious than sex crimes with child victims or in cases where the age gap between victim and offender is vast. Chapter 7 explores the evolving and contradictory views of underage women (i.e., in a legal sense these are statutory rape victims) involved in sexual relationships with older men. As the forthcoming discussion reveals in great depth, labeling these women "victims" is complicated, as is their own perception of the event over their life course.

No Big Deal

When talking about victims, offenders minimized the seriousness of their crimes. It was difficult to discern whether they actually believed what they had done was "no big deal" or whether these offenders employed a neutralization technique. Gresham Sykes and David Matza (1957) discovered that people attempt to downgrade the wrongfulness or deviance of something by describing it in more socially acceptable ways. Fifty percent of the offenders engaged in neutralizing or minimizing techniques at least one time during the interview. For example, Marcus, who was convicted of molesting a teenage male, described his crime as follows:

> It was not a big thing really, that I did. Basically, what happened is I was just touchin' his privates with my hand. But it ain't like I put my hand down through his pants or nothin' like that. I was just respondin' to him huggin' on me. It only happened two different times. The first time that it happened I was sorry and told him it should never have happened and then when he came back again with more [personal] troubles it happened again just touchin' him and then that was the end if it. And I paid a big price for it, you know. (All emphasis added)

Marcus engaged in neutralizing or minimizing techniques by using adjectives such as "just," "it" (meaning the sexual assault), and "only" to describe what he did to his victim. It was not possible to determine if Marcus used neutral and benign terms to describe his actions because he truly did not view his crime as serious or if he was just trying to present a more positive image of himself.

Larry was convicted of aggravated criminal sexual abuse for having sex with his underage female cousin. Although Larry was quick to take responsibility for what happened and actually turned himself in to the police prior to the victim's reporting the sexual assault, he nonetheless minimized the wrongfulness of his actions:

> You see, what happened is that I reconnected with this part of my family at a funeral [of another family member]. My uncle was a Vietnam veteran who was suffering from PTSD. He had financial problems and difficulties raising his daughter, my cousin. My uncle asked me to move in with them and help out with bills and stuff. My cousin lived there and a lot of drug abuse and substance abuse was goin' on, lot of dysfunction, he [the victim's father] was gone a lot, this and that, she was 16—looked older, *it was that kind of thing. We got closer than we should have.* I mean, we had sexual intercourse. I was on crack and some other drugs so *I was not in my right mind at the time.* I tried to get my cousin some help. I called her mother and said "Get her out of here." My cousin wanted to run away with me. She wanted to run away and get married. I am thinking *it,* what happened with us and all, was *no big deal* and this is getting way out of hand. So, I went to the police and told them "I had sex with a teenage girl." And I understand that legally she cannot consent so they arrested me. (All emphasis added)

Larry took responsibility for his actions while simultaneously minimizing the seriousness of what he did. Larry attempted to salvage his image as a "good guy" by placing the events in a context of a caring, helpful family member who simply "got closer [to his cousin] than he should have."

Gene, who was convicted of aggravated criminal sexual assault of an adult female, sounded similar in his attempts to minimize his wrongdoing:

> Gene: Alcohol is a part of this whole thing because it lowers my inhibitions . . . extremely. . . . I'm as normal a guy as you will find. I'm kinda like a shy person, but when I am drinking, I mean, I let everything loose. And I become extremely sexually active. I'm like a happy, a happy drunk, but in this, in the same sense I'm a dangerous drunk when it comes to the females.
>
> Interviewer: Do you mean you won't take no for an answer from a woman to any sexual advances you make towards her or do you mean something else when you say you can be a "dangerous drunk"?
>
> Gene: Yes, that is exactly what I am sayin'. When I get in that frame of mind I won't take no for an answer from her. And basically, in this case, what happened was . . . I mean, it wasn't a forceful thing, at all, ah, *basically all that happened* was that I tried taking

advantage of somebody while they were sleeping. And, as far as what I did, *all I did* was touching her privates in hopes of basically arousing her. I guess I might've done the wrong thing.

Taken collectively, the examples demonstrate that most sex offenders admit to only a certain degree of inappropriate conduct. For some, even this partial admission of responsibility may be an artifact of their probation and treatment requirement. As noted previously, a containment approach to sex-offender management dictates that offenders admit their role in committing sex crime(s) to probation officers and sex-offender treatment providers. If offenders fail to admit their guilt and to accept responsibility for their criminal wrongdoing, they are considered uncooperative and untreatable and therefore in violation of probation. It is also likely that offenders, like the rest of us, want to present the most positive image of themselves. Admitting only to less serious and less devious actions in these interviews may have allowed these men to save face about an embarrassing and shameful ordeal.

Accepting Responsibility

When asked to describe the events that led to their arrest, offenders often engage in victim blaming by projecting at least some of the responsibility for the crime onto the victim herself or himself. Offenders suggest that either the victim (including minors) initiated the sexual contact or that the victim wished for it to occur. In other words, offenders often deny the wrongfulness of their own behavior. However, there was a noticeable shift in how many of the offenders viewed their victims at the time of the interview compared to how they viewed them when the crime initially occurred. Slightly more than half of these men did in fact eventually accept full responsibility for the crime and talked at length about their remorse over the psychological trauma and harm they caused their victims. Taking personal responsibility for behavior and establishing victim empathy are other components to the containment approach to supervising sex offenders in a community-based setting. Research findings associate victim empathy and acceptance of responsibility with increases in desistance among sex offenders.[91]

The last two themes illustrate a shift in the way many of these offenders view themselves and their victims. Slightly more than 50 percent of the sex offenders interviewed in this study (16 of the 29 men) said they eventually reached a point where they accepted full responsibility for their behavior. Initially, the men did not believe they were completely or primarily at fault for what occurred with their victims. Rather, many of them described a transformation of thought influenced by treatment and personal introspection. The sincerity and reality of transformations are questionable when one is dealing with manipulative subjects. However, even the normally suspicious probation officers—for reasons that will be clearer in the following paragraphs—believe the changes described below are real. Jermaine, a man in his early twenties, was convicted of aggravated criminal sexual abuse of a 16-year-old female whom he had met only hours before their sexual encounter. Initially, Jermaine said he was hostile toward his victim (for misleading him into believing she was older than she really was), the police, and the probation department. However, Jermaine said he now understands things differently:

> I am guilty of not being smart, not being responsible, and not making good decisions. I see that now. I used to point the finger at her [the victim] and think this is your fault. I am the victim here! You lied to me. 'Cause of treatment and talking to my PO [probation officer] I now understand what *I* [emphasis original] did to cause this. *I* should have been more aware. *I* should have paid more attention to her age, to how she was acting. Heck, *I* should have actually found out how old she was before I had sex with her. I mean, I should have just been more responsible, more aware of things that go on in front of me instead of just let my mind and my actions go somewhere else.

According to probation and treatment records, Jermaine was extremely difficult to work with in the initial months of his probation term, as he felt he was treated unjustly by the criminal justice system that viewed him as a sex offender, a label he rejected. However, later reports showed gradual but significant improvement in his attitude, demeanor, and progress in treatment. The shift in his perspective on the crime appeared genuine. The motivations for Jermaine to misrepresent his true feelings about the event seemed minimal because at the time of the interview he had already successfully completed his treatment and was no longer required to report to probation. Perhaps the rehabilitation process worked for Jermaine and facilitated the goals of developing personal responsibility and victim empathy, which are crucial for lowering recidivism[92]

Shane was 19 years old when he was arrested for having sex with an acquaintance four years his junior. Shane said he met the victim while out "cruising" with friends one Friday night. He and his friends pulled up beside a car with several females inside. Shane says they asked the girls to pull the car over, and they complied. Shane said he started walking and talking with his victim, whom he said "looked older than me." This was Shane's reaction to learning her actual age:

> After hanging out some that night we all decided to go to one of the girl's parents houses to have a party. Somebody bought beer and there was other drinks too. And lots of other people and loud music. Me and her went upstairs to one of the bedrooms so we could talk and whatever. One thing led to another and we were fooling around and ended up having sex. Then, I noticed that she bled on the bed. And I thought, oh my god. And then this other girl's dad [another girl's parent and the homeowner] walks in on us and sees what is going on. At first I thought he was mad because I had had sex in his house. I can understand that. I'd be pretty upset too if my daughter had some girl over who had sex in my bed. And then the dad says "Do you know how old this girl is? She is only 15." I could have dropped to my knees in shame. I went to the cops and I said, "I just had sex with a minor, I didn't know she was a minor, and I want to do the right thing." The cops laughed at me and gave me a piece of paper and said here, go hang yourself with a confession. So I did a statement and I was arrested sometime later after they interviewed the girl and all. But I had to tell. I had to do the right thing after doing such a wrong thing.

Shane was one of the few offenders who accepted full responsibility for his actions from the beginning. This was rare within this group.

Finally, Bill, who was convicted of aggravated criminal sexual abuse of a minor female and possession of child pornography, had this to say about his actions:

> I didn't have any priors [prior convictions] when this happened. I had never done drugs or alcohol, none of that stuff. I crossed the line with this one, though. I met this girl on the Internet. I knew she was younger. I mean, I ain't going to lie to you, I knew all along she was a young girl. I didn't admit that at first to nobody, because I was ashamed, but I did know. I broke the law by talking her into having sex with me. It wasn't "rape" I guess because I didn't force her with anything but I did talk her into it with my words and she was too young to know what she was getting into. It's an ugly thing I did. I used to kid myself that I didn't do nothing wrong because she said okay to anything I asked her to do. But now I understand *exactly* [emphasis original] what I did wrong. I talked her into it. I

tricked her into it. And then I tricked myself so I wouldn't feel like
I was doing nothing wrong. I really crossed the line on this one.

Bill said that he wishes he could write his victim and let her know that she
was in no way responsible for her part in the sexual assault. He said he fears
that she still blames herself for his arrest because she cooperated with the
police and because Bill always told her they were doing "this" together. "I
made her think it was her doing too," Bill said.

Sex-offender research indicates that accepting individual responsibility
for the wrongfulness of their actions is essential to curb sexual recidivism
and reduce the number of victims.[93] If these offenders' perspectives are accurate and can be generalized to sex-offender populations at large, this study's
findings suggest that specialized treatment programs and probation departments with similar philosophies and techniques achieve this critical goal.

Victim Empathy

An integral component of reducing recidivism among sex-offender populations is getting offenders to understand the destructive emotional consequences their sex crimes have for victims and the victim's families. In the
therapeutic literature, this concept is known as victim empathy. Offenders'
sadness and remorse over the harm their actions caused their victims were
significant enough in 16 of the 29 interviews to be included in the victim
empathy section. Almost all of the offenders made statements such as "I'm
sorry for hurting [victim's name]," but an apology was not sufficient to war-
rant an inclusion in the victim-empathy theme. Rather, offenders were
required to engage in thoughtful discussions as to how their criminal behavior emotionally, physically, and/or sexually harmed their victims. Shelby is
a middle-aged man who was convicted of aggravated criminal sexual abuse
against a 13-year-old male neighbor. Shelby talks of the emotional aftermath
his victim is left to contend with as a result of his sexual victimization:

My heart hurts for what I have done to this boy. I was a victim of
sexual abuse when I was a young boy, by a Hispanic man who
worked on our farm, and I know, I know how this tears a boy up
inside. I can't sleep nights knowing I did the same thing to someone. I know I have scarred him. I put scars on him which I would
not want anyone ever to do to any kid, and yet, I hurt him. I can't
put into words how sorry I am for what I did to that boy. I hope he
is getting the help he needs. I am paying for his treatment through
my probation fees but I don't know if he is going or if it is helping.
But I hope it is.

Like many other convicted sex offenders, Shelby was sexually abused as a child, so he knows firsthand the pain and suffering that results from this victimization. Sexual assaults against male children, although less common than similar victimizations against female children, present unique challenges due to gender expectations and stereotypes that "real" men cannot be raped or that only effeminate men or "fags" get sexually assaulted. These fears keep many males, of all ages, from reaching out for help or reporting their victimizations to authorities.

Harry, who is convicted of a hands-off sex offense (i.e., voyeurism) against an adult female, says this about his victim:

> When I first started this probation thing, this court thing, treatment and all that business I somehow thought my case was different because I never put my hands on nobody in a sexual criminal way. I was peeping in this lady's bedroom window watching her all the time. The police saw me and arrested me. In her victim statement she said how scared and upset she is now all the time. I never understood that. I thought, Lady, I didn't even touch you or come in your house or nothing along those lines. But now I see more about what she is feeling. People feel violated and vulnerable when things like this happen. And they feel out of control of bad stuff. I hope she can start sleeping at night again because she said she couldn't anymore. I think what I did is just as bad as if I had touched her in a sexual way. I think she feels that much of a victim. I did that to her.

Harry's victim was the only one in the study who read her victim-impact statement aloud in court at his sentencing hearing. Harry said he later regarded the fear in her voice as one reason for his realization that her victimization was just as real as that of the victims of the other members of his sex-offender treatment group. In light of this fact, perhaps more victims should be encouraged to participate in oral or written victim-impact statements.

Larry, convicted of aggravated criminal sexual abuse for having sex with his underage female cousin, offered this comment when speaking about his victim:

> My cousin, she actually feels guilty for what happened to me. I am so sorry about that. It is really unfair to her. Actually, I think jail saved my life. I am thankful to her for cooperating with the police when they came to her. I can't see her or talk to her anymore

because the court said so, but if I could, I would scream out to her, "This is not your fault. You didn't do nothin' wrong. And I am so sorry for what I did to you. I made you grow up too fast." I was 29 and she was only 16. I would say to her, "You should have been allowed to be a kid for longer." The interviews with the police and all were real hard on her. They were real embarrassing and hard for her because they were arguing with her that she was not to blame for none of this but she didn't believe that. So the people who could have been helping her were arguing with her and making her feel she was wrong in her head. That messed with her as much as I did. She was like victimized by the system worse that she was victimized by me. She has to live with all this trauma now, thinking she was in love with me, that I left her, the police interviews, the embarrassment because it was in the papers. I have made her a victim of this forever. My sentence will end one day. Will hers? I pray it does.

Larry appears to appreciate the seriousness of his crime and the emotional devastation it caused his victim. He also touches on another important topic: the criminal justice system's response to victims of sexual assault and rape. A perception of the system's insensitivity and legacy of victim blaming contribute to the problem of underreporting by victims and the phenomenon of "second wounds" or "second victimizations," which describes system-related harms to victims. Victim empathy is the cornerstone of most sex-offender treatment programs because it is correlated with reductions in offending.

Sex-Offender Registration and Community Notification

The sex offenders speculated about whether they believed mandatory registration and community notification could deter sex offenders. Twenty-two of the 29 subjects (75 percent) indicate that it would not stop a motivated offender from victimizing someone. For example, Jose, convicted of having sex with an underage female three years his junior, states, "If you have problems, you are gonna commit sex offenses whether you are registered and on a public list or not." Similarly, Bobby, convicted of aggravated criminal sex abuse against his 14-year-old niece, says, "Registration is not gonna make a difference. I don't think putting your name on a list or on a . . . county web page is going to help make someone not offend or help keep the community safe." Finally, Will, who was convicted of aggravated criminal sexual abuse of a minor female, reports, "I don't think it will deter, no I don't. I don't think so because like, I knew about the list and being published on the Internet and all that stuff before I committed my thing [sex crime]. It didn't stop me."

These three men echo the sentiments on mandatory registration and community notification voiced by most of the sex offenders. It is plausible that offenders disliked the law because it, in fact, does accomplish its intended goal of limiting access to potential victims. There is some empirical indication that a deterrent effect might exist with these laws. However, other studies assert no such outcome, and in at least one instance sex-offender registration and community notification was correlated with an increase in the rates of sexual violence. Unless significant revisions to mandatory registration and community notification occur, these laws remain primarily a symbolic victory for victims.

Conclusions and Policy Recommendations

The first part of the chapter highlighted the high-profile nature of certain types of sex crimes and victims, as well as many of the attributes that distinguish sex crimes from other forms of violence. Additionally, an overview was provided of contemporary sex-offender laws and the science examining their impact on public safety. We then moved on to a micro-level analysis of sexual victimization by exploring the words and perceptions of nearly 30 convicted male sex offenders to learn what they said about their crimes, their victims, and the criminal justice system's response to sexual violence. Although the offenders often blamed their victim, the tendency toward victim blaming became less pronounced among offenders who were nearing completion of their probation and treatment programs. Personal responsibility and victim empathy, key concepts for increasing desistance among sex offenders, were more common among offenders who were further along in the probation sentences and treatment programs. Analysis of the interview data also reveal that men convicted of statutory rape were less inclined to accept full moral and legal responsibility for their crimes. Most of the offenders said that current sex-offender laws such as community notification were unlikely to deter offenders and protect victims. Modifications to many of the third-wave sex-offender laws were recommended.

With respect to the sex-offender laws discussed here, best practices dictate that they be reexamined against empirical data. This process would enhance their potential for increasing public safety and limit any unintended consequences that might inadvertently encourage victimizations. Generally, legislatures and other public officials embrace sex-offender laws because of their feel-good qualities even though they might not work as intended. For instance, many Florida lawmakers now realize that the state's "no-predator zones" are counterproductive to public safety, but even these legislative members are reluctant to support any repeals to the restrictions for fear of being seen as "pro-predator."[94] Furthermore, sex-offender registration without community notification may ultimately be more effective at decreasing victimization in that law enforcement officials will maintain valuable information, while the negative collateral consequences often associated with these laws can be avoided. Additionally, given that a small number of sex offenders are responsible for a disproportionate number of victimizations, direct and proactive arrest policies geared toward these recidivistic offenders are likely to be the most effective policing style for responding to these crimes. Further, empathetic police interviewing techniques are shown to increase the likelihood of sex-offender confessions. Finally, policing responses to sexual violence should include education for criminal justice agents, lawmakers, and the public so they become better informed about high-risk situations (i.e., acquaintance rape; child molestation by family members, associates, or friends) and how to better identify, protect, and respond to risks and sexual violations.

The civil commitment of sex offenders seems plagued with problems. Beyond the ethical and moral issues, there are practical questions about whether this legislation represents the best use of scare resources. Civil commitments are much more expensive than traditional imprisonment, and the money used to fund them could otherwise be used to administer prison-based sex-offender therapy, the successful completion of which is linked to reductions in future victimizations.[95] A community-based containment approach that is tiered so as to acknowledge that each sex offender represents a different amount of danger is recommended strongly.[96] Further, the funding for community-based treatment should be increased because outcome studies show that offenders who successfully complete these therapies recidivate less often and less quickly than similarly situated offenders who do not complete treatment.[97]

A more victim-oriented response to sexual offenders would encourage and systemically support the proper use of conventional criminal sanctions.[98] The key is to get criminal justice and court officials to zealously prosecute and appropriately sanction high-risk offenders. This goal may require more victim participation in all phases of the criminal process, and lawmakers and practitioners should be prepared to do whatever is necessary to support and encourage victim reporting, advocacy, testifying, and participating with victim-impact statements. In other words, if the criminal justice system were functioning correctly, these individuals would stay incarcerated in prison facilities (at a much lower fiscal cost) rather than wasting the scarce resources of the public mental health system through the use of Civil Commitment—potentially forever, and often in the complete absence of mental health therapy. If this protocol had been followed, Polly Klass and Megan Kanka's killers might still have been incarcerated at the time they sexually assaulted and murdered their young victims.[99]

We also investigated the role of GPS with sex offenders. Research indicates that it probably works well to augment existing probation and parole supervisory tools and a more cost-effective public safety policy.[100] However, best practices dictate that the public needs to be properly educated about the strengths and weaknesses of GPS tracking: it can be an invaluable tool to community supervision, but it is not a magic wand that ends sexual violence.[101]

The other policy issues we mentioned pertained to the second wave of sex-offender laws and were motivated by larger concerns of violence against women and children. An assessment of the rape reform legislation (e.g., rape shield laws, specialized investigation and prosecution units, evidentiary changes) indicates that in terms of benefit to victims, the laws achieved only minimal success.[102] Although the increases were not dramatic, generally, more rapists were sentenced to prison for their sex crimes after the implementation of reforms than before such legislation was in place.[103] However, a man who rapes a stranger is still likely to receive a longer prison term than a man who rapes someone he knows well.[104] Such findings provide yet more evidence that the criminal justice system continues to perceive crimes between known persons as less serious than crimes between strangers. Furthermore, one of the most disappointing outcomes associated with rape reform legislation has been its failure to make significant inroads toward encouraging victim reporting. Results indicate that the proportion of victims reporting their rapes to police did not rise sharply, as advocates and lawmakers had hoped.[105] But the reform movement did usher in extralegal improvements, including the growth of statewide and county-level sexual assault programs, rape crisis shelters, and emergency hotlines as well as the employment of hundreds of new rape victim advocates.[106] These hires occurred within the criminal justice system and beyond (i.e., victim-centered agencies and other related not-for-profit organizations). Sociologist and criminologist Susan Caringella further noted that the attention and public awareness associated with the rape reform movement also increased women's recognition of rape and legitimated the concept that women have complete autonomy over their own bodies and that forced sexual encounters are illegal.[107]

How Battered Women Lose: Unintended Consequences of Well-Intentioned Legal and Criminal Justice Policies

July 28, 2009—Governor Schwarzenegger line item vetoed the (California) Department of Public Health's Domestic Violence Program.... "We are appalled to see the Governor eliminate funding to vital programs that save lives," said Tara Shabazz, Executive Director of The California Partnership to End Domestic Violence (CPEDV). "State funding to domestic violence programs has been proven to save lives, and also millions of dollars in health care, law enforcement and other social costs. It is fiscally irresponsible to propose such cuts; the Governor is balancing the budget on the backs of our state's most vulnerable citizens." (StopFamily Violence.org: July 2009)

This chapter provides examples and raises questions related to the victim conundrum. In related to on battering and how the state responds to victims, civilly and criminally. As states update antiquated legal practices targeting victims' needs, it is critical to examine their consequences. Unintended side effects that seem benign, or even beneficial, on the surface may create tremendous obstacles for the victims they were intended to help. Our focus here is on issues in the national spotlight, some of which are not direct victim policies but rather are situations where policy efforts in one area collide with victims' circumstances in another area, creating unintended consequences so that victims are hurt or twice victimized.

Toward that end, we examine battered women and the effects of welfare reform, public housing initiatives, civil forfeiture cases, the Violence Against Women Act, and women arrested for domestic violence. The civil issues are examined first, and the remainder of the chapter focuses solely on one criminal issue: that of women arrested on domestic violence charges. We highlight this last issue, using data collected from female "offender" domestic violence treatment groups, as a way to examine how increased reliance on the criminal justice system to apprehend, punish, and treat domestic battery offenders affects victims, often adversely. The theme that we follow throughout the chapter is how unintended consequences of current policies harm victims of battering.

Welfare Reform and Its Effects on Domestic Violence

While intimate-partner violence cuts across race, ethnicity, sexual orientation, and social class, women of lower socioeconomic status bear the brunt of their impact, since a lack of economic resources is a primary reason that women remain in abusive relationships. More than 60 percent of women receiving welfare are victims of intimate-partner violence, compared to 22 percent in the general population.[1] In community-based samples that include both women who receive welfare and other low-income women, the rate of low-income battered women welfare recipients is higher than the rate found in samples of low-income women who are not on welfare.[2] Severity of violence is also more strongly associated with women who receive welfare.[3] In addition, battered women on welfare are more likely to experience adverse physical health, increased levels of drug and alcohol abuse, and mental health problems than low-income women who never received welfare.[4]

Thus, battered women living in poverty face numerous hardships when conforming to the new "welfare-to-work" policies enacted in the late 1990s and still in place today. The federal Personal Responsibility and Work Opportunity Reconciliation Act (PRWORA), which was passed in 1996 and reauthorized in 2002, replaced the former welfare program with the new Temporary Assistance for Needy Families (TANF). It requires recipients to work in exchange for assistance and limits the amount of time one can receive aid. In addition, PRWORA requires that the paternity of recipients' children be established and that child support be sought from the father.

Welfare reformers recognized that batterers interfere with their partners' attempts to fulfill new welfare requirements, such as attending school or getting a job, and that maintaining contact with the abuser or placing financial mandates upon him, such as child support, can be dangerous to victims.[5] Examples of batterers' interference with a woman's attempts to seek public aid include "making work-related threats; picking fights or inflicting injuries before important events such as interviews or tests; preventing her from sleeping; calling her repeatedly at work; saying negative things about her ability to succeed; or refusing to provide promised childcare at the last minute."[6] Research documents additional forms of sabotage: turning off alarm clocks, destroying clothes, disfiguring faces before job interviews, deliberately disabling the family car, and so forth.[7]

In addition, program staff "noticed that many of the abusers were unemployed or underemployed and reasoned that if the men were assisted with jobs or job training, then the unequal economic balance might be remedied, perhaps leading to less sabotage and violence."[8] Richard Tolman and Jody Raphael pointed out, "Most likely, the abusers implicitly knew that women with their own economic resources have the financial means to leave the relationship or might meet a man on the job who had more resources than they did" (2000: 667). Finally, studies demonstrated that between 35 and 56 percent of employed battered women were harassed at work—in person—by their abusive partner.[9] A welfare caseworker in Louisiana provided this example of batterer harassment: "I had a lady assigned to go to a job training program, but she couldn't go because even though she had a bond on the perpetrator, he was hanging around the place she was supposed to go for the training. I think she was dropped from TANF and sanctioned because she didn't attend."[10]

In discussing the connection between welfare and domestic violence, Andrea Lyon's (1999) research reveals that when factors such as length of stay on welfare and cycling (more than one episode of welfare relief) were examined, longer-term recipients were more likely to have experienced violence, and women with lifetime histories of violence were more likely to remain on welfare longer (a combined total of five years or longer). More specifically, in a sample of 3,147 domestic violence incidents reported to Salt Lake City police over three years, of those women victims who sought AFDC, 38 to 41 percent had their cases opened within a year (before or after) of the reported incident. These finding suggest a connection between domestic violence and welfare receipt. In the former case, welfare seems a strategic response to partner violence, and in the latter, seeking public welfare may help female gain independence following a reported incident; alternatively, the independence the women found through welfare contributed to subsequent retaliatory violence.[11] Similarly, Lisa Brush (2000) found that battered women obtaining protection orders dropped out of mandatory welfare-to-work programs at six times the rate of women who did not, reinforcing the evidence that battered women are at risk of noncompliance with welfare reform requirements for safety reasons. Still, many battered women find ways to work, often as a way to escape domestic violence.[12]

To address these problems of abuser interferences, the legislature passed an amendment to PRWORA, the Family Violence Option (FVO), which states may adopt. Participating states must do three things: (1) screen all public aid applications for domestic violence issues; (2) refer domestic violence victims to the appropriate social service agencies; and (3) provide a waiver of relevant program requirements (i.e., time limits, child support enforcement and paternity mandates, and work mandates if it jeopardizes her safety or if she is unable to comply because of domestic violence).[13]

While most states implemented Family Violence Options, findings indicate that eligible clients are not being fully informed of their rights as domestic violence victims or receiving the intended services and waivers.[14] For instance, in Maryland, caseworkers lacked training on how to identify and respond to domestic violence issues; in New York City, less than half of individuals self-identified as battered were referred to special domestic violence caseworkers, and only about one-third who were referred were granted Family Violence Option waivers.[15] In Wisconsin, about 75 percent of battered women on welfare were not told of available services such as counseling, housing, or the possibility of using work time to seek help. "In addition, while 26.8 percent reported they were afraid their former partner would harass them if the state attempted to collect child support, only 4.9 percent were told about the good-cause exception to the child support cooperation requirement."[16] Furthermore, only one in four battered immigrants in California received any information about domestic violence waivers for which they were eligible.[17] Finally, in Louisiana—consistently one of our nation's poorest states—none of the severely battered welfare recipients in the study received program requirement waivers or exemptions.[18] Frontline welfare caseworkers in Louisiana confirmed that exemptions to the welfare program were rarely given to battered welfare recipients.[19] While it is commendable that so many states passed family violence options (there are at least 39 participating states), poor caseworker training, the failure to disseminate needed information to victims or to properly screen clients for domestic violence, and agency-level structural obstacles undermine the formal policy's goal of allowing battered women who seek public assistance to avoid undue hardships.[20]

To be more precise, under the Welfare Reform Act of 1996/2002, expanded efforts are in place to establish paternity (through in-hospital genetic testing or through aggressive computer searches) and to garner wages and assets for purposes of child support. However, alerting abusers to victims' locations may reignite abuse or stimulate battles for custody and visitation that trigger regular and unsafe contact.[21] Furthermore, abusers often become angry and retaliate when subjected to such enforcement efforts.[22] Given what is known about offender retaliation, it is not surprising that so few battered women seek redress from these welfare program requirements. The rate of good-cause waiver requests is very low nationally and is most likely related to the lack of information about the option, the extensive documentation needed to obtain it,[23] and structural pressures on the welfare agencies.[24] In one study that investigated the implementation of the Family Violence Option, caseworkers confirmed nearly zero rates of waivers and exemptions for battered women. The authors found that "only one worker [out of 15] provided a good-cause waiver to a client because of domestic violence in the 2 years prior to the interview. Three of the workers were not aware that the policy existed or that domestic violence victims could be exempted from program requirements."[25] Obviously, there is a disconnect between the FVO's intention and its implementation.

The first scientific study to examine good-cause exceptions to the child support requirements for public assistance was conducted in four welfare offices in several Colorado counties.[26] We learned some important lessons. "Welfare reform has changed the intersection of domestic violence and child support. The time limits and work requirements that now shape public assistance also greatly increase the importance of child support."[27] Notwithstanding its importance, scant scientific research exists into the relationship between domestic violence and child support collection. The federal Office of Child Support Enforcement (OCSE) funded research to help fill the knowledge gap and to explore best practices for meeting the needs of domestic violence victims and increasing child support collection. The most extensive publication on the issue was based on studies conducted in Colorado, Massachusetts, and Minnesota.[28] Findings indicate that most of the welfare recipients who were victims of domestic violence rejected the good-cause waivers because the women needed and wanted child support.[29] In 1995 nearly 5 million custodial parents applied for public assistance, yet less than 9,000 claimed good-cause exemptions. This amounts to a national response rate of 0.17 percent. However, among the domestic violence victims in the three states studied, more than 18 percent of welfare applicants wanted a good-cause exemption. Analysis into the good-cause applications suggests that these recipients were more likely to have experienced a recent assault than the domestic violence victims who did not pursue the good-cause exemption and that these women were more likely than the other battered welfare recipients to have been severely beaten by the child's father.[30] Not only is the request rate for exemptions low; previous research in Colorado and New York suggests that only one in three of the domestic violence victims who seek an exemption are successful.[31]

Researchers attribute much of this slippage to the failure to complete the application process or the fact that the battered women lack documentation to support their claim of abuse. For instance, in these counties, applicants were allowed only seven days to complete the paperwork, which is unrealistic for low-income and poorly educated women who must obtain at least two medical, police, or court records. In addition, most of the victims never sought restraining orders, or if they did, sworn statements by victims did not serve as proof of abusers' violation of such orders.

In sum, the journey from welfare-to-work is especially difficult for battered women who face numerous obstacles by batterers who harass their partners or otherwise prevent them from working. These work-related threats and safety issues are exacerbated for women (and their children) who depend on public assistance in order to eventually leave a violent relationship. Establishing paternity and enforcing child support further heightens the dangerousness for many battered women who wish to avoid contact with their batterers. Although important measures such as the Family Violence Option have been instituted in an attempt to rectify the potentially harmful consequences of the new welfare requirements, more action to ensure that caseworkers and battered women are fully aware of these options and more flexibility in how victims verify prior abuse is necessary, permitting women to provide alternative forms of documentation of abuse is needed, and organizational barriers at the agency level that hinder exemption requests must be eliminated.

Battering and Public Housing

Domestic violence is cited as the primary cause of homelessness in many cities because victims who leave their abusers often have nowhere to go.[32] In addition, in violent relationships, the abusers typically control the household finances as one method of manipulating victims into powerless positions, leaving battered women with no means of securing first and last month's rent or security deposits if they do choose to flee. Isolation from friends and family members is a common abuser ploy as well, so that when victims are alienated and estranged from people who could help them—or friends and family are threatened by the abuser's violence—they have nowhere to turn.[33]

Following the nation's general "war on crime" policies, enforcement and prosecution agencies now use "three strikes" or "one strike" laws, instituted by state legislatures, to better combat repeat offenders.[34] These draconian laws were designed to end perceptions of "softness" in sentencing and to deter potential criminals by advertising the severe consequences of crime commission. For example, "one strike" laws against criminals residing in or visiting public housing aim to crack down on government assistance to citizens deemed undeserving. However, such laws create a new group of victims by permitting evictions of any resident or visitor engaged in criminal activity. Of the over 5 million people living in public housing in the United States, most are minorities, and most of the households are female-headed. In 2002, the U.S. Supreme Court upheld a federal housing law, the Anti-Drug Abuse Act of 1988 (revised 1994), designed to evict public housing tenants for any resident or guest arrested for drug-related or violent crimes.[35] This law unintentionally puts battered women at risk of losing their homes if they call police to report violence, essentially holding battered women responsible for their partner's abuse. Ironically, if they do not report the violence, they risk more beatings but can remain in public housing.[36]

The real-life implications of the Supreme Court decision were salient for Aaronica Warren, mother of an infant son, who lived in public housing in Ypsilanti, Michigan. Aaronica's ex-boyfriend beat her badly, yet she found the courage to call the police. About a week after reporting the battery, Aaronica received an eviction notice under this housing law. Even though the law was aimed at rooting out drug-related violence in federal housing projects, housing officials can evict any resident or visitor "who has been convicted of a felony that occurred there or nearby, as well as others who live in the household."[37] Aaronica's quagmire stems from the case *Department of Housing and Urban Development (HUD) v. Rucker*, which challenged the eviction of 63-year-old Pearlie Rucker, a great-grandmother who lived in public housing in Oakland, California. Pearlie, her mentally disabled daughter, two grandchildren, and one great-grandchild faced eviction because the daughter was found in possession of illegal drugs three blocks from Pearlie's apartment.[38]

The *Rucker* ruling is dangerous for battered women who are tenants in public housing, trapped in an abusive household with few options and no control over their violent partner or ex-partner. If a battered woman's partner is a drug user, the law assumes equal responsibility on her part. In *HUD v. Rucker* (2002), the U.S. Supreme Court found that the public housing agency's actions were consistent with regulations, holding that HUD "unambiguously requires lease terms that vest local public housing authorities with the discretion to evict tenants for the drug-related activity of household members and guests whether or not the tenant knew, or should have known, about the activity."[39] In fact, "implicit in *Rucker* is the idea that no matter the level of culpability, tenants who cannot control the criminal activities of household members or guests do not deserve to live in public housing."[40] This seems paradoxical, given that the goal of public housing is to create safe and affordable housing for low-income citizens, not to punish families in which one member or guest engages in crime.[41] Although it is difficult to know the extent to which battered women will be harmed by this Supreme Court decision, the implications are grave.

Here is another example. Tiffanie Alvera was evicted from her public housing apartment because of her landlord's concern that her husband's violence would endanger other tenants.[42] In August 1999 Tiffanie was violently assaulted by her then husband in the apartment they were sharing. Tiffanie's injuries were severe enough she required immediate medical treatment. "Within forty-eight hours of being rushed to the hospital, Alvera obtained a restraining order, notified her landlord of the restraining order, requested that her husband's name be taken off the lease, and applied for a move to a one-bedroom apartment."[43] At this point, she encountered barriers that confront any battered woman seeking public housing, beyond the long waiting list. For instance, there is an extensive application process for acquiring federally subsidized housing, and many applicants are rejected based on their credit or criminal histories. For battered women, good credit may be jeopardized by abusers' controlling economic tactics. Victims might have criminal records, reflecting activities where they participated in crime under duress or coercion by their abusers, especially since the passage of mandatory and pro-arrest laws (see subsequent discussion in this chapter and chapter 3), even though she may have acted in self-defense. And in some public housing jurisdictions, applicants must submit a letter of recommendation from respected community members: "For victims of domestic violence, these tasks may take an enormous effort. Victims may be cut off from the community, may have a deflated sense of self-worth, and may be unprepared to speak in their own defense."[44] Finally, very few public housing authorities offer priority housing for domestic violence victims, even though their lives, and those of their children, may be in danger.

Tiffanie was fortunate in that she obtained help from a lawyer familiar with filing disparate impact claims. This concept was initially raised in an amicus brief filed by the National Network to End Domestic Violence, which contended that "women are not engaging in criminal activity when they are beaten or abused in their home. Victims of domestic violence are not trying to threaten the health, safety or well-being of their neighbors."[45] This contention suggested that although the "one strike" law used in *Rucker* may seem gender-neutral on its face, the application of it could lead to a discriminatory outcome; since women are overwhelmingly the victims of domestic violence, eviction of families for crime may disproportionately punish women, as a class, for the offenders' actions. As Hirst argues, "Disparate impact claims have routinely been used to combat discrimination disguised by legitimate means. By showing that a neutral policy or practice may create an outcome that disparately affects members of a protected class, many plaintiffs have successfully changed such discriminatory practices."[46] Tiffanie's wrongful eviction was overturned by using such a disparate impact claim. The judge accepted the reasoning that the "one strike" law produced a disproportionately negative effect on women, since women comprise the majority of domestic violence victims; the judge also agreed that domestic violence does not create an unsafe housing environment. The success of a disparate impact claim in Alvera's case can guide other battering victims in wrongful eviction cases.

While welfare and housing reforms were not intended to further jeopardize battered women's safety and well-being, the examples discussed make it easy to see how policy efforts in one area can backfire in another and increase harm to women and their children.

Battering and Civil Forfeiture Laws

Another example of unintended consequences of new legislation involves "innocent" owners who seek to reclaim property seized through civil forfeiture laws. Following tough drug laws that stem from the "war on crime," illegal assets gained by drug dealing can be seized and confiscated. Often, these laws affect the wives and girlfriends of men engaged in drug crimes. In cases examined in the federal courts, the rulings indicate that female claimants must either demonstrate a lack of knowledge regarding the criminal use of property or launch a credible defense regarding an absence of consent to use property in an illegal fashion.[47] However, this is not how it typically works; in a number of cases, evidence of a wife's submission to her husband's power has been deemed insufficient to sustain a claim of nonconsent.[48] In one particular case, *U.S. v. 107.9 Acre Parcel of Land* (1990), a wife-claimant acknowledged participating in her husband's drug operation but argued that such cooperation was involuntary—that she pleaded with her husband to stop his illegal activities, and threatened to leave him, but because she was afraid of him ultimately did whatever he told her to do.[49] The court ruled in this case that a wife's submission to the demands of a husband involved in crime was not sufficient to reach the rigorous standard of legal duress and, as such, was insufficient to forestall forfeiture of jointly owned property to the government.

In another case, *U.S. v. Sixty Acres* (1990), the wife was ostensibly blamed for not leaving an unsavory domestic situation: her husband sold drugs to an undercover informant, which subjected their 60 acres of property to forfeiture. As part of her defense, she claimed that she lived in fear of bodily harm from her husband, but the court rejected this because she chose to take no action except to make verbal objections in "a bland and ineffective way, or to 'nag' her husband until he told her to 'mind her own business.'" The court held that because she was generally aware of the illegal activity, she did not meet the burden of proving she was an innocent owner; perhaps, the court explained, she should divorce to escape the forfeiture. Although the appellate court had evidence that her husband beat and threatened her and had killed his previous wife, she could not claim lack of consent under duress because the threat was not "immediate." Despite her fear that he would kill her too if she did anything other than submit to his wishes, the court was unconvinced of the severity of the coercive environment and thus offered her no protection.

Both of these civil forfeiture cases illustrate the victim-blaming ideology at work in domestic battery cases. The most striking defect in legal reasoning in this area involves the judiciary's naive social assumptions about how women ought to behave in their relationships. Nested within the court rulings is the erroneous assumption of symmetry of resources and power within a marriage or intimate relationships. Social and economic power in such relationships is rarely equally distributed. Yet judges repeatedly imply that wives should be accountable for their husbands' behavior and that wives share culpability due to their "failure" or inability to control their husbands.[50] These sexist assumptions translate into institutionalized victim blaming, further stripping victims of power and control and creating greater hardships for the children of these unions. Similar to the eviction of domestic violence victims from public housing discussed earlier in the section, battered women may be penalized for the criminal actions of their husbands.

The Violence Against Women Act: Civil Redress for Victims of Gender-Motivated Crimes

The Violence Against Women Act of 1994 (reauthorized by Congress in 2005 for fiscal years 2007 through 2011) created a federal civil rights cause of action for victims of gender-motivated crimes of violence.[51] This civil rights remedy was debated for over four years, as dozens of women, academics, medical professionals, and law enforcement officials testified before Congress regarding its necessity. It was controversial, since it designated sex crimes as "hate" crimes that violated victims' rights, permitting them to pursue compensatory and punitive damages.[52] Never before had crimes of rape and domestic violence been classified as gender-motivated civil rights violations.

Fewer than a dozen federal VAWA gender-motivated violence civil rights cases were filed nationwide, despite the belief that a federal law was warranted because state laws failed to adequately protect women targeted for violence simply because of their gender. Initially, a civil lawsuit was possible if it was a felony-level crime and the violence was motivated by gender animus. In terms of the first requirement, it was not necessary to have a criminal conviction of a gender-motivated crime of violence. This was significant, because victims are often reluctant to rely on formal criminal justice interventions.[53] The second requirement, that the act was committed because of the victim's gender, was more difficult to prove, particularly for cases that did not involve sexual assaults. The totality of the circumstances were evaluated, including the violent incidents, and the abuser's beliefs, statements, attitudes, gender slurs, and epithets were assessed to determine whether the resulting environment was threatening and intimidating, and, if so, whether this was due to the victim's gender.

However, this civil rights remedy proved problematic because not all sexual crimes are considered gender-motivated by all courts. This was the situation in the case that ultimately struck down the federal VAWA civil tort action, *Brzonkala v. Virginia Polytechnic*, in which a female college student was brutally gang-raped in her dormitory by two male university athletes. In 1994, Christy Brzonkala matriculated as a new student at Virginia Polytechnic Institute. That same month, she alleged that two male students who were attending the school on athletic scholarships repeatedly and forcibly raped her.[54] Following the rape, one of the rapists warned her, "You better not have any fucking diseases." Later, in the dormitory dining room, he announced publicly that he "liked to get girls drunk and fuck the shit out of them."[55] Christy filed a complaint using Virginia Tech's sexual assault policy. After this, she discovered that another male athlete was overheard telling one of the assailants that he should have "killed the bitch." As a result of the trauma, Christy stopped going to classes and eventually dropped out of school. The university's first disciplinary proceeding found one of the athletes guilty of sexual assault, but then a second disciplinary proceeding found that he had violated the school's Abusive Conduct Policy. Then the school reversed the results of both hearings and simply imposed deferred suspension until the athlete's graduation (allowing him to continue to play football for the school and keep his full athletic scholarship) and ordered him to attend a one-hour educational session.[56]

After learning of the university's final decisions, Christy filed suit against the two men based on the VAWA Civil Rights Remedy. This stimulated a flurry of court activity, moving the case from the district court, which ruled that the law was unconstitutional, to the Fourth Circuit Court of Appeals, which reversed the earlier decision. However, in a 7-4 vote, the circuit court also held that Brzonkola's complaint was not valid. The court found that "all rapes are not the same," some being more "egregious" than others. The federal district court judge stated that this date rape was less likely motivated by gender animus than stranger rape would have been.[57] On appeal, the Supreme Court affirmed the decision, declaring that the VAWA's Civil Rights Remedy is unconstitutional. The impact of the decision is that women (and men) are blocked from suing their attackers in federal court for damages resulting from injuries from gender-based violence. But in many jurisdictions, state-level hate crime legislation still provides legal redress for gender-based violence.

Taken together, the previous discussion of the effects of welfare reform laws, public housing "one strike" laws, civil forfeiture procedures instituted under the rubric of the "war on crime," and the Civil Rights Remedy of the federal VAWA illustrate a reluctance to address the needs of victims as well as a diminished willingness to protect female victims from males' sexual and physical violence against them. Although most of the policies were not created with victims in mind, when they are executed they often harm victims, resulting in a second victimization, as in the case of battered women. The VAWA Civil Rights Remedy offered one way to better address women's victimization, yet was struck down, leaving victims with traditional and largely ineffective options for pursuing justice. This ineffectiveness is one of the many reasons domestic violence survivors have difficulty escaping their abusive relationship. The victim conundrum for battered women continues to be explored in the next section.

Women and Domestic Violence: Why Do They Stay?

Researchers believe that this question is off point because it assumes that leaving puts an end to the violence, when instead it can actually make matters worse.[58] It also puts the responsibility on victims, who are expected to leave their homes, when it is the offenders who committed the crime. Moreover, many women do in fact leave. Some women leave after the first violent episode; for others it is a process that takes several attempts before they leave for good.[59] Or it may require exhausting other resources. For example, in a study of 251 battered women who voluntarily contacted a counseling unit attached to a county attorney's office, 71 percent left their batterers, and these women were also more likely to be employed, to have been in their relationship for a shorter time, and to have tried other coping strategies, such as filing assault charges and obtaining restraining orders.[60]

Studies based on interviews with battered women identified several factors that keep a woman in a battering relationship. The most important factors are the fear of the abuser's retaliation (against the woman herself or against other family members), economic dependency, child custody issues, and emotional/psychological bonding.[61] The time following separation is especially dangerous. Indeed, women are more likely to be murdered by their batterers after they leave the relationship.[62] Many battered women are trapped in relationships because they are economically dependent on their partners and lack alternative housing options.[63] Economic concerns are magnified if there are children to care for, and children further complicate leaving, given custody and visitation issues. When a battered woman leaves, her abusive spouse often fights for and wins custody or visitation rights, making it almost impossible for a woman to avoid contact with her batterer.[64] Furthermore, if the man inflicts abuse on the children, the woman may lose custody because she failed to protect them.[65]

Immigrant women face unique personal, institutional, and ideological barriers to leaving an abusive relationship.[66] In addition to economic impoverishment and child custody issues, they tend to be more isolated and dependent on their spouses because they often lack support networks or basic survival skills such as driving a car, and they frequently face a language barrier and cultural insensitivity as well. In addition, strict immigration and welfare policies may keep them trapped with "sponsor-spouses," and their backgrounds may cause them to view divorce as unacceptable.[67]

Finally, women's love for their partners does not automatically stop because that partner is a batterer.[68] Many battered women hope their partner will change. An early attempt to explain this phenomenon was Walker's (1984) cycle-of-violence model (the tension-building phase, the acute-battering incident, and the honeymoon phase), which points to the pattern of violent episodes interspersed with periods of affection and apology, sustaining the victim's hope that the violence will end.[69] However, critics have noted that the period of affection is itself a control tactic and that once domination is established, these loving periods decrease.[70]

Women Arrested for Domestic Battery: Victims, Offenders, or Something Else?

Before delving into the effects the justice system's involvement has on victims, we provide some background. As we mentioned in chapters 1 and 2, the social problem of domestic battery catapulted to the national scene in the 1970s with efforts of grassroots activists and victim advocates and with the success of civil liability suits against police departments who refused to treat domestic violence as a criminal offense. Many feminists and advocates for battered women (both men and women) fought tirelessly to get the criminal justice system to treat intimate-partner violence seriously, increase safety for women, hold offenders accountable for their violence, and rid the criminal justice system of gender bias.

As we mentioned in chapter 3, for the past two decades the entire system—the police, in particular—has been under siege to change its tolerant stance toward domestic battery. The system responded by enacting presumptive and mandatory arrest laws, establishing prosecutorial "no drop" policies in some jurisdictions, and designing treatment intervention programs.[71] Although mandating arrest communicates the seriousness of battering, opponents of arrest policies[72] note that relieving victims of their decision-making power by mandating arrest is patronizing to battered women and disempowering. Often, victims simply want the violence to stop in the given instance or fear the consequences that may accompany arrest, such as retaliation by their partner or loss of his income. Some believe that victim empowerment is best achieved by giving victims control over the outcome of the police or prosecutorial intervention and that a policy of victim preference is by far preferable to mandatory arrest.[73] Arrest may be effective only for employed suspects who would incur legitimate losses if arrested (such as the loss of a job or reputation).[74] In addition, police often circumvent such policies due to the inconvenience of case processing, belief in stereotypes regarding battered women, and dissatisfaction with limits placed on their discretion.[75] At a minimum, despite these criticisms and potential police bias against the poor and/or people of color, presumptive and mandatory arrest policies are a more satisfying criminal justice system response than the nonintervention that used to be the rule.[76] However, as these arrest laws grew in popularity, a concomitant increase in women arrested for domestic battery resulted.

Some jurisdictions recognized this unintended consequence and have either enacted "primary aggressor" laws or instituted new police training policies.[77] For instance, a 6 percent dual arrest rate reported in Dallas was reduced to 1 percent after police were trained to determine who was most culpable or most dangerous.[78] Nonetheless, battered women are now ensnared in pro-arrest policies, despite research showing that men who batter women account for over 90 percent of serious domestic violence incidents.[79] Nationwide statistics indicate that women prosecuted for domestic violence represent 5–10 percent of intimate-partner violence prosecutions, although this number is growing.[80] The forthcoming section covers in much greater detail the issue of men's and women's use of violence.

The remainder of the chapter concerns one issue, ostensibly about offenders, that is directly relevant to victims: the arrest of women for committing a domestic violent offense. In doing so, we question the effects of mandatory and pro-arrest statutes enacted over the past decade. The emphasis on arrest in cases of intimate-partner violence has resulted in increased arrest of battered women, but a more contextualized and thorough examination reveals that battered women typically use violence as a self-defensive measure or because there are no other means of escape.[81] In contrast, men use violence in relationships as a way to establish and maintain control over their partners. In many jurisdictions, the primary aggressor (typically the male) is not identified by police, and dual arrests (of both the victim and offender) have increased.[82] One consequence of these arrest policies is that battered women who have been arrested are required to attend "offender" treatment programs, which are designed to clinically intervene and control violent individuals who are truly guilty of domestic abuse.

Here is an example of a case in which a battered woman fought back in self-defense, only to end up arrested as a batterer. Since she was legally designated as an offender, she was assigned to a probation officer, who monitored her treatment in a batterers' intervention program. Beth's probation officer stated, "Beth cut her husband's throat so badly that he had to be Medivac-ed to the hospital; he almost died. He was constantly abusing her throughout their 6-year marriage and at the time of the stabbing, she said he was beating the crap out of her and she grabbed a knife—it was the first thing that was near her. . . . That's what she felt she had to do to get out of the situation." What is important to know in this case, and many others like it where the victims are arrested, is how the dynamics of abuse played out in the relationship prior to arrest. In violent relationships, men typically abuse women to gain control and maintain power over them. Often, he is in charge of the family's finances and dictates who she can talk to or visit, what she can wear, and so forth.

The women in our research, on the other hand, tend to use force either for self-defense, to protect themselves or their children, or out of frustration when they are at the ends of their rope and no other avenue of escape seems viable. Placing intimate violence in context helps to explain the different meanings, motivations, and consequences that acts of force have for men and women in intimate relationships. In Beth's case, because her husband was much larger and stronger than she was, she grabbed a knife so she could defend herself. Although this behavior is typical, such women end up charged with a felony because of their use of a deadly weapon, which equalized the physical power imbalance, whereas men are charged with a misdemeanor, since they used only their fists or feet.[83] In such cases a man may have a more visible and ostensibly serious wound, although the woman's intent many have been defensive, not malicious.

Differences in Men's and Women's Use of Violence

Do men and women use violence for the same reasons and with equal frequency? Much research has explored this gendered phenomenon by examining the rates of and reasons for partner abuse. Although early national surveys using the Conflict Tactics Scale (CTS) as a measurement instrument found that women reported using violence against male partners at rates equal to or slightly higher than the reverse,[84] most family violence scholars believe that intimate-partner violence is not an act of mutual battering (see chapters 2 and 3 for discussions of the methodological issues with the CTS). In fact, national survey results from the recent National Violence Against Women survey (NVAW), jointly conducted by the National Institute of Justice and the Center for Disease Control and Prevention, reveal that women are significantly more likely than men to be victimized by their intimate partners,[85] which is consistent with other national data from the NCVS.[86] Other studies that use the CTS and find support for mutual battering are largely dismissed once context is taken into account, once preemptive aggressive action is distinguished from self-defensive action, and once injury is considered.[87]

Other research reveals that there are indeed differences in the context and quality of violence used by women and men. As Andrea Lyon (1999: 257) contends, looking at "who hit" only reveals one aspect of the incident, and in order to fully understand the complexity of the whole context, the "why" and the "how" also need to be studied. Even Murray Straus (1993: 78), the author of the CTS, admits that men "typically hit or threaten to hit to force some specific behavior, pain, or injury," while "a woman may typically slap a partner or pound on his chest as an expression of outrage or in frustration because of his having turned a deaf ear to repeated attempts to discuss some critical event."[88]

Daniel Saunders (1986) found that most women in battered women's shelters reported using minor violence at some point in relationships as a means of self-defense or fighting back. Michele Cascardi, Dina Vivian, and Shannon-Lee Meyer (1991) interviewed 36 married couples and found that 58 percent of women who used severe violence attributed their actions to self-defense, compared to only 5 percent of the men; 50 to 80 percent of men who used severe violence did so in order to control their partners.

Using data collected from both partners of 199 military couples required to attend domestic violence treatment, Jennifer Langhinrichsen-Rohling,

Peter Neidig, and George Thorn (1995) found that although both husbands and wives used violence in 83 percent of the cases, the husband's violence was more severe, the husbands were less likely to be injured, and the husbands were far less likely to report any fear of their wives.

L. Kevin Hamberger, Jeffrey Lohr, and Dennis Bonge (1994) examined the motivations behind the violence of 75 women and 219 men arrested and court-referred into domestic violence counseling programs. They asked respondents, "What was the function, purpose or payoff of your violence?" Women's answers revealed that they used violence for self-defense, as protection from or retaliation for prior physical violence and psychological battering, or to escape violence. Men, on the other hand, used violence as a means of control and domination over their female partners. When women are the first to use violence, they are often using it as a tactical strategy to avoid getting hit themselves or in response to perceived threats of physical or sexual violence directed against them.[89]

In interviews conducted with criminal justice professionals and social service providers working directly with battered women arrested on domestic violence charges, Susan Miller (2005) found that women did not have the same power over men that men have over them. The men were rarely in fear of their lives. The women also did not control the men's autonomy, that is, whom they could call on the phone, whom they could socialize with, what clothing they could wear, whether they could visit with family members, or whether they had a curfew.

This evidence notwithstanding, some are not persuaded and maintain a gender-neutral stance, arguing that all violent acts and assaults, regardless of the context in which they are used, are criminal acts, independent of the assailant's gender, and that policies that fail to hold women accountable for violence they perpetrate should not be endorsed.[90] Often, the men most vocal about women's violence are ones embroiled in custody disputes during divorce proceedings; to strengthen their cases, such men frequently join father's rights groups that endorse this position.[91]

Concerns about gender neutrality and law enforcement get to the heart of the dilemma: Does equality demand that the law be applied uniformly, irrespective of gender? Like crimes should be treated in a like manner, but generally, a battering victim's use of violence is not the same as a batterer's use of violence. Therefore, due to this difference—and not because of gender—many feel that these cases should be handled differently. Similar to studies that explore why women use violence, additional studies that focus on arrested women reveal that they are often enmeshed in a pattern of violence that they typically did not initiate or control.[92] This possibility of differing contexts and motivations introduces serious policy implications for how women are treated and what kinds of intervention strategies should be used. This entails an understanding of the long-held recognition that intimate-partner violence is a major problem rooted in social and structural inequity in which power-control dynamics are used to allow one individual to gain mastery over another individual and within a relationship.

Arrest and prosecution may also increase the danger for victims of domestic battery. Some probation officers recognize that a woman on probation following a domestic battery arrest may still be in danger, or may be in even greater danger, if her partner is a batterer and she struck in self-defense or in an attempt to stop the violence from escalating.[93] Recent research conducted by Miller (2001; 2005) on women arrested for intimate-partner violence found that men manipulated the women and/or the criminal justice system: for example, some men challenge a woman's right to trial (rather than accepting a guilty plea) by claiming that the woman would lose her children if she lost at trial; self-inflict wounds so that police would view the woman as assaultive and dangerous; call 911 themselves, rather than letting women be the first to call, so that they could proactively define the situation; and capitalize on the outward calm they display once police arrive (the man's serenity highlights the woman's hysteria).[94] The treatment providers interviewed said that one of the most common statements they heard in treatment groups for male batterers was "Get to the phone first."

These mandatory arrest policies and their consequences raise multiple questions: What should the police do in situations where victims of domestic violence commit a violent act? Are police doing "too good a job" of making arrests and enforcing the law? Do police miss important contextual information by being incident-driven in their investigations? How should we evaluate the "success" of intimate-partner arrest policies? Are there actions that the police can take, such as determining the primary aggressor or uncovering the history of relationship abuse at the scene, that could have an effect on determining the course of action that police should follow? What should prosecutors do? If a battered woman does commit a violent crime, how should she be sanctioned by the courts? Many of these questions are addressed in the rest of this chapter.

Court Processing of Women Arrested for Abuse

Compounding the complexity of this issue, underscored by the questions posed above, is what happens to the victim after she is arrested as an offender.

In Miller's (2001; 2005) work, the issues raised by professionals in the field included women's unfamiliarity with the court process, limited knowledge of their options, and powerlessness in the process. Women's legal problems multiplied once they arrived at court. Many respondents advised women who acted in self-defense to hold out for a trial. However, the process was not that simple: most women were not accustomed to being charged as offenders, and they were mystified about the criminal justice process. Women were eager to get the case over with and return home, so they accepted a guilty plea without fully appraising the potential consequences of having a record. These consequences included being barred from certain employment opportunities, denial or loss of public housing, denial or loss of welfare benefits, problems related to immigration status, and issues related to custody hearings—all things that disproportionately harm women, since they tend to be the primary caregivers in relationships.[95] Women found the court process intimidating and stigmatizing:

> Women have an awful lot of pressure put on them when they get to the courts to just plea guilty. But the women don't seem to understand that there are reasons why they might not be guilty, even though they did scratch his face. I have even had clients whose partners were on top of them and they were pushing his face away and they broke his glasses and got scratches on his face and the next day the woman gets arrested. (Family court advocate)

In order to ensure the efficiency of case processing, public defenders and prosecutors acted less as adversaries than as a friendly courtroom workgroup members, thus possibly obscuring their real goals of a zealous courtroom pursuit of the truth in lieu of rushing women through the system.

> The public defenders are so accustomed to working with the Attorney Generals in negotiating the plea bargaining that they will really encourage the victim to go ahead and plea—it's just easier. It's faster and the victim will be taking a big chance in going into court and then if found guilty and then how about having a record. (Family court advocate)

Women were encouraged to plea guilty in exchange for getting into the First Offenders Program, which placed them under probation supervision and mandated their attendance at a 12-week treatment program.

> I think a lot of people get screwed in that way, since they are really encouraged to plea guilty then they have it on their record or they get this First Offenders Program through family court so that it won't end up on their record in the long run except for being arrested. It won't show up as a conviction so it won't affect their employment or if they were going to be found guilty then that's a good deal too, because then they are not going to have a conviction so that could affect them later. The whole thing is a big mess—who needs a record? and they don't know what is going to happen so they don't know if they should take the pleas. (Director of shelter)

Probation officers, treatment providers, shelter workers, and victim advocates felt that both public defenders and prosecutors took advantage of the women's confusion and manipulated them into decisions that benefited their own positions or the system's need to dispose of cases quickly.

> It's very dehumanizing. The women already feel stigmatized by having been arrested, they don't understand the process . . . and I'm not gonna tell you it's all that different for men. The process often takes place in a waiting room, you are told what can happen if you choose to plead not guilty and are found guilty, and then they are told what they can do if they plea guilty . . . so a lot of women are buying into it because it seems like the simplest thing to do. . . . they're afraid of going to jail. (Treatment provider)

These respondents also felt that the attorneys strong-armed the women into accepting a guilty plea in exchange for what was presented as an ideal opportunity: "The women hear about this wonderful offenders program where you go to treatment and you are on probation for a year and then your charges will be expunged off your record, so they agree to the program, but they just don't have a clear understanding of what they are agreeing to" (victims' services provider).

Shelter workers, victims' services personnel, and treatment providers believed that the women would be better off going to court with self-defense justifications: "At least three-fourths of the time if they had taken it on to trial, they could have gotten out of the charge and been found not guilty" (shelter director). However, social service providers and other battered women's advocates typically were not involved in the case at the arraignment stage, since the women were not yet identified as victims. Consequently, the women did not receive any alternative information or encouragement to plead not guilty. The arrested women were also concerned about the time and money the process took, and the First Offenders Program offered an attractive option just at the point when the women were most vulnerable. One of the treatment providers believed there was a problem with the way options were presented and that women gravitated toward life preservers thrown at them: "You're told that you have a choice of going to jail or staying with your family, and maybe that language is what makes the difference." Women easily capitulated once they were threatened with having a criminal record and possibly having their kids taken away from them. "And for all practical purposes, you deem the women powerless and they believe them-selves to be powerless. So consequently, if there's the remote chance that they are going to be convicted and they could lose their kids, they'll plead" (treat-ment provider).

Thus, in many cases the criminal justice system victimized battered women a second time. Battered women's confusion about their arrests was exacerbated by their lack of familiarity with the court process. Neither the arrested women nor the criminal justice system challenged the operating assumption of women's aggression once arrests were made.

Treatment Programs Designed for Female "Offenders"

One component of the social, legal, and political activism to address batter-ing is the development of treatment programs for abusers. Overwhelmingly designed for (heterosexual) men, these programs divert offenders from incarceration while they strive to reeducate and transform male batterers into peaceful, equality-embracing partners—a lofty goal for short-term pro-grams in which participation is court-mandated, not voluntary. However, as an unintended consequence of mandatory, preferred, and pro-arrest pol-icies aimed at deterring violence offenders, many battered women are now arrested and court-ordered to a treatment program designed for male abusers.[96] Domestic violence advocates and scholars are conflicted about these programs. Most agree that it is imperative to know who the batterer is and to send only that person to a treatment program.[97] For women who use violence but are victims of abuse, court-mandated programs seem inappro-priate. Sue Osthoff's view (2002: 1536) is unequivocal: "No one who is not a batterer should ever be required to attend a batterers' intervention program. Ever." Similarly, Shamita Dasgupta (2002) declares that it is illogical to label women batterers and follow the goals of batterer treatment programs designed to confront male privilege and resocialize participants to be nonviolent.[98] Although mandatory/pro-arrest policies aim to curtail discretion, and thus hopefully eliminate racism or classism by treating all perpetrators equally, it is possible that women who do not conform to gendered notions of "pure" or "good" victim (i.e., nice, delicate, passive) but, rather, are more "masculine" (i.e., mouthy, aggressive toward police, drunk) are the ones who face arrest.[99] If women use violence, they evoke different reactions, since the behavior contradicts gender-role assumptions.[100] Part of this incongruence is fueled by the way a battered woman is typically depicted by the media and legal system as passive and helpless.[101] If she does not conform to this expectation—if she is violent instead—it is scary and surprising. In addition, evidence suggests that battered women who use force are not safe; they face increased vulnerability to their partner's aggression.[102]

We investigated women's use of intimate-partner violence by analyzing transcripts from women's "offender" treatment groups.[103] In six months of participant observation of three different female "offender" treatment groups in one state, the authors observed 95 women who participated in the programs. Findings revealed three different types of behavior that led women to be charged with intimate-partner violence: truly violent behavior, defensive behavior, and frustration response behavior. The first category, *truly violent behavior*, included women who used violence in many circumstances, not just in intimate relationships: for example, against neighbors, other family members, strangers, or acquaintances. This accounted for the smallest number of women, roughly 5 percent of the program's clients. What was unique about this group was that the nature of their violence differed from that typically associated with "batterers." A batterer uses violence as a vehicle for getting his or her partner to do something.

However, from what was observed, the women who used aggressive violence against intimate partners did not have power over the men. The women were not able to control or change men's behavior; in fact, the male victims neither feared them nor changed their behavior out of a sense of intimidation, responses that would be typical for female victims abused by men. Linda's case typified this category. Linda was mandated to treatment based on three violent episodes; her current offense involved threatening a female neighbor for parking too close to her truck. Prior to this, Linda attacked her wheelchair-bound uncle during a family quarrel and attacked her live-in boyfriend due to jealousy over another woman. In group, Linda was argumentative and nonapologetic.

Another example is Tyra. She and her husband were separated at the time of the incident, and she had a drug addiction. Although she never physically hit him, she was arrested for terroristic threats. Tyra does not have a history of victimization, and she freely admitted that her husband, although emotionally distant and a workaholic, was not physically abusive. Here is how Tyra described the incident that brought her to group:

Tyra: I went out partying and never came home and my husband was a little upset, and I threatened him.

Facilitator: You threatened him? What did you threaten him with?

Tyra: That I was gonna get somebody to come there and kill him. I didn't strike him or nothin'. But he called the cops. The next day, they came to my work. I ended up with a year probation, this program, and drug counseling.

Tyra saw this as a wake-up call and now attends both Alcoholics and Narcotics Anonymous and is on probation for a year; she and her husband are attempting reconciliation.

An illustration of preemptive violence, one that followed a long history of victimization, is Dawn's story. Dawn and her husband have two children together. His abusive behavior toward her began when she was 5 months pregnant with their first child; he choked her, beat her, held guns to her head threatening to kill her, and drove cars at dangerously high speeds without letting her out. She had a civil protection order against him from one state, but he followed her to an adjoining state. Her mother and other family members encouraged her to try to make the marriage work, and they did reconcile; months later, she was pregnant with their second child. She left her son in his care, but when she came home, her husband was snoring on the couch while her son was screaming and crying; he mocked her and refused to answer any questions about their son. In the past, after he was violent and she called the police, he ran to the woods and hid, so he never was arrested. Suspecting the worse, afraid for her own safety, and mad as hell, she ordered him out of the house. Here are her words:

I went to the kitchen, I got a knife and threatened to kill him from the other side of the door. I didn't know what I was doing with the knife 'cause I really didn't want to hurt him but he went to grab for my hand and when I switched the knife over, it cut his thumb. He got that cleaned up and he went down to the gas station and called the police on me. They came and asked me if I had cut him. Actually, they said "stabbed" him. He also had lacerations on this chest and his back. I have no idea how they got there. I know that I didn't go do it with the knife. But they charged me with possession of a deadly weapon and assault in the second degree. They put me in handcuffs in front of my son.

These examples suggest that these women used violence in a response to an immediate incident, and the consequences were negligible. Although these men were victimized, their girlfriends and wives did not fit the pattern associated with male batterers. The women did not establish or reestablish control or power over their partner or former partner as a result of their actions. Only one woman had a long history of victimization.

The second category, *defensive behavior*, comprised the majority or about 60 percent of the women. These women were trying to get away or to leave in order to avoid their partner's violence. In many cases, particularly when there were children at home, the women were not able to get away; typically, a woman's violence occurred *after* her male partner was the first to use violence. The violence used by these women was in response to either an initial harm or a threat to them or their children, as can be seen in the following examples.

Patty returned to her abusive husband after a two-month separation; he begged her to come back after he was shot by a drunken friend, so she decided to try to make things work and they went out partying on his boat. When they got back home, her mother-in-law was there, and they don't get along, so Patty tried to leave. Here is her account:

> I tried to leave but he doesn't want me to leave, but I walked out the door and he jumps on me. I hopped in my car, and he moves behind my car and in front of my car and tries to break into the windows with a stick. So I put my car in drive and pinned him up against the garage wall. I didn't realize what I was doing until he looked at me and said "Patty, please go." I felt like total shit, I put my car in reverse and just left.

Patty was arrested the next day for assault with a deadly weapon and assault with intent to harm. Facing a possible jail term of 25 years, she hired an attorney and pled guilty to a lesser charge. She received probation, substance abuse treatment, and the First Offenders Program.

Wendy's experience mirrored that of many of the women in the group. Her ex-husband was abusive, striking both her and her son (by another man) for the several years they were together. As Wendy describes it: "He was pushing and beating on me and he would beat up my son all the time just because he [the son] was at home. He did drugs in front of them. I got sent to jail for not doing anything, for child endangerment." She was mad that she had been jailed for three days, and to make matters worse, when she got out of jail she found her husband at home with another woman:

> He started pushing and hitting me again, so I just hauled off and I struck him. And then I heard the cops come. My daughter had

called the cops and she said he is biting my mom. When the cops came, she told them to help me, but they let him tell the story instead. They saw that I had just come from jail.

Although her ex-husband had been physically abusive to her and the children, Wendy had never called the police or filed a protection order, so there was no paper trail that designated him as the batterer. The police did not investigate the circumstances of the prior arrest, the shared history, or the current incident.

Nicole's situation also involved her ex-husband and child. Tom, her ex-husband, asked Nicole for a Christmas suggestion for their daughter, and she said that sneakers were what the daughter wanted. Christmas came and went, and their daughter never received the present. Nicole spotted Tom at the shopping mall a few days after New Year's and asked him about it, insinuating that he spent the money to support his drug and alcohol addiction:

> Nicole: I said, "I am quite sure you wasted the money on your beer." He shoved me, hard, so when he shoved me, I just hit him. I didn't hit him hard, but he had said to me, "She [their daughter] deserves to suffer sometimes. Don't no kid deserve to have everything she want in life." Maybe that's true, but the point is that if he had told me that, I could've gotten her the sneaks.
>
> Facilitator: What did you hit him with?
>
> Nicole: A closed first. I punched him. I don't know actually where I hit him. I didn't hurt my hand, so it wasn't like I hit him real hard.
>
> Facilitator: What were things like when you were together?
>
> Nicole: We did drugs together. I stopped, and that busted him up. He hit me a lot. I hit him back, but actually I can't hurt him. He's bigger than me. I can only sting him, just like a little bit or nothing, get him away from me so I could leave.

Nicole was typical of women in this category who freely admitted to their violence and explained it within the context of ongoing abuse. These women saw their violence as an act of self-defense or a way to exit the hostile situation.

Terry was with her boyfriend as he drove his car. They were engaged in a verbal argument, and he began punching her as he drove. He accelerated, so she could not jump out. He grabbed her and put his arms around her neck in a choke hold, almost strangling her; she could scarcely breathe. Terry pushed him away. Despite the marks around her neck, she was arrested. Terry acknowledges that she was told that she did not have to plead guilty. However, she assumed that it was her fault and that pleading guilty and getting the First Offenders Program would allow her to avoid jail time. Terry describes herself as someone with a temper who has a lot of anger. She minimized his actions to the group, saying, "Since I know how he can get, I shouldn't be running my mouth. I have a problem with my mouth. He starts it; I finish it, because I have that much of a temper. I spent all these years trying to argue with someone that there's no sense in arguing with. I should know better." Quickly, the facilitator interjected, trying to put the violence into perspective for Terry: "When someone puts their hands around your neck, they are strangling you. It only takes seven pounds of pressure on the windpipe to kill you. And it only takes cutting off the oxygen to the brain for death; I think it's six minutes for a brain injury and anything under that you can be resuscitated hopefully."

What the incidents in this category demonstrate is that most women used violence to defend themselves or their children or to escape an impending violent attack—a possibility they knew was realistic, given their past experiences with the batterer. Most of the women had long histories of victimization, and most believed they had no choice but to fight back. Often, their social support networks and/or the criminal justice system failed to protect them. Many lived isolated lives, sometimes geographically exiled out in the country, and sometimes by design of the batterer, who had cut off the women's contact with friends and family. Children and drugs/alcohol were common factors. Often the women were arrested because the male batterer called the police, but just as likely another family member at the scene or a neighbor called. In all cases, the women were surprised and outraged at the arrest. The women in this category perceived their violence as a reasonable and justified action given the potential for harm to themselves or their children. Part of these women's disbelief at their own arrest stems from the fact that their abusers often escaped arrest after beating them, often in egregious ways.

The remaining 35 percent of the women comprise the final category, *frustration response ("end of her rope") behavior*. These women often had histories of domestic battery (with their current partner or in an earlier relationship) and reacted violently when nothing else seemed to stop his behavior. Typically, the women responded to stressful situations with partners that might lead to a mutually violent episode. These women were different from those in the first category (truly violent) because they overwhelmingly exhibited violent behavior with a partner who was abusive toward them emotionally, sexually, and/or physically. In some cases, the man was the primary aggressor, but the woman responded with violence.[104] Kelly exemplifies the women in the frustration response category. Kelly left an abusive 16-year marriage with Tim. When her new boyfriend, Gerald, started becoming emotionally abusive, she flashbacked to what emotional abuse had symbolized in her marriage, which was traumatic. (Tim's emotional abuse had typically led to both sexual abuse and physical battering.) Kelly hit her boyfriend with both hands, apparently causing no injury, but a neighbor called police to report the noise.

Another woman in this category, Eunice, reported a lengthy history of violent relationships with men. Eunice talks about the events leading up to her arrest:

> Eunice: I was charged with offensive touching. My husband and I got into an argument one night because the baby had a diaper rash and it was really, really late and he didn't feel like it was important to get the diaper rash medicine and I did and we got into an argument and it escalated. There was a lot of yelling involved and then I said that I was going to leave with the baby and he didn't want me to so he was standing there in front of the door, and I tried to move him out of the way. I scratched him.
> Facilitator: How did you scratch him?
> Eunice: With my nails. And someone heard the yelling and called the police. The police showed up and then I was charged.

Eunice was frustrated by her husband's behavior, which she portrayed as consistently neglectful, and admitted to causing his physical injury, albeit minor.

Sunny's experience is the final example for this category. From the time that she was 14 years old until she turned 24, she was a victim of many beatings (father, stepfather, boyfriends). Her current husband has physically assaulted her for the past two years. She explains, "I got to the point that . . . if you are gonna put your hands around me, choking me, or throwing me out of the car, I am not taking it no more." Although they reconciled after he beat her (because Sunny's mother would no longer let Sunny and the children stay with her), she was arrested for pushing him out of the doorway when she was trying to leave, similar to Eunice's case. She was attempting to leave because he was smoking pot in front of her three kids: her house became a drug hangout for her husband's friends, and she did not want her kids to be raised the (poor) way that she felt she was raised. Sunny decided that her children's safety was more important than "obeying" her tyrannical husband, so she risked further abuse by trying to leave.

For these women, their violence did nothing to change the abuse and power dynamics of their relationships. Without analyzing options or planning ahead, the women in this category responded to a violent environment with force, because much of the present situation was reminiscent of past abuse in their lives. The women's use of violence suggests that they were acting out older patterns where they used force as a reaction to conflict. In general, these women perceived that they had no other options—they either had not received or had not asked for help from the criminal justice system or their social support networks during earlier abusive incidents. They used violence as an expressive tool to demonstrate their outrage or frustration over a situation in which they felt powerless.

What these three paths to arrest indicate is that the truly violent woman is an anomaly. Of course there are indeed women who use violence against strangers and intimates, but they are rare, and the data demonstrate that considering context is vital to our understanding of the motivation and meaning behind women's force. Our examination of the cases revealed that most women used violence to thwart their husbands' or boyfriends' egregious actions, to defend themselves or their children, or because their current situation mirrored earlier circumstances in their lives where they perceived or experienced danger and violence. Although some battered women may be helped by court-mandated treatment programs (for instance, if those programs offered them information about resources that they would not get elsewhere), failing to understand the context of the relationship violence and coercing women to attend batterer groups (presented as gifts in exchange for guilty pleas) replicates the very system of power and control that antiviolence advocates and scholars seek to eradicate. It is time for some serious reflection about the appropriateness and potential misapplication of domestic violence arrest and punishment policies.

Conclusions and Policy Recommendations

This chapter explored the pitfalls and problems that developed when victims encountered new laws and policies. The effects of these reforms created new hardships or reinforced already untenable and dangerous positions for female victims of male violence. Throughout discussions in the chapter, it was obvious that the victim conundrum continues, leaving us struggling to untangle the puzzles.

We reexamined situations in which policy efforts in one area collide with victim circumstances in another, essentially creating second victimizations. It is no small matter that the lack of economic resources is a key reason that women stay in abusive relationships. This structural condition, poverty, influences both public housing residents and welfare-to-work participants. Moreover, many battered women work arduously to gain and maintain employment, despite their abusers' efforts to thwart them. The possibility of temporary exemptions to the stringent welfare-to-work requirements through the Family Violence Option needs to be more widely publicized both to recipients and to welfare caseworkers so that battered women's safety issues are better addressed. Research reveals that battered women are more likely to disclose abuse histories to on-site victims' advocates rather than to welfare caseworkers, so steps should be taken to ensure that such opportunities exist. In addition, as suggested by some researchers, greater flexibility in meeting the exception requirements is necessary, such as permitting sworn statements by family members, friends, or neighbors or having domestic violence professionals assess the applicant's situation instead of the current practice of accepting only official court documentation and formal criminal justice corroboration.[105] The Federal Office of Child Support Enforcement and others noted a critical need to better identify and serve domestic violence victims and the need to eliminate agency-level obstacles to victim support, such as poor caseworker training and inadequate resources.

In the public housing arena, it needs to be acknowledged that intimate-partner violence does not create an unsafe housing environment for others and that evicting battered women exacerbates their impoverishment. Domestic violence specialists should help interpret for landlords the unique situations faced by battered women and explain the difference between primary aggressive action and self-defensive action. Increased use of disparate impact claims as a tool to demonstrate how a law produces disproportionately negative effects on women should be considered in wrongful eviction cases, given the claims' early success in the courts. Finally, in terms of civil forfeiture cases, the nation as a whole is rethinking the draconian laws produced by various "wars" on crime or drugs. This trend is reflected by some courageous judges' refusal to impose mandatory penalties for "three strikes" laws for drug offenses, and there is some indication, at least at the state level, that the notion of the "innocent owner" in civil forfeiture cases is not viewed as culpable, as in cases past.

Another victim-relevant policy addressed here was the civil rights provision of the Violence Against Women Act. The demise of this civil remedy eliminated an opportunity for victims of gender-motivated violence to bring civil suit in federal court. A number of alternatives were proposed. It is important to note that critics (and the Supreme Court in the *Brzonkala* ruling) did not oppose the goal of the legislation per se, just the constitutional reasoning (Fourteenth Amendment) behind it.[106] Thus, one alternative is to use the Thirteenth Amendment as a constitutional vehicle to reenact civil remedies for victims of gender-motivated violence, since the Thirteenth Amendment provides Congress with the power to remedy occasions of involuntary servitude.[107]

Another option to the elimination of the federal civil rights remedy in VAWA is to increase state power in eradicating domestic violence; for instance, state legislation could allow a victim to obtain permanent injunctive orders that forbid a defendant from contacting her or him. This would extend most states' orders of protection, which currently last only for a specific amount of time.[108] Other state-level enhancements include permitting victims to collect damages from their attackers, including punitive damages and legal fees.[109] Finally, many states' statutes provide civil rights remedies for victims of gender-motivated violence in their bias crime laws. Over 27 states and the District of Columbia include gender in their bias crime laws, and though it is not widely used yet, this could be a fruitful avenue for victims to pursue.[110] Also, some federal legislation includes gender as a category needing protection.[111]

Finally, arrests of battered women raise the larger question of how mandatory policies (arrest and prosecution) feed into larger crime-control objectives and increase the power of the state. Regardless of one's political persuasion, fighting crime is a campaign pleaser, and funds flow into state budgets to help develop policies that are characterized by increased reliance on surveillance, control, and harsher punitive measure to shape social behavior.[112] Yet crime-control policy implementation comes at a cost. Overwhelmingly, research demonstrates that mandatory arrest and prosecution policies limit victim empowerment (albeit providing temporary respite from violence), increase the risk that battered women will be arrested on domestic violence charges, increase the risk of unwarranted removal of children by the state, and increase prosecution of female victims.[113] Some scholars argue that responses to domestic violence come at the expense of poor women, since the measures that render them less vulnerable to abuse, such as transportation, education, or job training, are not part of funded reforms.[114] Moreover, advocates for battered women spend the bulk of their time monitoring criminal justice interventions to domestic violence (by police and prosecutors) and conducting training sessions for criminal justice professionals. Thus, meaningful reforms to help economically poor battered women include increasing the number of free lawyers, increasing funds for emergency relocation and long-term housing, adding job training programs, and creating educational opportunities.[115]

An unintended consequence of the new mandatory arrest policies is to widen the net of domestic violence offenders. When discretion is removed or when contextual factors such as primary aggressor status are not fully examined, police arrest battered women. In other words, mandatory arrest policies increase the risk of arresting victims. The women described here demonstrate the "direct and collateral consequences of criminal arrests and convictions,"[116] which are particularly grave when victims are arrested mistakenly. While many advocates embrace a harsher criminal justice response to battering (largely to make up for years of indifference and trivialization), arrest policies that target the "wrong" offender were not the intended outcome. Given that the overwhelming majority of women arrested for domestic violence are not "batterers," approbation for a policy that is punitively based and not mindful of the circumstances in which intimate partner violence takes place is misguided.

Additional unintended fallout associated with these newer mandatory arrest and prosecution policies are their deleterious impact on victims' perceptions of empowerment. Faced with possible retaliatory violence, battered women may not report further violence, or they may not cooperate with police or prosecution efforts because, as in the dynamic with their abuser, victims often feel helpless and powerless to direct the outcome of their situation. To put it another way, rather than protecting and empowering victims, well-intentioned policies such as mandatory arrest and no-drop prosecution may unintentionally make matters worse for women. "Disempowering victims is the antithesis of the goal of most abused women and advocates. Those supporting this are probably unaware that they may be reinforcing the [societal] belief that the 'fickle' victim is the primary reason for the system's lack of responsiveness, rather than the system's inability to flexibly address individual victim needs."[117]

Another example of well-intentioned policies that have unexpected outcomes for victims is the advent of no-drop prosecution for domestic battery charges, which is designed to encourage aggressive prosecution and conviction in these cases.[118] However, what these policies gain in symbolism (i.e., woman battering will be zealously prosecuted, and the message that battering is wrong will be conveyed), they may lose in terms of deterring future violence. Therefore, it may not be surprising that the only prosecution policy associated with a decrease in incidents of domestic assault embraced the notions of victim empowerment for self-protection by allowing victims to drop criminal charges at will.[119] For this particular prosecution study, all victim-initiated domestic violence charges were allowed to be dropped if the victim believed that further prosecution of the case was unnecessary or if prosecution would increase the likelihood of revictimization by the abuser. (Cases resulting from police arrests were excluded, since victims cannot dismiss police charges.)[120] This finding suggests that criminal justice policies designed deliberately to discount a victim's preference for arrest or prosecution may not ultimately be in the best interest of some battered women.[121] Criminal justice personnel, and victims' services providers for that matter, need to recognize and acknowledge the rights of victims, respect their choices, avoid victim blaming, provide victims with options for informal and formal actions/redress, and work to actively support victims. Police need to enforce civil protection orders, and violations should be dealt with as a serious issue.

Battered women often say that they desire rehabilitation options for their abusers, thus they view arrests of their abusers as the vehicle that might be helpful in facilitating treatment for abusers' addiction or mental health problems.[122] Similarly, as mentioned briefly in chapter 5, analyses of program outcomes for sex-offender therapy indicate a reduction in sexual offending for men who successfully complete the stringent therapeutic process.[123] In terms of treatment programs designed for male batterers, models that use explicit confrontational techniques (i.e., confrontational group processes that force batterers to accept responsibility for their behavior) and offer longer-term programs and more in-depth counseling, such as EMERGE or AMEND, have demonstrated success.[124] Therefore, court-mandated treatment programs designed for men who batter and for male sex offenders have the potential to be one of the criminal justice system's most effective tools for reducing violence against women among recognized offenders.

Taken together, the victim issues raised in this section related to welfare reform, public housing, civil forfeiture, VAWA, and domestic violence arrest policies raise too many concerns and unintended consequences for them to be embraced wholeheartedly. At the core of these policies, victims' voices—their needs as well as the policies' effects on their lives—are absent. This needs to be rectified.

Assessing Where We Are, Where We Should Go, and How Best to Get There

7

> Let us make sure that we give our victims the right to be heard—
> not in some dispassionate way in an impact statement, but in a
> courtroom if they want to be heard, so that people can know what
> it's like to be a victim. Let us give them an opportunity to partici-
> pate, to be there, and to hold the criminal justice system at every
> level accountable. (U.S. Attorney General Janet Reno, New York
> City National Candlelight Vigil, April 25, 1993)

This final chapter raises unresolved questions about female victims and the politics of the victimization discourse, debating whether the responses are largely symbolic or whether they offer real reform. While we cannot address here all of the issues related to violence against women, we explore the most enduring victimizations and suggest a path for future research and practices. We also examine the policy outcomes associated with VAWA monies and review several promising state-level prevention programs aimed at reducing the victimization of women and children. In addition, we offer some overall recommendations regarding the future directions of the victims' rights movement aimed at ending violence against women. The concluding section of this chapter explores alternatives to victims' use of the formal criminal justice system, looking at the potential of restorative justice and other dispute resolution alternatives.

Reform or Rhetoric? The Politics of Victimization

The tenacity and endurance of offenders and their crimes of violence against women lead us to question the efficacy of criminal justice and legal responses as well as the potential of justice processes to end sexual assault and battering. In the past twenty years, many police and court procedures were scrutinized and overhauled, and many examples of victim advocacy, support, and legislation are now in place. Yet many problems remain intractable, no doubt because police, courts, and advocates lack the ability to create fundamental changes in social conditions that facilitate and perpetuate violence against women.

It is fashionable for social commentators to manipulate the message and attack the efforts of the victims' rights movement, and they are not without sound reasons. Concern about how legislators and conservative politicians have embraced victims' rights, especially at election time, is well placed. Helping victims is a crowd pleaser and aligns nicely with the punitive crime-control agenda of social and political conservatives.[1] It is also argued that officially sanctioned victim policy has a hidden agenda: to neutralize the anger and potential power of the victims' rights movement.[2] At least one scholar contends that the creation of a culture of victimhood can address the needs of individual victims, but this is accomplished at the expense of losing sight of larger policy and resource implications.[3] Victims' services agencies must strike a balance between one-on-one work with victims and their immediate needs versus playing a wider advocacy role and working for procedural, social, and political change.

In truth, trade-offs are necessary. Having a higher political profile elevates victimization to a larger, "worthy" social problem, which in turn attracts increased resources. However, politicians' motives are often questionable. Robert Elias (1990, 1993) contends that the victims' rights movement was co-opted by conservative groups, has been used to justify harsher penalties for offenders, has enacted legislation that authorities do not enforce, has failed to provide adequate funding for policy initiatives, and has rerouted funds earmarked for rehabilitation/treatment into crime-control efforts, all under the guise of "helping victims." For instance, politicians mount "wars" on drugs or crime and increase the severity of sentences, all in the name of victims, yet there is little evidence that the tactics protect victims more. These wars are expensive to conduct, do little to reduce victimization rates, and criminalize huge numbers of people without doing much to transform offenders' attitudes or behavior.[4] Treatment of offenders may produce long-term decreases in victimization (if the programs are adequately funded and administered), but in the short term, "wars on crime" primarily help politicians appear tough on crime and transform political candidates into elected politicians.[5]

At their inception, the rape and the battered women's movements were both fueled by grassroots participants and victims, who were joined by professionals (social workers, psychologists, and lawyers). The movements' early vision reflected both a sociopolitical analysis of women's subordinate status within gendered relationships and a belief in social change. Over time, the movements have undergone great changes, and the strong feminist or political principles and practices that marked the early efforts were incorporated into a more social service–oriented framework. This transformation is common: other analyses of state co-optation of "splinter groups" have revealed that often what is initially political work advocating broad social change gets reconfigured to provide victims with therapeutic assistance and other social provisions.[6] Not surprisingly, nonprofit victim service agencies that rely on government sources for much of their funding are inevitably constrained in terms of how outspoken they can be on policy issues. Research demonstrates that as dependency on the government for resources grows, victims' movements become tied to funding requirements and to satisfying bureaucratic exigencies.[7] For instance, in her analysis of the U.S. social welfare system, Nancy Fraser (1989) describes how political issues concerning different people's needs are transformed into legal, administrative, and/or therapeutic procedures.[8] This reconceptualization permits the state to appear responsive and benevolent to social concerns while still maintaining the power to determine the "needs" and "responses." This analysis can be easily extended to the rape and battered women's movements.

In this same vein, Frank Weed (1995) argues that changes stemming from the victims' rights movement are symbolic; he questions whether the rights of victims have really improved or whether the justice process simply appears more legitimate in victims' eyes. Numerous scholars believe that victims continue to be marginalized or completely ignored, and are revictimized as a result of system responses to their victimizations, a situation that is exacerbated for poor victims and/or victims of color. Part of these contradictions in rhetoric versus reality may reflect a distinction between practitioners working in the field and researchers working in the university setting: issues such as power imbalances in gender relations are more likely to be discussed by feminist movement workers and academics than by practitioners and researchers without a feminist orientation. Gillian Walker (1990) contends that this absorption of feminist concerns about gender, violence, and power into existing institutional structures inevitably occurs within patriarchal, capitalist societies as a result of governmental appropriation, manipulation, and depoliticization of the end-violence-against-women movement. State co-optation of movements like the anti-rape movement and the battered women's movement serves to "manage" and bureaucratize prevention and victim services—and, in doing so, may provide new laws and penalties and needed services, but generally does little to challenge or change gender relations.[9] "Therapeutic orientations eliminate wider political visions of social change and move, instead, to discourses associated with individualized medical-psychiatric care," as well as legal reforms.[10] This move from a feminist "political agenda of changing consciousness to a social service agenda of helping victims manage the trauma they experience" subtly— and successfully—displaces the critique of gender relations.[11]

Recall the voices of those commentators described in earlier chapters who rail at what they call a "victim culture." They are not so much denouncing the research as attacking a victim-oriented outlook. We have tried in this book to present balanced, scholarly evidence that reflects the enduring problem of violence against women in our society. The research findings and statistics are hard to dismiss. It is ironic to find that social conservatives now consider research too "pro-victim," given that in the 1970s, the liberal critics declared that the research was anti-victim.[12] We must move beyond a victim-culture debate.

Victim Paradoxes

We turn now from the politics of victimization to the complex and even contradictory perspectives on victims and victimizations. The topics we address in this conversation are sexual assault, sexual harassment (or gender harassment), and the meaning of abuse and how perceptions have changed over time. Furthermore, we acknowledge that the nature of who is considered a victim is fluid. Examples of this fluidity involve statutory rape (cases in which teenage girls date older men) and, later in the section, sexual (gender) harassment. Drawing on Sharon Lamb's (1999) book, we summarize a paradoxical conception of "statutory rape," based on research conducted by Lynn M. Phillips. Phillips's work demonstrates that listening to only one side of a statutory rape story, either the victim's version or the offender's, erases nuanced meanings and different perceptions of the same event. Thus, by acknowledging that alternative ways of looking at victims exist, it is possible to move beyond narrow definitions and meanings associated with such incidents. Unlike child abuse, rape, and battering, statutory rape typically involves willing participants and often "victim" initiation.[13] While the goal here is not to determine legality or even to decide whether statutory rape is inherently abusive, we do raise questions of power, consent, and coerciveness. Lynn Phillips (1997; 1999) found that teenage girls describe their experiences as chosen, and not traumatic but pleasurable. Teenagers describe themselves as more satisfied with the maturity and emotional intimacy of adult men, as well as the sense of respect and luxuries they receive from these men. Young women portrayed themselves as "active agents making constructive decisions to affirm their identities and bring them the benefits they sought from their relationships" and gaining access to wisdom and guidance they felt were lacking in their own homes.[14] The adult women interviewed, who had been involved with adult men when they themselves were teenagers, believed that although during their teen years they considered their involvement with adult men fun and exciting, in retrospect they can see more exploitation, manipulation, and coerciveness in the experience.[15] This raises a quandary: "If we were to listen only to young women's stories, we might conclude that adult-teen relationships are freely chosen, mutually beneficial, and therefore unproblematic. If we were to listen only to the voices of adult women . . . we might conclude that teen women are, in fact, overwhelmed victims who are preyed on by older men."[16] By taking both groups of women's perspectives into account, we get a more complete, albeit more complicated, picture of statutory rape, or at least a particular type of underage sexual activity, one that seems mutually consensual on its face. Also, in chapter 5 we presented the study showing how men convicted of crimes like statutory rape discuss the events leading up to their arrest and talk about their victims.

However, there is a meaningful difference between a situation in which both participants are in high school and consent to the sex (but one is underage while one meets the legal age of consent) and cases in which the male "perpetrator" who is of legal age evolves into a sex offender who will always prefer and prey on young women because they are less threatening than partners his own age. Thus, designating who is a victim may become even more ambiguous in already complicated situations, depending on the beliefs of the individuals involved—much more ambiguous than the labels conferred by the criminal justice system. Chapter 5 contains examples of statutory rape–like cases where young female victims, at least according to the men, were traumatized by the criminal justice system's response to what some of the victims perceived as consensual sexual relationships with older men; some of these men were regarded by the victims as boyfriends.

Nicola Gavey's (1999) work also addresses the confusion associated with victim identities and sexual assault. Specifically, she explores situations in which women's experiences meet legal definitions of attempted rape and/or date rape, yet the women choose to reject being labeled victims of rape. Partly, this rejection reflects women's understandings of what they believe constitutes "normal" (albeit coercive) heterosexual sex. Some of the women who were able to thwart men's sexually violent attacks felt empowered and proud of their abilities, not traumatized. This picture, of a triumphant woman who defends herself successfully against sexual assault, is not one typically highlighted in the rape literature. Entering into the contested area of the "date rape hype" debate, Gavey acknowledges that feminist research methods that classify attempted rapes, date rapes, and so forth in the general category of sexual assault succeeds in achieving an important goal: that of exposing the full range (and commonplace-ness) of sexual violence committed against women. At the same time, however, describing events as crimes and women who endure these crimes as victims without acknowledging that some women have alternative understandings of these events contradicts the feminist principle that one should not tell another's story; in other words, it may not be legitimate to label as "rape" experiences that women themselves do not describe in that way.[17] Highlighting women's success in avoiding rape is an important step in addressing overly deterministic models of victimization; it can be empowering to tell stories that reveal that rapists are not always successful. Gavey does not resolve this dilemma, but her insightful work highlights the situational complexity experienced by people who are ambivalent about their victimization and the ways that both researchers and practitioners struggle with how to best address their experiences.

The work done by both Gavey and Phillips highlights the problems inherent in establishing *who* is a victim and how should this label be conferred—by the victims themselves, advocates, or the legal system—and in understanding victims' interpretations of their experiences. Victims, as well as advocates and researchers, struggle to reconcile competing definitions and interpretations of events. Clearly, some victims experience more long-lasting harms of victimization, while others bounce back more quickly. Some of this resiliency depends on victims' interpretations of the events that occurred. Moreover, as we glean more intricate information from new research, we become more aware of the need for elasticity in recognizing the range of victims and discerning what responses are most appropriate to their needs (as advocates, policy makers, and so forth).

In another area, recent research has challenged traditional thinking about victimization under the rubric of sexual, or "gender," harassment, but based on socially constructed categories of acceptable femininity or masculinity. Here, the perpetrators are almost always men, a dynamic we also see in other group-perpetrator dynamics, such as gang rape or hate crimes. We make this exception—that of looking at gender harassment in which males are the victims—since it draws on sexist reasoning common to violence-against-women issues and underscores how important it is to challenge models of femininity and masculinity that perpetuate aggression, violence, and fear—factors that contribute to a culture tolerant of rape and battering. Since the 1980s, sexual harassment has become recognized as a set of sexist and demeaning behaviors that can be legally challenged, rather than simply endured and viewed as an inevitable part of school and work environments. Laws and policies address a range of negative conduct, from hostile environment to quid pro quo sex.[18] Thus, these gender-harassment cases challenge the assumption that women are somehow uniquely vulnerable to men's harassment and that only women are troubled by hostile work environments characterized by sexual innuendoes.[19] Research conducted by Deborah Lee (2000) examined workplace bullying of men by other men. She discovered that the most humiliating challenge to heterosexual men's identity is accusations of effeminacy. This is not unlike the 2009 phenomena of male-on-male rape in the Congo, a country where the government and Congo-Rwanda military are embroiled in a war with armed rebels. The country's sudden spike in men raping men is the source of concern for the Human Rights Watch, United Nations officials, and many Congolese aid organizations.[20] Experts regard this increased sexual violence against men as "yet another way for armed groups to humiliate and demoralize Congolese communities into submission."[21] Acceptable masculine behavior and appearance are rigidly defined, and if men do not meet these idealized standards, their masculinity is questioned. Although other research documents the sexual harassment of gay men, enforcement of narrow definitions of acceptable masculinity of heterosexual men is less examined.[22]

Male bonding between perpetrators, a dynamic strongly identified in other literature as instrumental to gang rapes committed against women and hate crimes committed against gays, is a key feature of masculinity harassment. For instance, at a Chevrolet dealership dominated by mostly male salesmen, the two male sales managers apparently would

> address salesmen as "little girls" or "whores." They would upbraid a guy by asking if he used tampons or tease him by saying that he had "to squat" when he urinated. The managers publicly derided struggling salesmen as "queers" or "steers"—because "steers try; bulls get the job done." To motivate the troops during sales meetings, they showed raunchy video clips, including one depicting a bull stepping on the genitals of a rodeo cowboy. [One] signaled his boredom with what a subordinate was saying to him by simulating masturbation

while the employee talked. He grabbed at male employees' genitals, sometimes making contact, sometimes, not, but mainly (or so it seemed to the men who got used to jumping out of his way or even running when they saw him) hoping to make them flinch.[23]

Ten of the salesmen filed a sexual-harassment lawsuit with the Equal Employment Opportunity Commission (EEOC), contending that the dealership created a hostile environment that discriminated against them as men. Thus, as the above examples of gender harassment and the earlier example of statutory rape indicate, the number and nature of victims expands as new understandings of sexual crimes' effects develop, and as new laws and policies are interpreted and enforced.

Policy reform in criminal justice and legal arenas are responses, not solutions. The reliance on criminal justice interventions, reflected in pro-arrest, no-drop, and evidence-based prosecution and VAWA projects, are limited in their ability to deter violence against women and challenge the gender-power relations that shore up these crimes. The next section questions the overreliance on the criminal justice system and proposes prevention projects as a way to create long-term change in social values that tacitly tolerate or facilitate violence against women.

Progress in Addressing Victims' Issues

Our intention in the preceding chapters was to provide a road map of sorts, one that told how and why the interest in victims and victims' rights began; what the main conflicts and debates surrounding victimizations are; how many female victims endure sexual victimization, physical violence, and stalking; and how they and the criminal justice system response to such experiences. We discussed the efficacy of many victim-centered policies and offered best practices. The unintended consequences associated with many of these laws were also examined. We also addressed how powerful social and cultural forces, such as the media, shaped the public's perceptions of victims and reflected public understandings about the extent and nature of crimes committed against women.

In the past twenty years, federal and state efforts to facilitate the victim's access to and participation in criminal justice proceedings have increased tremendously. Most of these efforts have centered on victims' rights to be present and heard at critical stages of the criminal justice process, such as prosecutorial charging decisions, plea negotiations, bail, pretrial-release hearings, trial, sentencing, and parole hearings. Concerns that the criminal justice workload would increase and that efficiency would be sacrificed have not been realized, nor have concerns that victims would use these new participatory rights to seek vengeance or retaliation against offenders. In fact, prosecutors and judges seem receptive to victims' comments and believe there is utility in knowing victim-impact information.[24] The sex-offender words contained in chapter 5 illustrate the transformative power of victim-impact statements in reshaping how offenders view their criminal behavior. However, victim-impact statements in particular have a limited effect on sentencing outcomes, which suggests that they are primarily symbolic in nature. One researcher suggested that including victims' input has only a "placebo value by creating the impression that 'something is being done.'"[25] Moreover, many victims do not take advantage of their rights to participate, despite some empirical findings that demonstrate that victim input can be powerful in discreet situations; for example, the presence of victim testimony is significantly associated with parole refusal decisions.[26] The unprecedented and successful attempt to reintegrate victims into a more participatory role in the criminal justice process is an important step forward in ensuring a balanced and just outcome.[27] Victims of sexual assault and rape, stalking, and battering—victims who often find the criminal justice process insensitive and too public—need to be fully supported in taking more active roles in exercising their participatory rights.

The enactment of legislation that provides victims' rights of participation in the justice process stemmed from the 1982 President's Task Force on Victims of Crime, which concluded the neglect of crime victims was a national disgrace. Similar to the explosion of constitutional, legislative, and judicial action discussed above, all 50 states instituted additional victim programs. The National Office for Victims of Crime (established in 1984) published a victims' rights manifesto, *New Directions from the Field: Victims' Rights and Services for the 21st Century* (1998). The almost 500-page document provides a comprehensive report and set of recommendations on victims' rights and services that have developed in the past 15 years in each state; it also offers global challenges for the nation to meet in its attempts to better assist victims in achieving justice and providing better services. Drawing on data collected from criminal and juvenile justice agencies, allied professionals, victims' services workers, and victims themselves, the report compiles hundreds of recommendations from the field. Here are the five key recommendations:

1. Enact and enforce consistent, fundamental rights for crime victims in federal, state, juvenile, military, and tribal justice systems, and administrative proceedings;

2. Provide crime victims with access to comprehensive, quality services regardless of the nature of their victimization, age, race, religion, gender, ethnicity, sexual orientation, capability, or geographic location;

3. Integrate crime victims' issues into all levels of the nation's educational system to ensure that justice and allied professionals and other service providers received comprehensive training on victims' issues as part of their academic education and continuing training in the field;

4. Support, improve, and replicate promising practices in victims' rights and services built upon sound research, advanced technology, and multidisciplinary partnerships; and

5. Ensure that the voices of crime victims play a central role in that nation's response to violence and those victimized by crime. (Office of Victims of Crime 1998: viii)

Although the 1998 report briefly mentions crimes of violence that are disproportionately committed against women, such as sexual assault or battering, these victimizations are not highlighted.[28] In addition, the thrust remains on evaluations of current reactive programs; less emphasis is placed on prevention and education efforts. While crimes committed against women generally remain submerged under general victim discussions, such as restitution and the barriers to its attainment, or victims' right to be present during criminal justice proceedings, there are a few exceptions. For instance, in a bulletin that examines enforcement of civil protection orders, relevant discussions of the full faith and credit provisions and the National Stalker and Domestic Violence Reductions Act (NSDVR Act) are included.[29] These provisions from the VAWA legislation and from laws passed in most states require that a protection order issued in another state must be enforced as though it were issued by the new state. This ensures enforcement of civil and criminal protective orders nationwide, even when victims cross state lines to escape abuse.[30] The NSDVR Act authorizes the inclusion of civil restraining and abuse prevention orders in all National Crime Information Center databases, yet only 19 states have started entering their protective orders since the FBI created the national registry in 1997.[31] The most recent statistics available are for the year 1998. That year the national registry contained slightly over 97,000 entries, which is estimated to be less than 5 percent of the 2 million orders qualified to enter the registry.[32] States need to participate more fully in these data collection efforts.

This report is helpful in presenting recommendations from practitioners in the field who work directly with victims, but it falls short of delivering specific policies for sexual assault, rape, stalking, and battering, and fails to evaluate research efforts of the victim programs that have developed in the last 15 years. Sadly, more than a decade after this 1998 report, OVC has published only descriptive, non-evaluative handbooks, brochures, or bulletins related to program models targeting violence against women and children.[33] The next section details some key victim-centered evaluations that were conducted on government-funded victim programs addressing violence against women.[34]

Policy Evaluations and Status of VAWA-Generated Programs

Over $1.6 billion has been allocated to VAWA-related programs.[35] As mentioned in chapters 2 and 6, the Clinton administration and Congress developed this bipartisan legislation (reauthorized in 2005 for fiscal years 2007 through 2011) to create a safer environment for women in their homes, on the streets, and in the criminal justice system. This widespread support was generated by a belief that male-on-female violence could be controlled by criminalizing certain behaviors, mandating criminal sanctions and treatment interventions, and providing criminal-justice agencies and victim advocates with the means to do their jobs effectively.[36] VAWA created two funnels through which monies flowed. One money funnel was designated for criminal justice intervention and was awarded to the U.S. Department of Justice. This money funded law enforcement and prosecution grants targeting domestic battery, sexual violence, and child abuse. Funds were earmarked to create or strengthen existing victims' services and police and prosecutors resources and to increase penalties for offenders, implement stalker and domestic violence reduction programs, and improve services for underserviced populations, such as battered immigrants and women of color.[37] In addition, legislation aimed at protecting battered women who move to a different state, bans on firearm possession for domestic violence offenders, establishment of the federal cause of action for gender-motivated violence, and the strengthening of restitution orders and extension of rape shield laws were also enacted.[38]

An economic analysis of the 1994 VAWA (before its reauthorization) revealed that it saved $16.4 billion in averted victimization costs.[39] The researchers measured costs as including direct property losses, medical and mental health care, police response, victims' services, lost productivity (workdays, school days, or housework days), reduced quality of life, and death, thus concluding that VAWA is cost-effective, affordable, and beneficial.[40] In other words, for each individual, the 1994 VAWA was "estimated to cost $15.50 per U.S. woman and would be expected to save $123 per U.S. woman in averted costs of criminal victimization."[41] It is also likely that the costs of victimization are underestimated for a variety of reasons: for example, repeated victimizations have a cumulative long-term negative effect on women's physical and psychological health, reducing their ability to pursue higher-quality and higher-paying educational and career opportunities.[42]

In 2001, the Urban Institute compiled a report on STOP (Services/Training/Officers/Prosecutors) grants, administered under VAWA funds.[43] The STOP and ARREST programs (grants to encourage arrest policies and enforcement of protection orders) make up the most heavily funded areas of VAWA. These grants provide funding to local communities and criminal justice agencies, while other VAWA-sponsored initiatives target federal-level issues, such as preventing interstate violations of restraining orders or creating a national domestic violence hotline.[44] Between 1995 and 2000, STOP grants received $672 million.[45] Congress continues to support STOP grant funding. For instance, in fiscal year 2008, the Office on Violence Against Women (OVW) granted more than $114 million in formula STOP grants, allocated to all 50 states.[46] The goals of STOP projects are to improve community-based victim services and to assist law enforcement and prosecutors in developing training programs, new policies, and protocols related to domestic violence, sexual assault, and stalking. Both victim-advocacy agencies and criminal justice agencies found that the STOP grants greatly enhanced each community's ability to meet the needs of victims of violent crimes against women.

The Urban Institute report is based on qualitative data gathered from surveys, telephone interviews, state performance reports, and on-site visits of grant recipients. There was also interest in obtaining statewide quantitative data that could address the hypothesis that arrest rates for crimes of violence committed against women were higher in STOP-funded jurisdictions and improved over time; however, *no* state was able to provide the necessary statistics (e.g., annual data that goes back to at least 1995, data covering at least 90 percent of the state's jurisdictions, and so forth),[47] whether or not the agencies received STOP funding. Inadequate and missing data remains an enormous problem; justice and advocacy agencies need to make more concerted efforts to collect statistics to use in evaluating whether their programs reduce battering, stalking, sexual assault, and rape.

The Urban Institute Report identified a disproportionate emphasis on projects developed and funded for battered women. Sexual assault projects received less attention and funding than domestic violence by law enforcement and prosecution agencies: only 7 percent of projects were focused primarily on sexual assault, while nearly 93 percent of STOP-funded projects focused primarily on battering.[48] Victims' services projects were only slightly more equitably distributed: about 75 percent of direct-service staff worked exclusively with victims of intimate-partner violence, and about 8 percent worked exclusively with victims of sexual assault. However, efforts are under way to prioritize monies directed at sexual assault victimization. The Violence Against Women Act of 2005 created the Sexual Assault Services Program (SASP), the first federal monies reserved exclusively to assist victims of sexual violence.[49] The 2005 version of VAWA appropriated $50 million for each of the fiscal years 2007 through 2011. The first appropriations under SASP occurred in 2008, when $9.4 million was allocated to fund programs for sexual assault victims. The official mission statement of SASP reads that it is "to provide intervention, advocacy, accompaniment, support services, and related assistance for adult, youth, and child victims, and those collaterally affected by sexual assault."[50]

In addition to victim-centered programs like those discussed above, over 600 state laws have been passed to help eradicate domestic violence, teen dating violence, sexual assault, and stalking.[51] The focus on sexual assault legislation includes defining sexual assault and its punishment and refining responses to federal laws that provided incentives for enactment of state-level sex-offender registration laws. Also addressed were repeals of various objectionable laws: those that permitted rape within the context of marriage, and those pertaining to statutory limitation provisions for rape, given the use of DNA to provide evidence long after the event. In terms of domestic violence legislation, changes in both criminal codes and criminal procedures were addressed, with many states increasing penalties for domestic violence crimes. States enacted laws that allow officers to make warrantless arrests in misdemeanor domestic violence cases and created mandatory or pro-arrest policies. In addition, 78 bills on stalking were passed by state legislatures; all states now have anti-stalking laws, and an increasing number of statutes have made stalking a felony.[52]

The Urban Institute report concludes with a series of recommendations for Congress to consider, including continuation and expansion of STOP funding; an increase in the number of projects that serve underrepresented populations, such as Indian victims living in urban areas; promotion of collaboration within local communities; expansion of funding for sexual assault projects; and development of better data and evaluation systems.[53] The report provides descriptions of the numerous and varied projects initiated state-by-state since 1995.[54] Many projects encompass routine efforts to implement more responsive programs for victims by advocates and criminal justice agencies, such as improving data collection efforts with arrest statistics, creating interagency units that bring together victim services with law enforcement and prosecution, and increasing training for criminal justice personnel. Additional projects include developing ways to allow violations of court orders to become part of the restraining order record, which helps with establishing stalking complaints and imposing harsher penalties, and adding a special victims' services position in the prosecutor's office to help victims navigate the court system. However, there are a number of innovative state programs that deserve a special mention in the following section.

Evaluation of Other VAWA-Sponsored Projects

In 2002, the National Institute of Justice funded a research project to study the *overall* effect of VAWA-supported programs.[55] Recall that the Urban Institute report discussed above focused *only* on the impact that STOP grants have had on helping communities respond more effectively to violence against women and how the criminal justice system has developed new policies and trainings as a result of these grants. The National Institute of Justice (NIJ) report, titled "Controlling Violence Against Women: A Research Perspective on the 1994 VAWA's Criminal Justice Impact," provides a comprehensive assessment of all facets of the act, which included mandatory research evaluations to study the impact of policy changes/reforms and new federal legislation[56] such as interstate domestic violence, interstate violation of a protection order, and additional rape shield evidentiary protections.[57] The NIJ research evaluators express similar concerns to those voiced in the Urban Institute report with respect to the heavy distribution of STOP grants focusing solely on domestic violence (about 50 percent); they noticed that just 12 percent of the grants focus exclusively on sexual assault and that even fewer focus on stalking.[58] As noted above, the 2005 version of VAWA created and funded the Sexual Assault Services Program to respond specifically to the needs of victims of sexual violence. In addition, both reports note the lack of attention directed toward preventing violence against women in the first place (i.e., general deterrence), since most of VAWA focuses on offenders who have already committed crimes against women.

According to 2004 and 2007 assessments from the U.S. Office of Management and Budget (OMB), an organization that evaluates all federal programs, VAWA is considered among the most successful of all the 1994 Crime Act programs, earning a score of "moderately effective," the next-to-highest ranking a program can receive.[59] OMB's (2007) primary recommendation for VAWA is to seek appropriate and independent evaluations to confirm the impact of its programming.

However, a true impact evaluation, in terms of assessing or measuring how these programs actually affect rates of violence against women, is difficult to perform because only a handful of grantee sites maintain meaningful statistics regarding their activities or changes in case processing (e.g., arrests, case dispositions) resulting from grant funds.[60] As such, assessments related to the efficacy of specific and general deterrence associated with VAWA reforms are problematic. Still, there is much to be optimistic about. For instance, VAWA has played a pivotal role in "encouraging and enabling the development of a critical mass of researchers to build knowledge on violence against women" by providing research funding and making the study of violence against women a mainstream and legitimate research agenda for scholars.[61] Furthermore, VAWA has profoundly changed how criminal justice agents view and respond to crimes of domestic battery, sexual assault, and stalking.[62] Finally, a 2009 study analyzed whether locales receiving VAWA monies experienced reductions in sexual violence and aggravated assault (as a measure of domestic battery) while controlling for other funding sources, meaningful demographic factors, and general crime trends that affect rates of violence. Results indicate that VAWA dollars are associated with meaningful reductions in the number of rapes and aggravated assaults, but not with other forms of serious violence.[63] These patterns held even after controlling for all other known factors that affect crime rates and other sources of justice funding. Although methodological constraints preclude the finding that VAWA funds caused the reductions in rape and aggravated assault, the results "are consistent with other research evaluating process and the cost/benefits of this funding."[64]

Examples of Other Projects That Address Violence Against Women

Numerous states have designed an array of programs that reflect the diverse needs of victims of violence against women. This section highlights programs funded by VAWA's STOP grants, as described in the Urban Institute Report.[65] These programs focus on improving evidentiary collection and support for victims of sexual assault and battering, addressing legislative initiatives and research efforts, reaching out to the needs of isolated or special populations, improving responses to stalking, and enhancing coordinated community approaches.

California designed a short-term project that focused on improving the evidentiary value of images of victim injuries and crime scenes of sexual assault by purchasing colposcopes and 35mm cameras for medical sites as well as distributing forensic camera kits to law enforcement agencies statewide.[66] One of the most widespread reform efforts aimed at increasing prosecution rates for crimes of rape is the Sexual Assault Nurse Examiner (SANE) program. There are nearly 500 SANE programs in existence across the nation.[67] Outcome studies show that they enhance the quality of forensic and other evidence of sexual assaults and provide immediate and ongoing support to survivors and case consultation to police and prosecutors. The specially trained forensic nurses also testify if a case goes to trial.[68] The program is also credited with reducing the "secondary victimizations" many rape victims experience through the reporting, investigation, and prosecution of sexual assaults.[69] The state of Montana purchased DNA equipment so that sexual assault evidence would no longer have to be sent out of state for testing; they also created a sexual/violent offender database and expanded police training on domestic violence and sexual assault crimes. Results included reductions in the number of dual arrests and stronger coordinated responses by law enforcement and victims' services providers to these changes in their operations (e.g., clearer police report writing, advanced investigative techniques, and photographing and documentation of bruises and wounds).[70] South Carolina also used funds to provide law enforcement officers with domestic violence kits that include a digital camera that records a victim's injuries and crime scene in an immediate, reproducible, and sharable form, a digital video camera for statements, and a voice-activated tape recorder that captures without prejudice excited utterances and spontaneous speech. As one can tell from the various states' programs that focus on improving evidence collection in South Carolina as well as other states, this aspect is crucial for victimless prosecution efforts, since victims often recant, especially if threatened with some form of retaliation from the abuser; in such cases the strength of the evidence becomes the deciding factor in the prosecution's failure or success.

The majority of states recognize the need to reach victims with diverse backgrounds and needs. For instance, California improved their identification and outreach program and direct services to isolated women of special populations, such as the elderly, recent immigrants, farm workers, Latinas, and American Indian tribes. Massachusetts also targeted special populations for services, including the elderly; the physically disabled; Asians; victims with substance abuse and mental health issues; the hearing-impaired; victims who are of the Christian, Jewish, or Islamic faith; incarcerated women; and women whose primary language is not English. Reaching historically underserved populations is a goal of New Jersey's programs, including services for Latinos, African Americans, South Asians, Koreans, Russian immigrants, Orthodox Jews, and rural victims. New Jersey formed partnerships with domestic violence and sexual assault experts in addition to welcoming the expertise of indigenous community organizations rooted in these racial/ethnic/religious communities. A program in Iowa established the first toll-free statewide hotline number with various language capabilities and the ability to route a victim to the newest domestic violence or sexual assault program. The state of Ohio identified groups of underserved victims and enhanced its services and cultural sensitivity training in different areas of the state; these groups include the hearing-impaired in Cincinnati, the Appalachian population in the southeast, migrant workers in the northwest, the Amish in the northeast, and African Americans in urban areas. A program in South Carolina exemplifies the utility of these diversity programs:

> A local law enforcement officer called on Acercamiento Hispano for translation assistance for a victim who spoke only a dialect of Russian. The translator was found, the woman received assistance, and, best of all, the woman was not further traumatized by her inability to communicate in English. Imagine the relief of a domestic violence victim who no longer has to depend on her abuser to intercede for her with the rest of the world.[71]

Finally, to highlight one more state, Wisconsin, multidisciplinary educational seminars were held to bring Hmong clan leaders together with law enforcement, prosecutors, and community members to discuss for the first time the legal and social issues related to domestic violence. They created a court and community interpreters' training program that bridges cultural gaps between victims' services providers, the criminal justice system, and the Hmong population, a prototype that can be used to address the needs of other underserved populations throughout the state.

Other innovative programs include Illinois's, which targets nonabusive women offenders who were victims of sexual or physical abuse. Another innovation in South Carolina is the use of GPS monitoring to locate offenders. The offender wears a "real-time" tamper-proof tracking device that activates the victim's pager and police department's 911 centers if the offender crosses an unlawful area identified earlier by the judge at the bond hearing. The use of GPS monitoring for purposes of tracking an offender's whereabouts was discussed in greater detail in chapter 5.

Many states focused their efforts on improving the coordination of responses by social service agencies and criminal justice system personnel. In Chicago, a citywide toll-free 24-hour hotline was created, staffed by certified domestic violence counselors, to act as a resource clearinghouse for police, prosecutors, hospitals, and victims. Many of Massachusetts's programs focused on greater coordination between agencies (a trend also seen in other jurisdictions across the country, such as in California, Arizona, Washington, and Minnesota). For example, in one rural community in Massachusetts, "forty-one police departments, four battered women's and sexual assault programs, the district attorney's office, legal services, the courts, and the batterers' intervention program collaborate to form a tight security net for victims, including bilingual/bicultural and physically disabled victims."[72]

Still other state efforts focused on addressing legislative initiatives, enhancing research opportunities, or improving criminal justice responses to violence committed against women. For example, within the district attorney's office in Iowa, a designated VAWA prosecutor was hired to pursue VAWA and Lautenberg matters, initiating rapid ATF intervention in Lautenberg cases.[73] In another Iowa county, one police department established a database program that allows tracking from the first 911 call and continuing through prosecution. They discovered in the first three-month evaluation of the program that officers were not making arrests on domestic violence calls as department policy required. New Mexico established a program that allows officers (with judicial approval) to issue emergency orders of protection on the scene during weekend and holiday hours. And Kansas developed stalking kits and stalking training for police officers and advocates.

The accomplishments of the various states' programs highlighted above using VAWA's STOP funding grants illustrate how important government funding is for establishing creative and important programs that play a role in addressing the needs of domestic battery, stalking, and sexual assault victims. Two significant points need to be made, however. First, these accomplishments are only the beginning. As the STOP Grants Administrator of Missouri points out, "It takes more than five years to establish a program. It takes more than five years to prove that a program is successful and will bring about systemic change. It takes more than five years to bring about societal change."[74] Funding must be continued in order for progress to be achieved and for any long-term progress toward the goal of eradicating violence against women. Second, not one of the state programs focused their efforts on prevention projects for youth, which many suggest is the key to ending violence against women. While some of this inattention is understandable—victims need immediate and ongoing assistance from direct service providers and criminal justice agencies—the current programs address only part of the problem. Resources are limited, and while the establishment of the programs described above is necessary, prevention and education strategies designed to play a role before violence occurs are also crucial in the fight to decrease domestic violence, sexual assault, and stalking.

Our next section explores how victims can increase their involvement in a way that supplements their reliance on the formal justice process.

Alternatives to Reliance on the Formal Justice System

In response to victim complaints about insensitive treatment from the criminal justice system, the use of informal resolution alternatives such as restorative justice (RJ) programs has increased in the past 20 years. Restorative justice is an umbrella term encompassing various programs that use forums to facilitate healing encounters between victims and offenders, often including the active participation by concerned community members.[75] One widely used program that exemplifies the goal of restorative justice is Victim-Offender Mediation (VOM). More than 300 communities across the United States offer VOM as an alternative to traditional criminal justice processes.[76]

In VOM programs, victims meet face-to-face with the person(s) who victimized them, providing victims with the opportunity to express the full impact of their crimes, receive answers to unresolved questions, receive apologies from offenders, and be directly involved in establishing offender accountability, most often by developing restitution plans.[77] The issue of guilt or innocence is not mediated; that is, there are clear victims and offenders, not "disputants," as in traditional mediation programs. There is no expectation that victims will compromise or decrease what restitution is necessary to manage their losses. Research shows that more than 95 percent of VOM sessions result in signed restitution agreements, victims are far more satisfied with the outcome than are victims who go through the formal court system, victims are significantly less fearful of revictimization, and offenders are more likely to complete restitution obligations and commit fewer and less serious crimes than their counterparts who go through the formal criminal justice system.[78] Emotional expressions are valued and healing is emphasized, key occurrences for the goal of victim empowerment. In addition, the community plays a role: strategies such as family group conferencing and sentencing circles are vital and offer the potential to attack root causes of battering, because of the belief that battering extends beyond the victim-offender dyad to include the community, its norms, and social inequities. In family group conferencing, support people such as family members or neighbors are invited to discuss the crime, interventions, and reparations. Sentencing circles are similar to family group conferencing, but they tend to focus more attention on community problems in which criminal activity is embedded.[79] Involving the community helps address diverse racial, ethnic, religious, or cultural factors that police and court officials may misinterpret or misunderstand.

However, the use of *traditional*, or *diversionary*, mediation models in cases of violence against women (sexual assaults, incest, and battering) has been criticized heavily for several reasons: they reinforce the view of sexual assault and intimate-partner violence as private matters; the power imbalance inherent in intimate-partner violence or rape remains unaddressed; reparation of the relationship could take precedence over repairing harms caused by the relationship; and they require no stipulation that the violence must end.[80] But these critiques focus mainly on *diversionary* restorative justice programs, in which offenders receive lighter sentences or consequences through their participation. Much of the criticisms can be avoided through the use of *postconviction* RJ programs, which share the goal of victim healing as a central focus but do not offer offenders a sentence of program participation in lieu of punishment. Typically, in postconviction RJ programs, victims have the opportunity to tell their stories about the violence they experienced, which can be very empowering for battered women or incest victims formerly cowed into silence through intimidation and fear or for a rape victim who remains gripped by terror. In addition, because the therapeutic postconviction RJ process often involves the presence of other people, they offer the opportunity for heightened condemnation of the crime in a public forum.

Three RJ programs that address violence against women are discussed by Mary Koss and her colleagues; Mark Umbreit and his colleagues; and Susan L. Miller. Koss and her team designed and implemented a diversionary RJ program that responds to victims and first-time offenders of acquaintance rape, indecent exposure, and peeping; the program has been in operation in Arizona for several years now.[81] Umbreit and his colleagues conduct ongoing research and work with victims of violent crimes.[82] And Miller has conducted an analysis of a program that uses postconviction therapeutic models for victims of rape, domestic violence, and incest.[83] Evaluations of these programs thus far reveal success in victim empowerment, satisfaction, and healing, as well as in offender rehabilitation. Internationally, there is more enthusiasm for and use of RJ programs with crimes involving violence against women; for instance, both Australia and New Zealand use RJ programs for juvenile sexual offenders or family violence. While there are no results yet on long-term effectiveness, the goals of greater victim input, satisfaction, and empowerment are being met.

Because RJ programs emphasize victim healing and empowerment and involve the community in regulating the behavior of abusers, many scholars are starting to reconsider them and acknowledge that they may be appropriate in cases of violence against women.[84] Such programs bring both formal and informal social controls to bear in the effort to stop battering. The hope is that victim-centered responses reduce victim trauma and honor victims' expressed preferences—all of which could ultimately increase reporting of sexual violence and other forms of violence committed against women. However, it is clear that any RJ program to address violence against women must ensure that agreements are based on victims' consent and equity, and that they occur within a safe context, handled by facilitators knowledgeable about power and control dynamics implicit in sexual and physical violence committed against women. Furthermore, resulting plans must be carefully monitored well into the future, and if the need arises, resorting to the formal justice process should be an option.

Thus, while restorative justice has the potential for achieving satisfying outcomes in cases of rape and battering, it remains to be seen how well it is suited to these kinds of crimes in terms of doing justice and protecting victims. Clearly, more theoretical development needs to be done and evaluative research needs to be conducted in order to assess the appropriateness of restorative justice programs for female victims of male violence.

Looking Ahead: The Potential for Preventive and Educational Programs

In order to create any meaningful transformation, the state needs to move beyond efforts to pacify activists or win elections for politicians and stop relying exclusively on criminal justice options to challenge violence against women. Bringing about long-term change requires turning our attention to prevention practices and policies, and to education efforts, which are important steps toward addressing the structural causes of violence against women. Prevention that is aimed at general deterrence (keeping potential offenders from committing acts of violence in the first place) has received much less attention by VAWA and state/federal action than specific deterrence (keeping criminals from committing additional illegal acts). Still, there are promising areas of general prevention of violence against women, such as school-based education programs and other youth projects. As mentioned earlier in this chapter, when one looks at the massive report from the Victims of Crime office, *New Directions from the Field: Victims' Rights and Services for the 21st Century* (1998), little is said about organizations dealing explicitly with female victims of male violence, such as rape crisis centers or battered women's shelters. Rather, the bulk of the recommendations refer to general victim services such as restitution, compensation, and civil remedies. It is only in the Education Section that the report finally highlights a prevention program that does not rely exclusively on criminal justice intervention: the development of school- and university-based victim education programs. The consistent goals across these programs are to inform young people about victims' rights and to assist young victims in developing skills to aid in their healing. At the college and university level, the emphasis was on developing curriculum to train students and advocates about victims' needs in general, and about specific needs for victims of child abuse, battering, and so forth. Only one sexual assault prevention program was highlighted: Santa Monica, California, helps secondary school students to develop and practice effective communication and self-protection skills. Other prevention efforts related to violence against women and children included checking the records of anyone who applies for work in a school (looking for arrests or convictions of sexual assault, child molestation, porn offenses; this is legally required in only 21 states); installing lighting and emergency phone systems on college campuses and controlling building access and establishing security patrols; developing violence prevention programs and anti-gun violence programs that provide alternatives to violent behavior; developing speaker programs for high school and college students using sexual assault survivors; using peer educators to teach nonviolent conflict resolution tactics, especially in multicultural communities; and requiring new students' names to be forwarded to the National Center for Missing and Exploited Children to determine if these names matches those of known missing children.

The Victims of Crime Office report (*New Directions from the Field*) encourages the development of K–12 programs that offer crisis counselors to victims and witnesses, and programs that address child abuse, incest, sexual assault, drunk driving, gang involvement, and hate crimes. Age-appropriate sexual assault and dating violence awareness and prevention programs were urged, especially given that the research literature demonstrates that the majority of rape victims are victimized before the age of 18 and most never reported the crime to police. Finally, the report spoke of the need to better define dating violence and sexual assault and to train faculty and staff how to best respond to such incidents. In addition, scholars elsewhere believe a way to decrease sexual assault and rape is to focus on moving boys away from a definition of masculinity that "centers on toughness, power, dominance, eagerness to fight, lack or empathy, and a callous attitude toward women."[85] Masculinity, then, must be redefined to include caring, nurturance, and empathy so that these coexist with positive "masculine" characteristics such as courage, initiative, and adventurousness for both boys and girls. It is hoped that this redefinition will not only help boys develop nonviolent ways, but will also facilitate greater self-esteem and autonomy for girls.[86] Egalitarian models of play expand narrow confines of approved behavior and toys and stress interpersonal communication skills. The goal of these early programs is to cease the perpetuation of models of masculine and feminine behavior that foster aggression, violence, and fear. In fact, Australia, New Zealand, and Canada all have mandatory educational programs: the subject of family violence is addressed in the school curriculum. These efforts are crucial in addressing prevention of violence against women, providing better safety for female victims, and developing youth programs that teach better communication skills and nonviolent ways to resolve conflict.

The next prevention program we discuss is designed for elderly battered women, a group that is significantly underresearched even though the National Center on Elder Abuse reports a 150 percent increase in reported cases of elder abuse since 1986.[87] This elderly abuse prevention experiment was conducted in New York City and utilized educational platforms and a coordinated community response in an attempt to reduce incidents of battering and to better understand the violent victimization of mature women (age 65 and older).[88] Elderly women face unique challenges, such as being physically dependent on their abuser due to health problems, which complicates attempts to locate alternate housing or safe-place shelters.[89] In this particular study, several public housing projects were randomly selected to receive educational material describing battering and giving area phone numbers for victim assistance. Brochures and posters were placed in common areas of the building, such as the lobby and laundry facilities. Community presentations were held at senior centers and other area locations. Some of the households that reported elder abuse to police were singled out to receive a home visit from a police officer and a domestic violence counselor.[90] Researchers expected that households would become less violent once the level of abuse education and contact with the victim and offender increased. However, the opposite occurred: elderly tenants who received public education and were selected for follow-up home visits reported significantly higher levels of physical abuse than families that received only one form of intervention (education *or* follow-up visits) or no intervention at all. In the end, researchers surmised that the combination of interventions may have had the unintended consequence of inciting the abusers, resulting in more, not less, violence in the homes. Elder abuse victims may be more dependent on their abuser, both physically and financially, than younger victims of abuse, and therefore may have fewer opportunities to leave the situation.[91] This possibility suggests that programs for elderly battered women may require different considerations and interventions. Moreover, the women in this study were 66 percent African American and 30 percent Latina, which suggests that programs need to be mindful of differences among victims and their responses.[92]

Finally, we point to a promising development in terms of expanding the traditional reactionary intervention-focused criminal justice response: the Center for Disease Control efforts to address intimate-partner sexual and domestic violence through their public health initiative.[93] Approximately $2.6 million in funds were made available for program development the first fiscal year (2002), with a commitment to fund projects for three years; 14 states have received such funding. The CDC's purpose is to stimulate the development and implementation of activities to prevent domestic violence that can be integrated into coordinated community responses or similar community-based collaborations at the state and local levels.

A number of state programs, funded by the CDC effort, addresses the population of adjudicated juvenile delinquents. Their goal is to educate male and female adolescents under state jurisdictions (such as those in juvenile residential facilities or halfway houses, or under house arrest) about intimate-partner domestic violence prevention. These programs for youth at high risk of engaging in intimate-partner violence educate the participants about causes, forms, and consequences of this behavior and challenge them to establish and maintain healthy relationships.[94] Other programs target underserved populations; the state of Delaware, for example, is in the process of developing a program to meet the needs of Latin Hispanic women and children who live in the most rural part of the state. Other underserved communities, such as Native Indian Americans and migrant workers, are targeted across the nation. Some projects are designed to reach a school-based population: for example, the state of Delaware was awarded a grant to address dating violence among teenagers. Funds for this program go toward the Delaware Safe Dating Theater Project (DSDTP), which combines peer leadership training about the issue of dating violence with a dramatic play presented to youth from 8th to 12th grade. The peer leaders assist professional staff in responding to any teens who seek assistance, and a second theater presentation, which is developed and performed by students, provides additional opportunities to influence the culture of the entire school. This program creates opportunities for dialogue among peers and caring adults in their everyday environment, establishes a way for youth to become empowered to educate their peers, and creates an opportunity for referrals for those students who have previously been or are currently in an abusive or potentially abusive situation. This kind of out-of-the-box thinking is crucial if we want to address primary prevention issues, particularly given that approximate one-third of high school and college-age youth experience dating violence.[95] For instance, in a study following 111 females for five years, from 8th to 12th grades, 23 percent reported sexual coercion or abuse by dates or boyfriends, 15 percent reported unwanted vaginal intercourse with dates or boyfriends, and 10 percent reported other forms of sexual assault (i.e., being fondled or forced to perform oral sex).[96]

Let's not let boys and men off the hook! Many prevention programs are aimed at potential victims, such as telling young women not to drink and flirt or accept rides with strangers, installing blue-light systems on college campuses, advocating self-defense courses or carrying pepper spray, and so forth. By contrast, national groups such as Men Can Stop Rape and "1 in 4" were formed to mobilize men to prevent men's violence against women. According to its mission statement, Men Can Stop Rape aims to "empower male youth and the institutions that serve them to work as allies with women in preventing rape and other forms of men's violence. Through awareness-to-action education and community organizing, we promote gender equity and build men's capacity to be strong without being violent."[97] Involving men (and educating boys) in the fight against male violence committed against women is crucial. Changing values and raising awareness are essential tasks in the effort to eliminate rape, sexual assault, and battering and all factors that foster aggression and violence against women.

Today there is also a greater understanding of risk factors for both victims and perpetrators, knowledge that can be used to created meaningful prevention programs. For instance, risk factors for adolescent dating violence (for victims and perpetrators) identified by the Centers for Disease Control and Prevention National Center for Injury Prevention and Control and the Constitutional Rights Foundation Chicago include acceptance of abusive behaviors; desire to maintain control in a relationship; having friends engaged in abusive relationships; having sexually aggressive peers; age disparity between dating partners; heavy alcohol or drug use; belief in traditional sex roles and gender stereotypes; beliefs in rape myths (often victim-blaming myths); and observing or experiencing abuse in one's family.[98] According to research posted on the National Youth Violence Prevention Resource Center Web site, characteristics that have been identified as protective factors include a sense of purpose and belief in a positive future; a commitment to education and learning; the ability to act independently and feel a sense of control over one's environment; the ability to solve problems; conflict resolution and critical thinking skills; the presence of meaningful, supportive relationships with adults; and participation in activities where youth have choices, decision-making power, and shared responsibility, thereby helping them to develop new skills and develop self-confidence, and providing a chance for them to make a difference.[99] Again, addressing these issues early in people's lives can create positive values and thus have a profound effect on achieving long-term goals of ending violence against women.

The goal to bring prevention and, ultimately, social change back into efforts to address violence against women is noteworthy, since most funding and energies are used to address criminal justice intervention issues (i.e., training for police and prosecutors, changes in arrest policies, court-mandated batterer treatment programs). Social change holds the key to our long-range goal to end violence against women—and echoes the vision of the grassroots rape crisis and battered women's movements of the 1970s. Some reformers and scholars suggest that a more comprehensive and promising approach to ending other forms of sexual victimization, especially child sexual abuse, is to recontextualize it within a public health model, where prevention on all levels is the key to ending violence.[100] Researchers need to work closely with practitioners to achieve understandings about which programs work toward achieving this goal.

Conclusions and Policy Recommendations

When violent acts committed against women are framed as crime issues without a concomitant focus on victims, solutions are limited to strengthening law enforcement, enacting harsher sentences, and other criminal justice procedures. While these options are essential as one component of a larger strategy, framing the issue solely in terms of criminal justice intervention limits our range of solutions. Whenever we look only to a criminal justice model to address these issues, we reduce options and limit effectiveness, since many factors related to violence against women are systemic to our culture and require us to reexamine our social values and priorities. Furthermore, the extant literature indicates that traditional criminal justice responses to violent crimes are ineffective and often counterproductive. We need multiple and layered solutions that put victims at the center. Responsive strategies alone, such as the creation and improvement of victim services and criminal justice reforms, will not do the trick. Education and prevention programs (i.e., primary, secondary, and tertiary) need to be part of the mix. Prevention efforts include victim-centered, situational, and community-level prevention strategies.[101]

In this book, we have sought to articulate the various questions that exposed the paradoxes and tensions associated with the policies and visions of the end-violence-against-women movement. Although relying on the state to fix the problems gives political currency both to social conservatives and to liberals, the trade-off is that the state strengthens its control over policies and enhances its crime-control agenda. Yet even within this politically charged environment, glimmers of hope exist, as well as real progress in addressing victims' issues in a way that is empowering and satisfying to individuals and to communities. Grassroots activism, the increasing number of battered women's shelters and rape crisis centers in all 50 states, the media, and legislation like VAWA have moved victims' issues into the national consciousness. Statistics generated by research on rape, sex offenders, battering, and stalking make the incidence and prevalence of violence against women and children undeniable. Much progress has been made, and much has been learned, but there is still a long road ahead in our fight to eradicate violence against women. Clearly, a one-size-fits-all mentality is short-sighted: it does not always best serve victims' needs and may actually result in further harm. Victim empowerment programs attempt to rectify this problem by offering a variety of choices, thus respecting the autonomy of women and the individuality of victims' needs. Victims' assessment of their own safety and understanding of how the impact of applying sanctions affects their lives is crucial.

Feminist scholars recognize, however, that change at a systemic level is necessary before significant reductions in violence against women can be achieved. For instance, there are currently many exciting education programs under way, designed to prevent the next generation of young people from becoming victims and perpetrators of sexual assault, rape, and battering. Perhaps this is the most promising strategy in our battle to eradicate violence against women.

Despite the concern about the overreliance on the criminal justice system to solve the violence-against-women problem, much has been accomplished that has furthered knowledge and created tangible help for victims. The efforts discussed in these chapters need to continue. We hope that all of this book's readers are now better informed about the issues, and that some of them have been convinced to join in the fight. Only when we improve institutional responses but also simultaneously challenge the social and political factors that facilitate interpersonal violence will crimes of violence committed against women be extinguished.

Notes

CHAPTER 1

1. Karmen 2007.
2. Ibid.
3. Ibid.
4. Shichor and Tibbetts 2002: ix.
5. Ibid.: 5.
6. Ibid.: 1; Karmen 2007.
7. Mendelsohn 1940; Von Hentig 1948; Wolfgang 1958.
8. Karmen 2001: 99.
9. Shichor and Tibbetts 2002: 1.
10. Mendelsohn 1940.
11. Meadows 2001: 20–21.
12. Sellen and Wolfgang 1964.
13. Shichor and Tibbetts 2002: 1–3.
14. Estrich 1987; Belknap 2006: 238.
15. Lerner and Miller 1978.
16. Janoff-Bulman 1992: 62.
17. Kappeler, Sluder, and Alpert 1998.
18. Ryan 1971.
19. Best 1999: 99.
20. Cole 2007: 21.
21. Sykes 1992: 134.
22. Dershowitz 1994: 45.
23. Ibid.: 8–11.
24. In addition, victimization of the elderly and disabled tends to overrepresent females, but this abuse includes institutional personnel and nonstranger perpetrators

and can often include other family members, which complicates our focus on crimes committed by mostly men against women.

25. Renzetti 1992; Girshick 2002.

26. Girshick 2002: 164.

27. Elliott (1996) as cited in Perilla et al. 2003: 20.

28. Perilla et al. 2003: 20.

29. Ibid.

30. Although feminist theories of rape and battering typically focus on heterosexual couples and erase lesbians (Renzetti 1999), a number of studies have been conducted with lesbians who sexually violate or assault their partners, and findings indicate that the prevalence rates of violence in lesbian couples equal or exceed those in heterosexual couples (see Renzetti 1992; Margolies and Leeder 1995; Waldner-Haugrud, Gratch, and Magruder 1997; Waldner-Haugrud 1999; Girshick 2002). However, making generalizations about lesbians' use of force is fraught with problems, given that the samples used are typically small and collected from clinical settings and from lesbian bars or events or oversample white and middle-class women. The studies also suffer from the use of unclear definitions of what constitutes abuse and from methodological issues related to sampling: the samples are nonrandom due to the invisibility of lesbians as a whole and the fact that lesbians have to explicitly self-identity and disclose their sexual orientation in order to be included in a study (Perilla et al. 2003; see also Burke and Follingstad 1999; Turrell 2000; Giorgio 2002). Future research on victimization will be helped by the work conducted with lesbians who experience violence from their partners or former partners. As Nancy Worcester (2002: 1401) states, "Unlike those working on heterosexual domestic violence, people working on lesbian intimate violence have always had to look at how any behavior can be used as power and control, how any behavior can be used as a survival tactic, and the fact that victims may well identify as abusers."

CHAPTER 2

1. Task Force 1992: ii.

2. Clark, Biddle, and Martin 2002: 417–428.

3. Cosgrove-Mather 2003.

4. In 2002 the convictions in this case were overturned. Five men of color (black and Hispanic) were originally convicted of the rape and beating after confessing to police. The confessions were always controversial, but it was the confession made by another convicted rapist that he was the real offender and DNA test results linking him to the crime that were the basis for the conviction reversals (Cosgrove-Mather 2003).

5. Best 1999: 116.

6. Meloy and Miller 2009.

7. Bulkeley and Thomson 2004.

8. Fitzpatrick 2006.

9. Domestic partner amendment 2005.

10. For example, a new study shows a related long-reaching impact of banning same-sex marriage for thousands of Hispanic/Latino same-sex households in Florida (Ciancitto and Lopez 2005).

11. Schlattner and Linehan n.d.

12. Benedict 1992.

13. Dershowitz 1994.

14. Westervelt 1998.

15. Ibid.: 3.

16. Ibid.

17. Lamb 1996: 8; Lamb 1999.

18. Caputi 1993: 5–15.

19. Karmen 2007.

20. Ibid.

21. Wolf 1993: 135–136. Some of the confusion over "feminist" voices in this dialogue stems from the very different definitions people have of "feminism" in particular (see Kaminer 1993). For example, in contrast to her "victim feminism," Naomi Wolf's "power feminism" "encourages us to identify with one another primarily through the shared pleasures and strengths of femaleness, rather than primarily through our shared vulnerability and pain. It calls for alliances based on economic self-interest and economic giving back rather than on a sentimental and workable fantasy of cosmic sisterhood" (Wolf 1993: 53).

22. Sykes 1992.

23. Sykes 1992: 12, 15.

24. Sykes 1992. See also Hoff Sommers 1994.

25. Sykes 1992. This case is not as meritless as it may sound. The victim had third-degree burns around her groin, inner thighs, and buttocks, and endured seven days in the hospital and multiple skin grafts. Company documents revealed that McDonalds received at least 700 reports of coffee burns in the past decade, and its settled claims arising from injuries amounted to over $500,000 (Gerlin 1994).

26. Sykes 1992.

27. Ibid.: 185.

28. Not all of the books that appeal to a mass-market audience that present an alternative (more politically liberal) perspective are addressed in this chapter, because they tend to focus less on violence against women (for example, see June Stephenson's 1995 book, *Men Are Not Cost-Effective*, and Mariah Burton Nelson's 1995 book, *The Stronger Women Get, The More Men Love Football*).

29. See Walker 1984.

30. Roberts 2003: 27, 135–156.

31. Ibid.

32. Downs 1996.

33. Mahoney 1994: 59.

34. Ferraro 2003.

35. Lewin 1992: E6.

36. Mahoney 1992: 1283–1319; Schneider 2000; Ferraro 2003.

37. Gondolf and Fisher 1988: 11.
38. Ibid.
39. Mahoney 1994: 59–92.
40. Ibid.: 62.
41. hooks 1989, as cited in Mahoney 1994: 62.
42. Koss, Gidycz, and Wisniewski 1987: 162–170; Mahoney 1991: 1–94; Schechter 1982.
43. Karmen 2007.
44. Ibid.
45. Gilbert 1991: 54.
46. DeKeseredy and Kelly 1993: 137–159; Koss and Cook 1993: 104–119; Schwartz and Pitts 1995: 9–31.
47. In fact, Hoff Sommers goes as far as to challenge the prevailing "assumption" that America is still patriarchal. Everyday realities suggest otherwise: men comprise 86 percent of Congress (Belkin 2003), while only eight Fortune 500 companies have female CEOs, and women comprise only 29 percent of the nation's lawyers and judges (U.S. Department of Labor 2004). In 1999 the Maryland Appellate Court had to formally rule that the use of the word "babe" was not permitted during legal proceedings, since male attorneys and judges continued to address female attorneys that way ("Babe" banned 1999). Despite notable exceptions, women overall continue to comprise the smallest number of positions of power in commerce, government, and legal occupations.
48. Malamuth 1986.
49. Hoff Sommers 1994: 219
50. Lamb 1999: 107.
51. As cited in Sykes 1993: 179.
52. Lamb 1996: 107–108.
53. Schwartz and DeKeseredy 1997: 24. Gilbert 1991.
54. See Miller 2005.
55. Karmen 2001.
56. Kimmel 2002: 1336–1367; Osthoff 2002: 1521–1544; Saunders 2002: 1424–1448; Worchester 2002: 1390–1415. Moreover, research demonstrates that women comprise the overwhelming majority of battering victims; often, even women arrested on domestic violence charges have used violence for self-defensive reasons, and not as primary aggressors (Osthoff 2002).
57. Miller and Meloy 2006.
58. Pearson 1997: 120.
59. Johnson 1995; Miller 2001; Miller 2005; Miller and Meloy 2006.
60. Barrett, Miller-Perrin, and Perrin 2004.

CHAPTER 3

1. See Decker, as cited in Miller, N. 2001: 13; see Moultrie 2001.
2. See chapter 4 for more information on the factors associated with media interest in crime and victimization.
3. Rennison and Welchans 2000.

4. Bureau of Justice Statistics 2007.
5. Rennison and Welchans 2000.
6. Martin 1976.
7. Dobash and Dobash 1979; Martin 1976.
8. Pagelow 1984.
9. Dobash and Dobash 1979.
10. Martin 1976; Pagelow 1984.
11. Dobash and Dobash 1979.
12. Pleck 1989: 28.
13. Ibid.
14. Ibid.
15. Buzawa and Buzawa 2003.
16. Pleck 1989.
17. Buzawa and Buzawa 2003.
18. Pleck 1989.
19. Although wife beating was officially against the law in this period, certain appellate court rulings in the mid- to late 1800s reflected judicial reluctance to interfere in the private sphere. A husband's right to "use toward his wife such a degree of force as is necessary to control an unruly temper and make her behave herself" was upheld by North Carolina Supreme Court in *State v. Black*, where the court refused to "invade the domestic forum or go behind the curtain." This case actually overturned a guilty finding by a lower court. In *State v. Rhodes* the North Carolina Supreme Court upheld a case where a husband was found not guilty of an act that would have "constituted a battery if the subject of it had not been the defendant's wife." The court noted that although state law did not recognize the right of the husband to whip his wife, state government would not interfere with "family government." In *State v. Oliver*, the court noted that unless there was serious injury, malice, or cruelty, "it is better to draw the curtain, shut out the public gaze and leave the parties to forgive and forget." While judges sometimes made unqualified references to "old laws" that permitted wife beating, no American judge ever endorsed the so-called rule of thumb, which was thought to permit a husband to beat his wife with a stick no thicker than his thumb (Pleck 1989: 32).
20. After the start of the 1900s, the perception of violence in the home being a serious crime generally declined as law-and-order concerns gave way to social casework methods and the more humane treatment philosophy to deal with social problems (Pleck 1989).
21. Belknap 2001.
22. Schechter 1982.
23. Garner and Clemmer 1986; Zorza 1992.
24. *Scott v. Hart*, U.S. Dist Ct. for the Northern Dist. of Calif. C76–2395 (1976).
25. *Bruno v. Codd*, 47 N.Y.2d 582, 393 N.E. 2d 976, 419 N.Y.S. 2d 901 (1979).
26. Karmen 2001; Zorza 1992.
27. *Thurman v. City of Torrington, Conn.*, 595 F. Supp. 1521 (1984).
28. Zorza 1992.

29. Buzawa and Buzawa 2003; Zorza 1992.
30. Sherman and Berk 1984.
31. Despite problems in carrying out the experimental design, the findings from this research were widely cited as proof of a deterrent effect of arrest. The Minneapolis study spawned replications in six other cities (the Spouse Assault Replication Program, SARP), which resulted in conflicting findings, and problems with research methods remained. The findings suggested, however, that married, employed offenders may be more likely to desist from violence following an arrest than offenders who have lower stakes in conformity. The most recent reanalysis of the SARP data generally finds a modest deterrent effect for arrest compared to other interventions as a group, but factors such as the offender's age and prior criminal record remain important in future offending (Maxwell, Garner, and Fagan 2001).
32. Buzawa and Buzawa 1993; Stanko 1989.
33. Ferraro and Pope 1993.
34. See Buzawa and Buzawa 2003; Felson and Ackerman 2001; Jones and Belknap 1999.
35. Buzawa and Buzawa 2003.
36. Ford and Breall 2003.
37. Worden 2000.
38. Spohn and Holleran 2001.
39. Ford and Breall 2003.
40. Ibid.
41. Worden 2000; Buzawa and Buzawa 2003; Gover, MacDonald, and Alpert 2003; Mirchandani 2006; Gover, Brank, and MacDonald 2007; Mirchandani 2008.
42. See Healey, Smith, and O'Sullivan 1998.
43. Ferraro and Johnson 1983: 325–337; Logan, Shannon, Walker, and Faragher 2006; Logan and Walker 2009.
44. Harrell and Smith 1996: 214–242.
45. See Keilitz 2001; Holt et al. 2002.
46. Worden 2000.
47. Buzawa and Buzawa 2003.
48. Worden 2000.
49. Brownmiller 1975.
50. Ibid.
51. Ibid.
52. Russell 1990.
53. Small and Tetreault 1990.
54. Barshis 1983.
55. Small and Tetreault 1990.
56. Karmen 2007.
57. Estrich 1987.
58. Karmen 2007.
59. Ibid.

60. Martin 2005.
61. Brownmiller 1975.
62. Scully 1995: 197–215.
63. Bureau of Justice Statistics 2006.
64. Spohn 1999; Taslitz 1999.
65. Caringella 2009.
66. *Brown v. State*, 106 N.W. 536 (Wis. 1906), as cited in Spohn 1999.
67. *People v. Murphy*, 108 N.W. 1009, 1011 (Mich. 1906), as cited in Spohn 1999.
68. Karmen 2007; Spohn 1999; Taslitz 1999.
69. Wriggins 1983: 116.
70. LaFree 1980; Walsh 1987; Zatz 2000: 518–519.
71. See George and Martinez 2002.
72. Ibid.
73. Wriggins 1983: 117.
74. Horney and Spohn 1991: 117–153; Taslitz 1999.
75. Caringella-MacDonald 1988; Karmen 2007; Caringella 2009.
76. Horney and Spohn 1991: 117–153.
77. Bachman and Paternoster 1993.
78. Caringella 2009: 34.
79. Ibid.
80. Ibid.
81. Finkelhor and Yllo 1983: 119–131.
82. Russell 1982.
83. Russell 1990; Bergen 1999; Bergen 2006.
84. DeKeseredy, Rogness, and Schwartz 2004: 675–691.
85. Bergen 2006.
86. Bennice and Resnick 2003: 231.
87. Spohn and Horney 1996.
88. Caringella 2009: 60–61.
89. Baum, Catalano, Rand, and Rose 2009.
90. Ibid.
91. Ibid.
92. Ibid.
93. Ibid.
94. Ibid.
95. Office for Victims of Crime 2002.
96. Sinwelski and Vinton 2001: 46–65.
97. Office for Victims of Crime 2002.
98. Ibid.
99. Miller, N., 2001.
100. Baum, Catalano, Rand, and Rose 2009.
101. Ibid.
102. Rasche 1995.
103. Rantala and Edwards 2000.

104. Justice Research and Statistics Association (JRSA) (n.d.).
105. Ibid.
106. Gelles and Straus 1988.
107. Ibid.
108. Straus, Gelles, and Steinmetz 1980.
109. Gelles 2000: 784–804.
110. Gelles and Straus 1988.
111. Ibid.; Hamptom and Gelles 1994.
112. Gelles 2000: 784–804.
113. Gelles and Straus 1988.
114. Hamptom and Gelles 1994: 105; Mahoney, Williams, and West 2001.
115. Straus 1979: 75–88.
116. Straus, Hamby, Boney-McCoy, and Sugarman 1996: 283–316.
117. Ibid.
118. Kimmel 2002: 1336–1367.
119. Dobash, Dobash, Wilson, and Daly 1992: 71–91.
120. DeKeseredy and Schwartz 1998.
121. Bachman and Saltzman 1995.
122. Bureau of Justice Statistics 2006.
123. Rennison and Welchans 2000.
124. Ibid.
125. Bachman 2000: 839–867.
126. Bachman and Saltzman 1995.
127. Ibid.
128. Tjaden and Thoennes 1998a; Tjaden and Thoennes 1998b; Tjaden and Thoennes 2000.
129. Tjaden and Thoennes 1998a; Tjaden and Thoennes 2000.
130. Tjaden and Thoennes 1998a: 4–5; Tjaden and Thoennes 2000.
131. Tjaden and Thoennes 2000; Tjaden and Thoennes 2006.
132. Tjaden and Thoennes 2006.
133. Ibid.
134. Tjaden and Thoennes 1998a: 13.
135. Ibid.: 3–4.
136. Ibid.: 8–9.
137. Tjaden and Thoennes 2000; Tjaden and Thoennes 2006.
138. Rennison and Welchans 2000.
139. Ibid.
140. Tjaden and Thoennes 1998a: 6.
141. Belknap 2006.
142. Koss, Gidycz, and Wisniewski 1987: 162–170.
143. Ibid.
144. Koss and Cook 1998, as cited in Karmen 2007.
145. Koss and Cleveland 1997.
146. Koss and Cook 1998, as cited in Karmen 2001.

147. Fisher, Cullen, and Turner 2000.
148. Ibid.
149. Ibid.
150. Tjaden and Thoennes 1998b; Tjaden and Thoennes 2000; Tjaden and Thoennes 2006.
151. Tjaden and Thoennes 1998b.
152. Tjaden and Thoennes 2000; Tjaden and Thoennes 2006.
153. It is often reported that stalking typically occurs when a woman attempts to leave an abusive partner, so the NVAW survey explicitly examined the timing of stalking in a relationship. Interestingly, it is not only after a relationship ends that women find themselves stalked by their partners, although many do. Twenty-one percent of the female victims said that the stalking occurred before the relationship ended, 43 percent said it occurred after, and 36 percent said it occurred both before and after the relationship ended.
154. Tjaden and Thoennes 1998b: 8; Tjaden and Thoennes 2000; Tjaden and Thoennes 2006.
155. These abusive acts included: had a hard time seeing her point of view; was jealous or possessive; tried to provoke arguments; tried to limit her contact with family and friends; insisted on knowing where she was at all times; made her feel inadequate; shouted or swore at her; frightened her; prevented her knowledge of or access to family income; prevented her from working outside the home; insisted on changing residences even when she didn't need or want to (Tjaden and Thoennes 1998b). Finally, stalking experiences were accompanied by negative mental health consequences for victims; 30 percent of the female stalking victims sought psychological counseling as a result of their stalking victimization (Tjaden and Thoennes 1998b: 11).
156. Fisher, Cullen, and Turner 2000.
157. Browne 1987: 17, emphasis in original.
158. Dobash and Dobash 1984.
159. Dobash and Dobash 1984: 269–288.
160. Browne 1987.
161. Ibid.: 13.
162. Johnson 1995: 283–294; Johnson and Ferraro 2000.
163. See Bennice and Resick 2003; Bowker 1983a; Frieze 1983; Frieze and Browne 1989; Meyer, Vivian, and O' Leary 1998; Pagelow 1981; Pagelow 1984; Shields and Hannecke 1983; Walker 1984.
164. Frieze 1983.
165. Ibid., as cited in Pagelow 1984: 428.
166. Pagelow 1984: 429, emphasis in original.
167. Pagelow 1981.
168. Bowker 1983b. Frieze and Browne 1989: 163–217.
169. Meyer, Vivian, and O'Leary 1998.
170. Ibid.: 423–424.
171. Ibid.: 428.

172. Russell 1982, 1990.
173. Finkelhor and Yllo 1983.
174. Ibid.: 119–131.
175. Mahoney, Williams, and West 2001: 143–178.
176. DeKeseredy 2000: 728–746; Gordon 2000.
177. DeKeseredy 2000; Desai and Saltzman 2001.
178. Gordon 2000: 747–783.
179. Stets and Straus 1990, as cited in Gordon 2000.
180. Follingstad, Rutledge, Berg, Hause, and Polek 1990: 107–120.
181. Ibid.
182. Foa and Rothbaum 1998, as cited in Campbell and Wasco 2005.
183. Gordon 2000; Desai and Saltzman 2001: 35–52.
184. Smith 1994; Johnson 1998: 23–51; Desai and Saltzman 2001: 35–52.
185. Fisher, Cullen, and Turner 2000.
186. Bachman and Saltzman 1995.
187. Hanmer and Saunders 1984.
188. Desai and Saltzman 2001: 35–52.
189. Ibid.
190. Mahoney, Williams, and West 2001: 143–78.
191. Yoshihama 1999.
192. Rasche 1995: 246–261.
193. Ibid.
194. Ibid.
195. Ibid.; Richie 2000.
196. Girshick 2002.
197. Dasgupta 2002; Raj and Silverman 2002.
198. Raj and Silverman 2002: 367–398.
199. Johnson 1998; Campbell and Dienemann 2001.
200. Johnson 1998: 23–51.
201. Campbell and Dienemann 2001: 57–72.
202. Tjaden and Thoennes 1998a, 1998b.
203. Saltzman, Fanslow, McMahon, and Shelley 1999.
204. Desai and Saltzman 2001: 35–52.

CHAPTER 4

1. Chermak 1997: 711.
2. Jewkes 2004.
3. Ryan and Wentworth 1999.
4. Ibid.
5. Caringella-MacDonald 1998.
6. Ardovini-Brooker and Caringella-MacDonald 2002; Moorti 2002; Meyers 2004.
7. Granted, there are times when attention to specific individual details is necessary in newscasts: "To be of real benefit to the community, crime coverage must educate, it must empower readers and viewers" (Cote and Bucqueroux 1996: 2).

If a serial rapist attacks women as they leave the campus library to return to their dormitories, the media has a moral obligation to public safety to investigate and report on all of the known facts and circumstances of each assault so that students can take every precaution to procure their personal safety. When public safety is not an issue, however, the normative practice of making the victim's activities the crux of news reporting suggests, albeit covertly, that *she* did something wrong.

8. Benedict 1992; Karmen 1984; Lerner 1965; Meyers 1997; Russell 1984; Russo 1997.
9. Within academic writings about crimes of sexual violence, Lamb (1996: 122) argues that a pseudo-objectivity is adopted, since academics choose words that sound more objective than evocative.
10. Benedict 1992.
11. Ibid.
12. Lamb 1996.
13. Ardovini-Brooker and Caringella-MacDonald 2002.
14. Penelope 1990: 209.
15. Lamb 1996.
16. Scheppele and Bart 1983: 67.
17. Karmen 1990: 3.
18. Johnson 1989: 330.
19. Meili 2003.
20. Lipschultz and Hilt 2002; Zalin 2001.
21. Tiegreen and Newman 2009: 1.
22. Chermak and Weiss 2005; Dowler 2003; Meyers 1997; Ryan and Wentworth 1999.
23. Howitt 1998; Tiegreen and Newman 2009.
24. Dart Center 2006, as cited in Sheley and Ashkins 1981.
25. Dorfman, Thorson, and Stevens 2001.
26. Zalin 2001.
27. Lauritsen 2003: 3.
28. Sorenson, Peterson Manz, and Berk 1998.
29. Ibid.
30. Dorfman, Thorson, and Stevens 2001.
31. Benedict, 1997; Chermak and Weiss 2005; Meyers 1997.
32. Dart Center 2006, as cited in Kitzinger 2004.
33. Byerly and Ross 2006: 40.
34. Ibid.
35. Caringella-MacDonald 1998.
36. A notable exception to this occurred during the O. J. Simpson murder trial. When the media learned that prior to her murder Nicole Brown Simpson had been a victim of domestic abuse during her marriage to O. J., it catapulted the topic into the national spotlight in an unprecedented way. The media attention to domestic violence was probably deemed newsworthy and relevant more because it involved a black celebrity with a white wife as opposed to the well-documented fact that abused women are most likely to be killed by the abuser *after* they leave the relationship (Campbell 1992; Wilson and Daly 1993; Belknap 2006). Furthermore,

research finds that the media are more likely to report on domestic violence cases that result in a homicide (Family Violence Prevention Fund 2003).

37. Buzawa and Buzawa 2003.
38. Zalin 2001.
39. Bullock and Cubert 2002.
40. Kelley 2009
41. Ibid.: 1.
42. Ibid.
43. Ibid.: 2.
44. Ibid.
45. Ardovini-Brooker and Caringella-MacDonald 2002; Meloy and Miller 2006; Moorti 2002; Meyers 2004.
46. Byerly and Ross 2006: 43.
47. Ardovini-Brooker and Caringella-MacDonald 2002; Byerly and Ross 2006; Meloy and Miller 2006; Meyers 2004; Moorti 2002.
48. Sorenson, Peterson Manz, and Berk 1998; Rodgers and Thorson 2001.
49. Barlow, Barlow, and Chiricos 1995.
50. Lule 2001.
51. Berkow 1992, as cited in Lule 2001: 360.
52. Stanko 1992.
53. Chermak and Weiss 2005; Leonard 2003; Meyers 1997; Spears and Seydegart 1993; Wood 2004.
54. Chermak and Weiss 2005; Leonard 2003; Meyers 1997; Spears and Seydegart 1993; Wood 2004: 79.
55. Messner and Solomon 1993. The story was covered almost entirely in the sports section of the newspaper.
56. Newspaper sports departments are more masculine-identified than other news reporting department (Messner and Solomon 1993). For instance, the Association for Women in Sports Media estimate that only about 300 of the 10,000 sports reporters and journalists in this country are female (Nelson 1991).
57. Messner and Solomon 1993.
58. Mills 1988: 229, as cited in Messner and Solomon 1993: 345.
59. Leonard 2003.
60. Ibid.
61. Messner and Solomon 1993; Meyers 1997; Wood 2004.
62. Hanmer and Maynard 1987: 3.
63. Byerly and Ross 2006; Chermak 1995; Jewkes 2004; Leonard 2003; Meyer 1997; Spears and Seydegart 1993; Wood 2004.
64. Spears and Seydegart 1993.
65. Spears and Seydegart 1993.
66. Belknap 2006.
67. Wood 2004.
68. Spears and Seydegart 1993; Wood 2004.
69. Wood 2004: 104.
70. Chermak 1995.

71. Stanko 1998.
72. Cote and Bucqueroux 1996: 2.
73. Belknap 2006; Meyers 1997; Stanko 1998.
74. Belknap 2001; Dobash 1979; Hanmer and Maynard 1987; MacKinnon 1993; Meyers 1997; O'Toole and Schiffman 1997; Scully 1994; Walker, Madden, Vásquez, VanHouten, and Ervin-McLarty: 2006.
75. Scherer 2003: 2.
76. Cote and Bucqueroux 1996; Hackney 2003; Scherer 2003.
77. Parade Magazine 1997.
78. Cote and Bucqueroux 1996.
79. Cote and Bucqueroux 1996; Hackney 2003; Scherer 2003.
80. Scherer 2003:1
81. Oukrop 1982: 21.
82. Karmen 2001.
83. Scherer 2003.
84. Cohen 1991; Dershowitz 1988; Kantrowitz, Starr and Friday 1991.
85. Kelly (n.d.).
86. Kelly (n.d.).
87. Kelley 2009.
88. Cote and Simpson 2000; Scherer 2003.
89. Rhode Island Coalition of Domestic Violence (n.d.).
90. Kawamoto 2005: 3.
91. Brooks 1997.
92. Brooks 1997.
93. Brooks 1997: 70.
94. Kawamoto 1995.
95. Kawamoto 1995: 11.
96. Ford, Bachman, Friend, and Meloy 2002.
97. Kawamoto 1995.

CHAPTER 5

1. On October 1, 1993, 12-year-old Polly was abducted at knife point, during a slumber party, from the bedroom window of her Petaluma, California, home. The community response and media coverage to Polly's disappearance was unprecedented. Thousands joined in the search for Polly, and the girl's disappearance became international news. The nationwide search for Polly went on for several weeks, until police made an arrest in the case and the killer led authorities to the body. Richard Allen Davis, a convicted child molester, was eventually convicted and sentenced to death for Polly's kidnapping, rape, and murder (*U.S. News*, September 26, 1996). Elizabeth Smart's kidnapping is discussed in chapter 4.
2. Davey 2009.
3. Interstate Commission for Adult Offender Supervision 2007; Meloy and Coleman 2009; Meloy, Miller, and Curtis 2008; Meloy, Saleh, and Wolff 2007; Scott and Gerbasi 2003.
4. Griffin, Miller, Hoppe, Rebideaux, and Hammock 2007.

5. Snyder 2000.
6. Ibid.
7. Lieb, Quinsey, and Berliner 1998; Salter 2003.
8. Center for Disease Control and Prevention 2007.
9. Lieb, Quinsey, and Berliner 1998.
10. National Center for Victims of Crime and Crime Victims Research and Treatment Center 1992.
11. Greenfeld 1997.
12. Freedman 1987; Sutherland 1950.
13. Weisburg 1984.
14. These laws were not only examples of America's commitment to rehabilitation but were also experiments in expanding the power of the state to deprive an individual of his or her liberty in the absence of due process and other constitutional protections afforded under criminal law (Moreno 1997).
15. Lieb, Quinsey, and Berliner 1998.
16. Finkelhor 1984.
17. Spohn and Horney 1992.
18. Dorsett 1998.
19. Hendricks had a sexually violent history dating back to 1955, when he pled guilty to indecent exposure. In 1956, he served a brief period of incarceration for another incident of "lewdness" against a female child. In 1960, he sexually assaulted two young boys and was sentenced to two years in prison. Seven years later, the state of Kansas convicted Hendricks for sexually molesting two more children (a male and female), for which he served another short incarceration. In 1984, Hendricks was charged again for child molestation, this time against two 13-year-old boys. Although the defendant met the criteria outlined in the Habitual Criminal Act (three prior felony convictions), the state opted not to pursue Habitual Criminal charges, which could have tripled his sentence. Rather, the defendant pled guilty to two less serious offenses and received the minimum sentence on each count. The judge sentenced Hendricks to 5 to 20 years in prison, and at the end of his sentence the state of Kansas tried to get Hendricks civilly committed. The court ordered him to undergo a psychological evaluation, the results of which indicated that Hendricks met the clinical diagnosis of pedophilia and was "mentally abnormal." A lengthy legal battle ensued, but in 1997, in a 5–4 decision, the U.S. Supreme Court upheld the constitutionality of the Kansas law that solidified the legal practice of preventive detention of dangerous sex offenders. By underscoring the potential role of treatment, the justices ruled that the legislation was regulatory in nature, not punitive, even though many states that commit offenders under these laws do not offer them therapy.

Several other high-profile cases during this era also fueled disdain for and fear of sex offenders. For instance, the tragic 1990 sexual assault and murder of a 7-year-old Tacoma, Washington, boy by a recently paroled sex offender, the 1994 rape and murder of young Megan Kanka in New Jersey, and the abduction and the 1993 rape of Stephanie Schmidt in Kansas by an ex-convict who had recently been released from prison were catalysts to the enactment of civil sex-offender legislation.

20. La Fond 2000. The definition of a mentally ill sex offender, for purposes of preventive detention, is legislatively vague and varies from state to state. Still, current preventive detention practices unilaterally permit sex offenders to be classified as legally sane for the purposes of prosecution, conviction, and penalty; yet, as they near the completion of their sentence, the state can petition the court alleging that the offenders are mentally disordered and dangerous and should therefore be committed.

21. See Janus 2000; La Fond 2000; Lieb and Matson 1998 for a thorough review of earlier versions and rehabilitative goals of sexual psychopath laws.

22. Ibid.; Alexander 2004; LaFond 2000.

23. Griffin, Miller, Hoppe, Rebideaux, and Hammock 2007.

24. These sanctions apply only to criminals being processed in the federal court system and only to offenders convicted of sex crimes.

25. This latter provision is a spin-off of the sentencing scheme commonly known as the "three strikes" laws, which call for lifetime prison terms for three-time-convicted felons.

26. Meloy, Miller, and Curtis 2008. GPS (Global Positioning System) is a worldwide navigational system that operates using orbiting satellites that track a cell-phone-sized receiver's location, updating the position every few seconds (Brown, McCabe, and Wellford 2007).

27. Meloy, Miller, and Curtis 2008.

28. Ibid.

29. Ibid.

30. Meloy 2006.

31. New Jersey State Parole Board 2007.

32. Lewis 1988.

33. The minor differences between the two groups were not statistically meaningful (ibid.).

34. Schram and Milloy 1995.

35. Adkins, Huff, and Stageberg 2000.

36. Ibid.

37. Barnoski 2005.

38. These results reached the threshold of statistical significance at the .01 level (ibid.).

39. Ibid.

40. Walker, Madden, Vásquez, VanHouten, and Ervin-McLarty 2006.

41. Duwe and Donnay 2008.

42. Prescott and Rockoff 2008.

43. Ibid.: 34.

44. Meyer III, Molett, Richards III, Arnold, and Latham 2003.

45. Ibid.

46. Janus 2003; Levenson 2004a.

47. Levenson 2004b.

48. Ibid.
49. Ibid.
50. Schram and Milloy 1998.
51. Hanson and Bussiere 1998.
52. Milloy 2003; Milloy 2007.
53. Meyer III, Molett, Richards III, Arnold, and Latham, 2003.
54. Gookin 2007.
55. Ibid.
56. Janus 2003.
57. Ibid.
58. Friedland 1999.
59. Ibid.; Cohen and Jeglic 2007.
60. Doyle 2004.
61. Meloy 2006.
62. Griffin, Miller, Hoppe, Rebideaux, and Hammack 2007.
63. *Seattle Times*, May 8, 2003.
64. Barnhardt 2003.
65. Langan and Levin 2002.
66. Minnesota's sex-offender residence restriction law applies only to offenders on supervised release. The state of Colorado does not have a state-level sex-offender restriction law. They do, however, authorize their probation and parole officers to implement residence restrictions when deemed necessary (personal correspondence with Kim English, October 31, 2007).
67. Duwe, Donnay, and Tewksbury 2008; Minnesota Department of Corrections 2007.
68. Minnesota Department of Corrections 2007: 2.
69. Colorado Department of Public Safety 2004; Minnesota Department of Corrections 2003, 2007.
70. Skipp and Campo-Flores 2009.
71. See Tewksbury and Mustaine 2006.
72. See Levenson 2006; Levenson and Cotter 2005; Levenson and Hern 2007; Zandbergen and Hart 2006.
73. Durling 2006; Levenson and Cotter 2005; Levenson and Hern 2007; Meloy 2006; Sample and Streveler 2003; Tewksbury and Lees 2006; Zandbergen and Hart 2006.
74. See Braithwaite 1989; Kruttschnitt, Uggen, and Shelton 2000; Laub, Nagin, and Sampson 1998; Laub and Sampson 2001; Wolff, Meloy, Saleh, and Shi 2005.
75. Zandbergen and Hart 2006.
76. Skipp and Campo-Flores 2009.
77. Zandbergen and Hart 2006.
78. Ibid.: 20.
79. Skipp and Campo-Flores 2009: 3.
80. Zandbergen and Hart 2006: 20.

81. Brown, McCabe, and Wellford 2007.
82. Renzema and Mayo-Wilson 2005; Brown, McCabe, and Wellford 2007.
83. Brown, McCabe, and Wellford 2007.
84. Koch 2006: 2.
85. Brown, McCabe, and Wellford 2007.
86. Koch 2006: 2.
87. Meloy 2006.
88. English, Pullen, and Jones 1997; Stalans 2004.
89. Stalans 2004.
90. Pseudonyms are used for all offenders' names.
91. English, Pullen, and Jones 1997.
92. Berliner, Schram, Miller, and Milloy 1995; Hanson and Bussiere 1998; Marques, Day, Nelson, and West 1994; Marshall and Pithers 1994; Prentky, Lee, Knight, and Cerce 1997.
93. Berliner, Schram, Miller, and Milloy 1995; Hanson and Bussiere 1998; Marques, Day, Nelson, and West 1994; Marshall and Pithers 1994; Prentky, Lee, Knight, and Cerce 1997.
94. Skipp and Campo-Flores 2009: 3.
95. Berliner, Schram, Miller, and Milloy 1995; Hanson and Bussiere 1998; Prentky, Lee, Knight, and Cerce 1997.
96. Meloy, Saleh, and Wolff 2007.
97. Janus 2003; Meloy 2006.
98. Dorsett 1998.
99. Richard Allen Davis, the individual convicted in California of the highly publicized sexual assault and murder of Polly Klass, had previously served 15 years in prison for sex crimes dating back to 1973. However, because of plea negotiations, he was able to avoid convictions for the specific sex offenses, which would have required him to register. And Leroy Hendricks, the defendant who fought the constitutionality of sexually dangerous persons' civil commitment statutes in Kansas, was himself released from custody many times after accepting plea negotiations for reduced charges. Furthermore, it must be acknowledged that since sex crimes are severely underreported and few offenders are ever caught, registration legislation applies to only the small percentage of offenders who are apprehended and convicted of committing specific sex crimes.
100. Meloy and Coleman 2009.
101. Brown, McCabe, and Wellford 2007.
102. Caringella 2009.
103. Bachman and Paternoster 1993.
104. Greenfeld 1997. For our purposes here, this category refers to *any* intimate relationship, past or present, between the victim and offender.
105. Bachman and Paternoster 1993.
106. Caringella 2009: 26–27.
107. Ibid.

CHAPTER 6

1. NOW Legal Defense and Education Fund 2003.
2. Lloyd 1997; Marshall and Honeycutt 1999; Tolman and Raphael 2000.
3. Marshall and Honeycutt 1999.
4. Allard, Albelda, Colten, and Cosenza 1997; Curcio 1996; Tolman and Raphael 2002.
5. Pearson, Griswold, and Thoennes 2001.
6. NOW Legal Defense and Education Fund 2003: 2.
7. Raphael 1995; Raphael 1996.
8. Raphael 1996.
9. NOW Legal Defense and Education Fund 2003.
10. Lindhorst and Padgett 2005.
11. Brandwein 1997a, Brandwein 1997b as cited in Lyon 1999.
12. Lloyd 1997; Raphael 2000.
13. Lindhorst and Padgett 2005.
14. Pearson, Griswold, and Thoennes 2001.
15. NOW Legal Defense and Education Fund 2003.
16. Ibid.: 3.
17. Ibid.
18. Lindhorst and Padgett 2005.
19. Ibid.
20. See Lindhorst and Padgett 2005; Pearson, Griswold, and Thoennes 2001.
21. Raphel 1996.
22. Pearson, Thoennes, and Griswold 1999: 428–429.
23. Pollack 1996.
24. Lindhorst and Padgett 2005.
25. Ibid.: 421.
26. See Pearson, Thoennes, and Griswold 1999.
27. Pearson, Griswold, and Thoennes 2001: 188.
28. See ibid.
29. Ibid.
30. Ibid.
31. Pearson, Thoennes, and Griswold 1999.
32. See U.S. Conference of Mayors 2006; U.S. Conference of Mayors 2007.
33. Public housing options cannot meet the demand; for instance, "Cleveland's Section 8 program is currently closed because there are no vouchers available to the burgeoning number of families in need. Kansas City accepts 120 new applicants for assisted housing every day. Philadelphia has only been able to meet twenty-four percent of its residents' housing needs, San Antonio has only met ten percent, and Washington, D.C. has only met thirty-one percent" (Hirst 2003, p. 136).
34. Danner 1998.
35. Schram 2002.
36. See Hornstein, Kaye, and Atkins 2002.
37. Schram 2000.

38. Hornstein, Kaye, and Atkins 2002.
39. *HUD v. Rucker*, 122, S.Ct. 1230 (2002).
40. Hirst 2003: 140.
41. Ibid.: 141.
42. Ibid.
43. Ibid.: 131.
44. Ibid.: 137.
45. Ibid.: 141.
46. Ibid.: 143.
47. See Massey, Miller, and Wilhelmi 1998. There is some evidence that some state courts are doing a better job in determining "innocent" owners and targeting enforcement efforts accordingly (see NJ case law).
48. Massey, Miller, and Wilhelmi 1998: 23.
49. *U.S. v. 107.9 Acre Parcel of Land*, 1990.
50. Massey, Miller, and Wilhelmi 1998.
51. See Violence Against Women Act (42 U.S.C. § 13981).
52. Brooks 1997: 70.
53. Atkins, Jurden, Miller, and Patton 1999: 74.
54. This case was particularly messy since it involved a "date" or "acquaintance rape," a type of sexual assault that does not neatly correspond to what many consider a "real rape" (see Estrich 1987).
55. NOW Legal Defense and Education Fund 2003.
56. Ibid.
57. 132 F.3d 949,949, 4th Cir. (1997).
58. Browne 1987.
59. Pagelow 1984.
60. Strube and Barbour 1984.
61. Belknap 2001; Ferraro 2001.
62. Wilson and Daly 1993.
63. Ferraro 1983; Pagelow 1981.
64. Ferraro 2001.
65. Ibid.
66. Dasgupta 2004.
67. Ibid.
68. Browne 1987; Ferraro 1983; Ferraro 2001; Pagelow 1981.
69. Ferraro 2001.
70. Dutton 1992; Ferraro 2001.
71. Iovanni and Miller 2001; Pence and Paymar 1993.
72. See Buzawa and Buzawa 1993.
73. Ibid.
74. Zorza 1992.
75. Ferraro 1989.
76. Miller 2000; Zorza and Woods 1994.
77. Ibid.

78. Martin 1997.
79. Dobash, Dobash, Wilson, and Daly 1992; Pagelow 1992.
80. Hooper 1996.
81. Miller 2001.
82. Ostoff 2002.
83. Miller 2001.
84. Gelles and Straus 1985; Straus and Gelles 1986; Straus and Gelles 1990; Straus, Gelles, and Steinmetz 1980.
85. Tjaden and Thoennes 1998: 7.
86. Bachman and Saltzman 1995.
87. Taking Johnson (1995) and Johnson and Ferraro's (2000) work into account, categories of offenders are distinguishable. These researchers differentiate between minor relationship violence, which is not connected to a general pattern of control, and what they call intimate terrorism, in which violence is only one of a repertoire of tactics in a general pattern of control. A third category, violent resistance, encompasses self-defensive action and is most often used by women.
88. See also Mullender 1996.
89. Bowker 1983b; Browne 1987; Feld and Straus 1989; Hanmer and Saunders 1984.
90. Lyon 1999, as cited in Straus 1993.
91. Rosen, Dragiewicz, and Gibbs 2009.
92. Barnett and Thelen 1992; Cascardi, Vivian, and Meyer 1991; Hamberger and Potente 1994; Marshall and Rose 1990.
93. Mullender 1996: 209.
94. Miller 2001: 1354, 1368.
95. Ibid.
96. Ibid.
97. See three special issues of *Violence Against Women*: Bible, Dasgupta, and Osthoff 2002; Dasgupta, Osthoff, and Bible 2002; Dasgupta, Osthoff, and Bible 2003.
98. See Pence and Paymor 1993 for a discussion of male treatment programs.
99. Osthoff 2002; Gilbert 2002: 1271, 1287.
100. Dasgupta 2002: 1379.
101. Ferraro 2001.
102. Bachman and Carmody 1994; Feld and Straus 1989; Gelles and Straus 1988.
103. Miller and Meloy 2006.
104. The Domestic Abuse Project in Minnesota designates a similar category to the frustration response category described above, one they call, "Never Again." This motivation is often characteristic of women who have had long or repeated relationships in which they were battered. They adopted a survival mode of thinking—"No one is ever going to hurt me that way again"—and used violence to decrease their chances for further victimization (Domestic Abuse Project 1998). The research team did not observe this kind of motivation very often. However, prior abuse often manifests in a mindset of defiance and a refusal to accept further victimization or abuse.
105. Tolman and Raphael 2000.

106. Hagan 2001.

107. Hagan (2001: 938) argues: "Domestic violence consists of the violent acts of one man against one woman, and when it manifests as a cycle of abuse, it results in a form of slavery to the victim. Once the cycle of domestic violence begins, it is likely to escalate until the legal system intervenes or one of the participants is dead. Domestic violence is a system of dominance and subservience, often a personal scale, and represents the reduction of women to the status of material possession. It results from an abuser's need for domination, coercion, degradation, and control. A man who abuses women often engages in such behavior because he believes that his wife or girlfriend, in essence, is a possession that he has a right to control. Once a pattern of violence is established, the victim essentially becomes captive to her abuser, feeling the need to request permission to leave or make any personal decisions, lest she pay the price for disobedience. A woman who finds herself in this situation may feel she cannot leave due to the man's threats of further violence or even death." (See Hagan 2001 for the legal reasoning behind why battered women can be viewed as living in involuntary servitude with their abusers).

108. Hagan 2001.

109. Ibid.

110. Goldscheid 1999; Hagan 2001.

111. See the Federal Hate Crime and Prevention Act of 1999.

112. Coker 2001: 802.

113. Han 2003; Miller 2001; Osthoff 2002; Coker 2001.

114. Schneider 2000.

115. Coker 2001.

116. Maguigan 2003: 427.

117. Buzawa and Buzawa 2003: 199.

118. Ibid.

119. Ford 1993.

120. Ibid.

121. Ford, Bachman, Friend, and Meloy 2002.

122. Hoyle and Sanders 2000.

123. Ford, Bachman, Friend, and Meloy 2002.

124. See Healy and Smith 1998.

CHAPTER 7

1. Maguigan 2003.

2. Williams 1999.

3. Ibid.: 9.

4. Williams 1999: 68.

5. Elias 1993; Jones 1996; Phipps 1988.

6. See Matthews 1994 for a discussion of the rape crisis movement; Miller and Barberet 1994 for a discussion of the battered women's movement; Staggenborg 1988 for a discussion of the pro-choice movement.

7. Fraser 1989; Miller and Barberet 1994.

8. Fraser 1989: 154.

9. See Matthews 1994.

10. Dobash and Dobash 1992: 291–292.

11. Matthews 1994: 1–2.

12. Karmen 2001.

13. Phillips 1997.

14. Phillips 1999: 89, 93.

15. Ibid.

16. Ibid.: 99–100.

17. Gavey 1999: 68.

18. Ferraro 2003: 125.

19. Ehrenreich 2002.

20. Gettleman 2009: A1.

21. Ibid.

22. Epstein 1996.

23. Talbot 2002: 53–54.

24. Tobolowsky 1999.

25. Walsh 1986: 1139.

26. Tobolowsky 1999.

27. For advantages and disadvantages of victims' participatory rights, see Tobolowsky 1999.

28. In 1994, then Attorney General Janet Reno sought assistance from members of the American Society of Criminology to report the major research findings and controversies in 12 identified crime areas and submit them to her for policy consideration. One of the 12 task forces examined violence against women, particularly in regard to rape and battering, and offered the following suggestions: increase criminal justice system accountability to expose discretionary decision making; expand victim compensation; expand victim advocacy; increase outreach to minorities; increase training of criminal justice officials; increase public awareness of rape and battering through media campaigns, films, and town hall meetings; change cultural values that support a violent prone society; and improve measurement of victimizations to facilitate more research on the implementation of reforms (NIJ 1996). Many of the policy suggestions raised in this 1996 report are covered in later VAWA-initiated programs and are reflected in policy changes.

29. Office for Victims of Crime 2002.

30. Ibid.

31. Ibid.

32. As of July 2009 the Office for Victims of Crime note these figures as the most recent available for review.

33. As noted on April 17, 2009, via the Office for Victims of Crime online publications.

34. We chose to examine programs funded by the government rather than attempt a summary of all of the research that addresses violence against women. For

instance, the monthly journal *Violence Against Women* is devoted to publishing research on this issue, and numerous nonspecialty journals also publish articles in this area.

35. Moore Parmley 2004, as cited in Boba and Lilley 2009.
36. Ford, Bachman, Friend, and Meloy 2002.
37. Campbell 1996.
38. Violence Against Women Office 1996.
39. Clark, Biddle, and Martin 2002.
40. Ibid.: 417.
41. Ibid.: 423.
42. See report in Laurence and Spalter-Roth 1996 on the long-term impact on earnings potential for battered women.
43. Burt, Zweig, Andrews, Van Ness, Parikh, Uekert, and Harrell 2001.
44. Ford, Bachman, Friend, and Meloy 2002.
45. The median grants are slightly more than $30,000; some grants are as low as $500, and others as high as $5 million (Burt, Zweig, Andrews, Van Ness, Parikh, Uekert, and Harrell 2001: 6).
46. Department of Justice Press Release 2008.
47. Law enforcement data included numbers of domestic violence and sexual assault complaints, number of repeat calls about the same offender, number of arrests for domestic violence and sexual assault, and number of arrests for domestic violence–related homicides with a male perpetrator and female victim. Prosecution data included numbers of cases charged with domestic violence or sexual assault offenses, number of cases settled by a plea to a lesser domestic violence or sexual assault charge, number of cases settled by a plea to a different charge, number of cases going to trial on these charges, and number of cases resulting in conviction (Burt, Zweig, Andrews, Van Ness, Parikh, Uekert, and Harrell 2001: xii).
48. Burt, Zweig, Andrews, Van Ness, Parikh, Uekert, and Harrell 2001: xii.
49. Sexual Assault Services Program 2008.
50. Ibid.: 1.
51. National Domestic Violence Hotline.
52. Burt, Zweig, Andrews, Van Ness, Parikh, Uekert, and Harrell 2001: xiii.
53. Ibid.: xvi.
54. See ibid.: 119–227.
55. Ford, Bachman, Friend, and Meloy 2002.
56. VAWA wanted to ensure that state efforts to control violence against women, such as the issuance of a restraining order, were respected across the country and that it became a federal crime to cross state lines or enter or leave Indian country for the purpose of causing harm or harassing or intimidating a domestic partner (interstate domestic violence) (Ford, Bachman, Friend, and Meloy 2002). Unfortunately, the efficacy of such efforts is unknown because, to date, *no* research has been conducted on the specific deterrent effects of this body of federal legislation.
57. Ford, Bachman, Friend, and Meloy 2002.
58. Ibid.

59. Office of Management and Budget 2004, 2007.
60. Ford, Bachman, Friend, and Meloy 2002.
61. Ibid.: 36.
62. Ibid.
63. Boba and Lilley 2009.
64. Ibid.: 182.
65. Burt, Zweig, Andrews, Van Ness, Parikh, Uekert, and Harrell 2001.
66. Ibid.
67. Campbell, Bybee, Ford, and Patterson 2008.
68. Ibid.
69. Campbell, Wasco, Ahrens, Sefl, and Barnes 2001; Campbell and Raja 2005; Campbell, Townsend, Long, Kinnison, Pulley, Adames, and Wasco 2006.
70. Burt, Zweig, Andrews, Van Ness, Parikh, Uekert, and Harrell 2001:
71. Ibid.: 206.
72. Ibid.: 166.
73. The Lautenberg Amendment (Domestic Violence Gun Ban), signed into law in 1996, mandates that individuals convicted of a misdemeanor involving domestic violence can never own or acquire a firearm of any type.
74. Burt, Zweig, Andrews, Van Ness, Parikh, Uekert, and Harrell 2001: 174.
75. Van Ness and Strong 1997; Presser and Gaarder 2004.
76. Umbreit 2000.
77. Ibid.: 1.
78. Ibid.
79. Presser and Gaarder 2004: 409.
80. Ibid.
81. Hopkins and Koss 2005.
82. Umbreit, Vos, Coates, and Brown 2003.
83. Miller (Forthcoming, 2011).
84. For additional sources see Umbreit 2000; Presser and Gaarder 2004.
85. Miedzian 1993: 156.
86. See Buchwald, Fletcher, and Roth 1993.
87. Ibid.
88. Davis and Medina-Ariza 2001.
89. Ibid.
90. Unlike more traditional forms of battering, where the abuser is most likely to be an intimate partner, two-thirds of elders are abused by their grown children or grandchildren (Davis and Medina-Ariza 2001).
91. Ibid.
92. Ibid.
93. The CDC uses the abbreviation IP-DV (intimate-partner domestic violence) to describe situations in which one partner in an intimate relationship uses physical violence, sexual violence, threats of physical or sexual violence, psychological/emotional abuse, stalking, and/or economic abuse to establish a coercive pattern of power and control over his or her partner.

94. Delaware Coalition Against Domestic Violence 2002.
95. Levy 1998.
96. Telljohan, Price, Summers, Everett, and Casler 1995.
97. See wysiwyg://22/http://www.mencanstoprape.org.
98. See www.cdc.gov/ncipc/default.htm; www.crfc.org.
99. See www.safeyouth.org/scripts/index.asp.
100. Smallbone, Marshall, and Wortley 2008.
101. Ibid.

References

Adkins, G., Huff, D., and Stageberg, P. (2000). Iowa sex offender registry and recidivism. NCJ-202847. Des Moines: Iowa Criminal and Juvenile Justice Planning Agency. Retrieved June 25, 2007, from http://www.ncjrs.gov/app/abstractdb/AbstractDBDetails.aspx?id=202847.

Allard, M. A., Albelda, R., Colten, M.E., and Cosenza, C. (1997). *In harm's way? Domestic violence, AFDC receipt and welfare reform in Massachusetts.* Boston.

Alexander, M. A. (1999). Sexual offender treatment efficacy revisited. *Sexual Abuse: A Journal of Research and Treatment, 11*(2), 101–116.

Alexander, R. J. (2004). The United States Supreme Court and the civil commitment of sex offenders. *Prison Journal, 84,* 361–378.

Amir, M. (1971). *Patterns of forcible rape.* Chicago: University of Chicago Press.

Ammerman, R. T., and Hersen, M. (1992). Current issues in the assessment of family violence. In R. T. Ammerman and M. Hersen (Eds.), *Assessment of family violence: A clinical and legal sourcebook* (3–10). New York: Wiley.

Anon. (1994). Choice of language shapes views, defines limits, and can alter reality. *Media Report to Women, 22*(2), 1.

Aos, S., Phipps, O., Barnoski, R., and Lieb, R. (2001). The comparative costs and benefits of programs to reduce crime. Washington State Institute for Public Policy, Olympia. Retrieved June 1, 2006, from, http://www.wsipp.wa.gov/rptfiles/costbenefit.pdf.

Ardovini-Brooker, J., and Caringella-Macdonald, S. (2002). Media attributions of blame and sympathy in ten rape cases. *Justice Professional, 15*(1), 3–18.

Association for the Treatment of Sexual Abusers (ATSA). (2007). Facts about sex offenders. Retrieved November 11, 2007, from http://www.atsa.com/ppOffenderFacts.html.

Atkins, D. G., Jurden, J. G., Miller, S. L., and Patton, E. A. (1999). Striving for justice with the VAWA and civil torts actions. *Wisconsin Women's Law Journal, 14,* 69–104.

"Babe" banned. (1999, June 6). *Arizona Daily Star.*

Bachar, K., and Koss, M. P. (2001). From prevalence to prevention: Closing the gap between what we know about rape and what we do. In C. M. Renzetti, J. L. Edleson, and R. K. Bergen (Eds.), *Sourcebook on violence against women* (117–142). Thousand Oaks, CA: Sage.

Bachman, R. (2000). A comparison of annual incidence rates and contextual characteristics of intimate-partner violence against women from the National Crime Victimization Survey (NCVS) and the National Violence Against Women Survey (NVAWS). *Violence Against Women, 6*(8), 839–867.

Bachman, R., and Carmody, D. C. (1994). Fighting fire with fire: The effects of victim resistance in intimate versus stranger perpetrated assaults against females. *Journal of Family Violence, 9*(4), 317–331.

Bachman, R., and Paternoster, R. (1993). A contemporary look at the effects of rape law reform: How far have we really come? *Journal of Criminal Law and Criminology, 84*(3), 554–574.

Bachman, R., and Saltzman, L. E. (1995, August). *Violence against women: Estimates from the redesigned survey.* NCJ-154348. Washington, DC: U.S. Department of Justice.

Bandura, A. (1973). *Aggression: A social learning analysis.* Englewood Cliffs, NJ: Prentice Hall.

Barlow, M. H., Barlow, D. E., and Chiricos, T. G. (1995). Economic conditions and ideologies of crime in the media: A content analysis of crime news. *Crime and Delinquency, 41*(1), 3–19.

Barnett, O., Miller-Perrin, C., and Perrin, R. (2004). *Family violence across the lifespan: An introduction.* Thousand Oaks, CA: Sage.

Barnett, O. W., and Thelen, R. E. (1992). Gender differences in forms, outcomes, and motivations for interpartner aggression. Unpublished manuscript, Pepperdine University, Malibu, California.

Barnhardt, L. (2003, May 20). Effort aims to iron out AMBER Alert System's Wrinkles; Minimizing false reports of missing children. *The Baltimore Sun.*

Barnoski, R. (2005). Sex offender sentencing in Washington State: Has community notification reduced recidivism? Washington State Institute for Public Policy, Olympia. Retrieved May 23, 2006, from http://www.wsipp.wa.gov/rptfiles/05 08-1202.pdf.

Barshis, V. (1983). The question of marital rape. *Women's Studies International Forum, 6,* 383–393.

Basow, S. (1992). *Gender: Stereotypes and roles* (3rd ed.). Pacific Grove, CA: Brooks/Cole.

Baum, K., Catalano, S., Rand, M., and Rose, K. (2009). *Stalking victimization in the United States.* NCJ-224527. Washington, DC: Office of Justice Programs, U.S. Department of Justice.

Belkin, L. (2003, October 26). The opt-out revolution. *New York Times Magazine,* Section 6, pp. 42–47, 58, 85–86.

Belknap, J. (2001). *The invisible woman: Gender, crime, and justice* (2nd ed.). Toronto, Canada: Wadsworth.

Belknap, J. (2006). *The invisible woman: Gender, crime, and justice* (3rd ed.). Belmont, CA: Wadsworth.

Belknap, J. (2007). *The invisible woman: Gender, crime, and justice* (4th ed.). Toronto, Canada: Wadsworth.

Bem, S. L. (1974). The measure of psychological androgyny. *Journal of Consulting and Clinical Psychology, 42*(2), 155–162.

Bem, S. L. (1993). *The lenses of gender: Transforming the debate on sexual equality.* New Haven, CT: Yale University Press.

Benedict, H. (1992). *Virgin or vamp: How the press covers sex crimes.* New York: Oxford University Press.

Bennice, J. A., and Resick, P. A. (2003). Marital rape: History, research, and practice. *Trauma, Violence, and Abuse, 4*(3), 228–246.

Bergen, R. K. (1996). *Wife rape: Understanding the responses of survivors and service providers.* Thousand Oaks, CA: Sage.

Bergen, R. K. (1999). Marital rape: Violence against women online resources. Retrieved September 15, 2003, from http://www.vaw.umn.edu/documents/vawnet/ctscritique/ctscritique.pdf.

Bergen, R. K. (2006). Marital rape: New research and directions. Harrisburg, PA: Applied Research Forum, National Online Resource Center on Violence Against Women. Retrieved April 5, 2009 from http://new.vawnet.org/category/Main_Doc.php?docid=248.

Berger, P., and Luckmann, T. (1967). *The social construction of reality.* New York: Anchor Books.

Berliner, L., Schram, D., Miller, L. L., and Milloy, C. D. (1995). A sentencing alternative for sex offenders: A study of decision making and recidivism. *Journal of Interpersonal Violence, 10*(4), 487–502.

Best, J. (1999). *Random violence: How we talk about new crimes and new victims.* Berkeley: University of California Press.

Bible, A., Dasgupta, S. D., and Osthoff, S. (Eds.). (2002). Women's use of violence in intimate relationships, Part 1 (Special issue). *Violence Against Women, 8*(11).

Boba, R., and Lilley, D. (2009). Violence Against Women Act (VAWA): A nationwide assessment of effects of rape and assault. *Violence Against Women, 15*(2), 168–185.

Bohm, R. (1986). Crime, criminal and crime-control policy myths. *Justice Quarterly, 3,* 191–214.

Bowker, L. H. (1983a). *Beating wife beating.* Lexington, MA: Lexington Books.

Bowker, L. H. (1983b). Marital rape: A distinct syndrome? *Social Casework, 64,* 347–352.

Braithwaite, J. (1989). *Crime, shame and reintegration.* Cambridge: Cambridge University Press.

Brandwein, R. A. (1997a, March). *Navigating change: Understanding the links between welfare reform and family violence.* Paper presented at the 43rd annual program meeting, Council on Social Work Education, Chicago, Illinois.

Brandwein, R. A. (1997b, June). *The use of public welfare by family violence victims: Implications of new federal welfare "reform."* Paper presented at the Fifth International Family Violence Research Conference, New England Center, Durham, New Hampshire.

Brener, N. D., McMahon, P. M., Warren, C. W., and Douglas, K. A. (1999). Forced sexual intercourse and associated health-risk behaviors among female college students. *Journal of Consulting and Clinical Psychology, 67*(2), 252–259.

Brooks, R. (1997). Feminists negotiate the legislative branch: The Violence Against Women Act. In C. R. Daniels (Ed.), *Feminists negotiate the state: The politics of domestic violence* (65–81). Lanham, MD: University Press of America.

Brown, T., McCabe, S., and Wellford, C. (2007). *Global Positioning System (GPS) technology for community supervision: Lessons learned.* Washington, DC: National Institute of Justice, U.S. Department of Justice.

Browne, A. (1987). *When battered women kill.* New York: Free Press.

Browne, A. (1997). *When battered women kill* (2nd ed.). New York: Free Press.

Brownmiller, S. (1975). *Against our will: Men, women and rape.* New York: Simon and Schuster.

Brundson, C., and Morley, D. (1978). *Everyday television: Nationwide.* London: FBI.

Brush, L. D. (2000). Battering, traumatic stress, and welfare-to-work transition. *Violence Against Women, 6*(10), 1039–1065.

Buchwald, E., Fletcher, P. R., and Roth, M. (Eds.). (1993). *Transforming a rape culture.* Minneapolis: Milkweed.

Bulkeley, D., and Thomson, L. (2004, November 15). "Amendment Test Looms." *Deseret Morning News.* Salt Lake City, UT. Retrieved June 1, 2010, from http://www.deseretnews.com/article/1,5143,595105511,00.html.

Bullock, C., and Cubert, J. (2002). Coverage of domestic violence fatalities by newspapers in Washington State. *Journal of Interpersonal Violence, 17*(5), 475–499.

Bureau of Justice Statistics (2006). Criminal victimization in the United States. Statistical Tables (Table 42). Retrieved August 23, 2008, from U.S. Department of Justice, Office of Justice Programs, Bureau of Justice Statistics, http://www.ojp.usdoj.gov/bjs/pub/pdf/cvus/current/cv0642.pdf.

Bureau of Justice Statistics. (2007). *Homicide Trends in the U.S.: Intimate homicide.* Retrieved December 20, 2007, from U.S. Department of Justice, Office of Justice Programs, Bureau of Justice Statistics, http://www.ojp.usdoj.gov/bjs/homicide/intimates.htm.

Burke, L. K., and Follingstad, D. R. (1999). Violence in lesbian and gay relationships: Theory, prevalence, and correlational factors. *Clinical Psychology Review, 19*(5), 487–512.

Burt, M. R., Zweig, J. M., Andrews, C., Van Ness, A., Parikh, N., Uekert, B. K., and Harrell, A. V. (2001). *2001 Report: Evaluation of the STOP grants to combat violence against women.* Washington, DC: Urban Institute.

Busch, R. (2002). Domestic violence and restorative justice initiatives: Who pays if we get it wrong? In H. Strang and J. Braithwaite (Eds.), *Restorative justice and family violence* (223–248). Cambridge: Cambridge University Press.

Buzawa, E. S., and Buzawa, C. G. (1993). The scientific evidence is not conclusive: Arrest is no panacea. In R. J. Gelles and D. R. Loseke (Eds.), *Current controversies on family violence* (337–356). Newbury Park, CA: Sage.

Buzawa, E. S., and Buzawa, C. G. (2003). *Domestic violence: The criminal justice response.* Thousand Oaks, CA: Sage.

Byerly, C. M., and Ross, K. (2006). *Women and media: A critical introduction*. Malden, MA: Wiley-Blackwell.

Cahn, N. R. (1991). Civil images of battered women: The impact of domestic violence on child custody decisions. *Vanderbilt Law Review, 44*, 1041–1097.

Cal. Supr. Ct. L.A. County (2001). *People v. Poynton*, GA038353.

Campbell, B. J. (1996). A message from Violence Against Women Office Director, Bonnie J. Campbell. *Violence Against Women Act NEWS, 1*(1).

Campbell, J. (1992). If I can't have you, no one can. In J. Radford and D. E. Russell (Eds.), *Femicide: The politics of woman killing* (99–113). New York: Twayne.

Campbell, J. C., and Dienemann, J. D. (2001). Ethical issues in research on violence against women. In C. M. Renzetti, J. L. Edleson, and R. K. Bergen (Eds.), *Sourcebook on violence against women* (57–72). Thousand Oaks, CA: Sage.

Campbell, R., Wasco, S., Sefl, T., and Barnes, H. (2001). Preventing the "second rape": Rape survivors' experiences with community service providers. *Journal of Interpersonal of Violence, 16*(12), 1239–1259.

Campbell, R., and Raja, S. (2005). The sexual assault and secondary victimization of female veterans: Help-seeking experiences with military and civilian social systems. *Psychology of Women Quarterly, 29*, 97–106.

Campbell, R., and Wasco, S. M. (2005). Understanding rape and sexual assault: 20 years of progress and future directions. *Journal of Interpersonal Violence, 20*(1), 127–131.

Campbell, R., Townsend, S. M., Long, S. M., Kinnison, K. E., Pulley, E. M., Adames, S., and Wasco, S. M. (2006). Responding to sexual assault victims' medical and emotional needs: A national study of the services provided by SANE programs. *Research in Nursing and Health, 29*, 384–398.

Campbell, R., Bybee, D., Ford, K., and Patterson, D. (2008). *Systems change analysis of SANE programs: Identifying the mediating mechanisms of criminal justice system impact*. Washington, DC: U.S. Department of Justice.

Caputi, J. (1977). The glamour of grammar. *Chrysalis,4*, 35–43.

Caputi, J. (1993). The sexual politics of murder. In P. B. Bart and E. G. Moran (Eds.), *Violence against women: The bloody footprints* (5–15). Newbury Park, CA: Sage.

Caringella, S. (2009). *Addressing rape reform in law and practice*. New York: Columbia University Press.

Caringella-Macdonald, S. (1998). The relative visibility of rape cases in national popular magazines. *Violence Against Women, 4*(1), 62–80.

Carter, S. (n.d.). TV coverage of victims in three Michigan markets. Michigan State University, School of Journalism. Retrieved December 15, 2003 from http://victims.jrn.msu.edu/research/carter1.html.

Cascardi, M., Vivian, D., and Meyer, S. L. (1991). *Context and attributions for marital violence in discordant couples*. Paper presented at the 25th Annual Convention of the Association for the Behavioral Therapy, New York, New York.

Cavender, G., Bond-Maupin, L., and Jurik, N. C. (1999). The construction of gender in reality crime TV. *Gender and Society, 13*, 643–663.

Centers for Disease Control and Prevention (2007). Sexual violence: Fact sheet. Retrieved August 11, 2007, from http://www.cdc.gov/ncipc/factsheets/svfacts.htm.

Chancer, L. (1998). Gender, class, and race in three high-profile crimes: The cases of New Bedford, Central Park, and Bensonhurst. In S. L. Miller (Ed.), *Crime Control and Women: Feminist Implications of Criminal Justice Policy* (72–94). Thousand Oaks, CA: Sage.

Chermak, S. (1995). *Victims in the news: Crime and the American news media*. NCJ-169626. Boulder, CO: Westview Press.

Chermak, S. (1997). The presentation of drugs in the news media: The news sources involved in the construction of social problems. *Justice Quarterly, 14*(4), 687–718.

Chermak, S., and Weiss, A. (2005). Maintaining legitimacy using external communication strategies: An analysis of police-media relations. *Journal of Criminal Justice, 33*(5), 501–512.

Cianciotto, J., and Lopez, L. (2005). *Hispanic and Latino same-sex households in Florida*. New York National Gay and Lesbian Task Force Policy Institute. Retrieved July 15, 2008, from http://www.buddybuddy.com/latin-00.pdf.

Clark, K. A., Biddle, A. K., and Martin, S. L. (2002). A cost-benefit analysis of the Violence Against Women Act of 1994. *Violence Against Women, 8*(4), 417–428.

Cohen, M., and Jeglic, E. L. (2007). Sex offender legislation in the United States: What do we know? *International Journal of Offender Therapy and Comparative Criminology, 51*(4), 369–383.

Cohen, R. (1991, April 21). Should the media name the accuser when the crime being charged is rape? *New York Times*, p. E4.

Coker, D. (2001). Crime control and feminist law reform in domestic violence law: A critical review. *Buffalo Criminal Law Review, 4*, 801–860.

Cole, A. M. (2007). *The cult of true victimhood: From the war on welfare to the war on terror*. Palo Alto, CA: Stanford University Press.

Colorado Department of Public Safety (2004). *Report on safety issues raised by living arrangements for and location of sex offenders in the community*. Denver, CO: Sex Offender Management Board.

Cook, P. W. (1997). *Abused men: The hidden side of domestic violence*. Westport, CT: Praeger.

Cornell, D. (1991). *Beyond accommodation*. New York: Routledge.

Cosgrove-Mather, B. (2003). Central Park Jogger reveals identity: Writes in new book of horror at reopening of case. Retrieved August 5, 2009, from http://www.cbsnews.com/stories/2003/03/28/national/main546571.shtml.

Cote, W., and Bucqueroux, B. (1996). Covering crime without re-victimizing the victim. Paper presented at Nation Newspaper Association's Annual Convention, Nashville, Tennessee. Retrieved January 24, 2007, from http://victims.jrn.msu.edu/public/articles/nashvill.html.

Cote, W. E., and Simpson, R. (2000). *Covering violence: A guide to ethical reporting about victims and trauma*. New York: Columbia University Press.

Crenshaw, K. (1997). Intersectionality and identity politics: Learning from violence against women of color. In M. L. Shanley and U. Narayan (Eds.), *Reconstructing political theory: Feminist perspectives*. University Park: Pennsylvania State University Press.

Cuklanz, L. M. (2000). *Rape on prime time: Television, masculinity, and sexual violence.* Philadelphia: University of Pennsylvania Press.

Curcio, W. (1996). *The Passaic City study of AFDC recipients in a welfare-to-work program: A preliminary analysis.* Available from the Passaic City Board of Social Services, Paterson, NJ.

Daly, K. (2002). Sexual assault and restorative justice. In H. Strang and J. Braithwaite (Eds.), *Restorative justice and family violence* (62–88). Cambridge: Cambridge University Press.

Daly, K., and Chasteen, A. (1997). Crime news, crime fear, and women's everyday lives. In M. Fineman and M. McCluskey (Eds.), *Feminism, media, and the law* (235–248). New York: Oxford University Press.

Danner, M. J. E. (1998). Three strikes and it's women who are out: The hidden consequences for women of criminal justice policy reforms. In S. L. Miller (Ed.), *Crime control and women: Feminist implications of criminal justice policy* (1–14). Thousand Oaks, CA: Sage.

Dasgupta, S. D. (2002). A framework for understanding women's use of nonlethal violence in intimate heterosexual relationships. *Violence Against Women, 8*(11), 1364–1389.

Dasgupta, S. D. (2004). On violence against women's 10th anniversary: A birthday wish. *Violence against Women, 10*(12), 1401–1406.

Dasgupta, S. D., Osthoff, S., and Bible, A. (Eds.). (2002). Women's use of violence in intimate relationships, Part 2 (Special issue). *Violence Against Women, 8*(12).

Dasgupta, S. D., Osthoff, S., and Bible. A. (Eds.). (2003). Women's use of violence in intimate relationships, Part 3 (Special issue). *Violence Against Women, 9*(1).

Davey. M. (2009). Case shows limits of sex offender alert programs. *New York Times.* Retrieved September 2, 2009, from http://www.nytimes.com/2009/09/02/us/02offenders.html.

Davis, R. C., and Medina-Ariza, J. (2001). Results from an elder abuse prevention experiment in New York City. Research in Brief. Washington, DC: U.S. Department of Justice, Office of Justice Programs, National Institute of Justice.

DeKeseredy, W. S. (2000). Current controversies on defining nonlethal violence against women in intimate heterosexual relationships. *Violence Against Women 6*(7), 728–746.

DeKeseredy, W. S., and Kelly, K. (1993). The incidence and prevalence of women abuse in Canadian university and college dating relationships. *Canadian Journal of Sociology, 18*, 137–159.

DeKeseredy, W. S., and MacLeod, L. (1997). *Woman abuse: A sociological story.* Toronto: Harcourt Brace.

DeKeseredy, W. S., and Schwartz, M. D. (1998). Measuring the extent of woman abuse in intimate heterosexual relationships: A critique of the Conflict Tactics Scales. *Violence Against Women Online Resources.* Retrieved September 15, 2003, from http://www.vaw.umn.edu/documents/vawnet/ctscritique/ctscritique.pdf.

DeKeseredy, W. S., Rogness, M., and Schwartz, M. D. (2004). Separation/divorce sexual assault: The current state of social scientific knowledge. *Aggression and Violent Behavior, 9*, 675–691.

Delaware Coalition Against Domestic Violence (2002). *Prevention enhancement RFP*. Wilmington, DE: DCADV.

Department of Justice Press Release (2008, September 29). Office on Violence Against Women awards $114 million to support comprehensive crime prevention. U.S. Department of Justice, Office on Violence Against Women. Retrieved June 25, 2009, from http://www.ovw.usdoj.gov/docs/fy08-stop-awards-ann.pdf.

Dershowitz, A. (1988). *Taking liberties: A decade of hard cases, bad laws, and bum raps*. Chicago: Contemporary Books.

Dershowitz, A. M. (1994). *The abuse excuse: And other cop-outs, sob stories, and evasions of responsibility*. Boston: Little, Brown.

Desai, S., and Saltzman, L. E. (2001). Measurement issues for violence against women. In C. M. Renzetti, J. L. Edleson, and R. K. Bergen (Eds.), *Sourcebook on violence against women* (35–52). Thousand Oaks, CA: Sage.

Dobash, R. E., and Dobash, R. P. (1979). *Violence against wives: A case against the patriarchy*. New York: Free Press.

Dobash, R. E., and Dobash, R. P. (1984). The nature and antecedents of violent events. *British Journal of Criminology, 24*(3), 269–288.

Dobash, R. E., and Dobash, R. P. (1992). *Women, violence and social change*. New York: Routledge.

Dobash, R. P., Dobash, R. E., Wilson, M., and Daly, M. (1992). The myth of sexual symmetry in marital violence. *Social Problems, 39*, 71–91.

Domestic Abuse Project (1998). *Women who abuse in intimate relationships*. Minneapolis: DAP.

Domestic partner amendment used in defense against domestic violence charges. (2005, January 1). Retrieved June 1, 2010, from http://www.freerepublic.com/focus/f-news/1322321/posts.

Dorfman, L., Thorson, E., and Stevens, J. E. (2001). Reporting on violence: Bringing a public health perspective into the newsroom. *Health Education & Behavior, 28*(4), 402–419.

Dorsett, K. (1998). *Kansas v. Hendricks*: Marking the beginning of a dangerous new era in civil commitment. *Depaul Law Review, 48*, 113–159.

Dowler, K. (2003). Media consumption and public attitudes toward crime and justice: The relationship between fear of crime, punitive attitudes, and perceived police effectiveness. *Journal of Criminal Justice and Popular Culture, 10*(2), 109–126.

Downs, D. A. (1996). *More than victims: Battered women, the syndrome society, and the law*. Chicago: University of Chicago Press.

Doyle, J. (2004, July 11). *Treatment for rapists, molesters under fire cost, legality and effectiveness at issue in extended program*. Retrieved January 5, 2007, from http://www.sfgate.com/cgi-bin/article.cgi?file=/chronicle/archive/2004/07/11/MNGB57ILU41.DTL.

Durling, C. (2006). Never going home: Does it make us safer? Does it make sense? Sex offenders, residency restrictions, and reforming risk management law. *Journal of Criminal Law and Criminology, 97*, 317–380.

Dutton, M. A. (1992). *A model for assessment and intervention: Empowering and healing the battered woman*. New York: Springer Publishing.

Duwe, G., and Donnay, W. (2008). The impact of Megan's Law on sex offender recidivism: The Minnesota experience. *Criminology, 46*, 411–446.

Duwe, G., Donnay, W., and Tewksbury, R. (2008). Does residential proximity matter? A spatial analysis of sex offense recidivism. *Criminal Justice and Behavior, 35*(4), 484–504.

Ehrenreich, N. (2002). Subordination and symbiosis: Mechanisms of mutual support between subordinating systems. *UMKC Law Review, 71*, 251–324.

Elias, R. (1990). Which victim movement? In A. J. Lurigio, W. G. Skogan, and R. C. Davis (Eds.), *Victims of crime: Problems, policies, and programs*. Newbury Park, CA: Sage.

Elias, R. (1993). *Victims still*. London: Sage.

Elliott, P. (1996). Shattering illusions: Same-sex domestic violence. In C. Renzetti and C. H. Miley (Eds.), *Violence in gay and lesbian domestic partnerships* (1–8). Binghamton, NY: Harrington Park Press.

English, K., Pullen, S., and Jones, L. (1997). *Managing adult sex offenders in the community—A containment approach*. National Institute of Justice—Research in Brief. Washington DC: U.S. Department of Justice, Office of Justice Programs, National Institute of Justice. Retrieved March 15, 2007, from www.ncjrs.gov/pdffiles/sexoff.pdf.

Epstein, D. (1996). Keeping them in their place: Hetero/sexist harassment, gender, and the enforcement of heterosexuality. In J. Holland and L. Adkins (Eds.), *Sex, sensibility and the gendered body*. Basingstoke, England: Macmillan.

Estrich, S. (1987). *Real rape*. Cambridge, MA: Harvard University Press.

Family Violence Prevention Fund (2003). Intimate partner violence goes underreported in California newspapers. Retrieved June 20, 2004, from http://endabuse.org/programs/display.php3.

Farrell, W. (1999). *Women can't hear what men don't say*. New York: Tarcher/Putnam.

Feld, S. L., and Straus, M. A. (1989). Escalation and desistance of wife assault in marriage. *Criminology, 27*, 141–161.

Felson, R. B., and Ackerman, J. (2001). Arrest for domestic and other assaults. *Criminology, 39*(3), 655–675.

Ferraro, K. J. (1983). Negotiating trouble in a battered women's shelter. *Urban Life, 12*, 287–306.

Ferraro, K. J. (2001). Woman battering: More than a family problem. In C. Renzetti and L. Goodstein (Eds.), *Women, crime, and criminal justice: Original feminist readings* (135–153). Los Angeles: Roxbury.

Ferraro, K. J. (2003). The words change but the melody lingers: The persistence of the battered women's syndrome in criminal cases involving battered women. *Violence Against Women, 9*, 110–129.

Ferraro, K. J., and Johnson, J. M. (1983). How women experience battering. *Social Problems, 30*(3), 325–337.

Ferraro, K. J., and Pope, L. (1993). Irreconcilable differences: Battered women, police and the law. In N. Z. Hilton (Ed.), *Legal responses to wife assault: Current trends and evaluation* (96–123). Newbury Park, CA: Sage.

Fineman, M. A., and Mykitiuk, R. (1994). *The public nature of private violence: The discovery of domestic abuse.* New York: Routledge.

Finkelhor, D. (1984). *Child sexual abuse: New theory and research.* New York: Free Press.

Finkelhor, D., and Yllo, K. (1983). Rape in marriage: A sociological view. In D. Finkelhor, R. J. Gelles, G. T. Hotaling, and M. A. Straus (Eds.), *The dark side of families: Current family violence research* (119–131). Beverly Hills: Sage.

Finkelhor, D., and Yllo, K. (1985). *License to rape: Sexual abuse of wives.* New York: Holt, Rinehart, and Winston.

Fisher, B. S., Cullen, F. T., and Turner, M. G. (2000). *The sexual victimization of college women.* NCJ-182369. Washington, DC: U.S. Department of Justice.

Fitzpatrick, M. (2006, February 2). *Quest news action WI, HRC release. Vol. 13, No. 1, Wisconsin marriage benefits.* Retrieved June 1, 2010, from http://www.quest-online.com/NewFiles/QuestXIII1.html.

Follingstad, D. R., Rutledge, L. L., Berg, B. J., Hause, E. S., and Polek, D. S. (1990). The role of emotional abuse in physically abusive relationships. *Journal of Family Violence, 5*(2), 107–120.

Ford, D. A. (1991). Prosecution as a victim power resource: A note on empowering women in violent conjugal relationships. *Law and Society, 1*(2), 313–334.

Ford, D. A. (1993). *The Indianapolis domestic violence prosecution experiment* (Final report submitted to the National Institute of Justice). Indianapolis: Indiana University–Purdue University Indianapolis, Department of Sociology.

Ford, D. A. (2003). Coercing victim participation in domestic violence prosecutions. *Journal of Interpersonal Violence, 18*(6), 669–684.

Ford, D. A., Bachman, R., Friend, M., and Meloy, M. (2002). *Controlling violence against women: A research perspective on the 1994 VAWA's criminal justice impacts.* Research in Brief. Washington, DC: National Institute of Justice, U.S. Department of Justice, Office of Justice Programs.

Ford, D. A., and Breall, S. (2003). *Violence against women: Synthesis of research for prosecutors.* NCJ-199660. Rockford, MD: National Institute of Justice/NCJRS.

Fraser, N. (1989). *Unruly practices: Power, discourse and gender in contemporary social theory.* Minneapolis: University of Minnesota.

Freedman, E. B. (1987). Uncontrolled desires: The response to the sexual psychopath, 1920–1960. *The Journal of American History, 74*(1), 83–106.

Friedland, S. I. (1999). On treatment, punishment, and the civil commitment of sex offenders. *University of Colorado Law Review, 70,* 73–155.

Frieze, I. H. (1983). Investigating the causes and consequences of marital rape. *Signs, 8,* 532–553.

Frieze, I. H., and Browne, A. (1989). Violence in marriage. In L. Ohlin and M. Tonry (Eds.), *Crime and justice: An annual review of research,* vol. 11 (163–217). Chicago: University of Chicago Press.

Garner, J., and Clemmer, E. (1986). *Danger to police in domestic disturbances—a new look.* Research in Brief. Washington, DC: National Institute of Justice, U.S. Department of Justice.

Gavey, N. (1999). 'I wasn't raped, but . . . ': Revisiting definitional problems in sexual victimization. In S. Lamb (Ed.), *New versions of victims: Feminists struggle with the concept* (57–81). New York: New York University Press.

Gelles, R. J. (2000). Estimating the incidence and prevalence of violence against women: National data systems and sources. *Violence Against Women, 6*(7), 784–804.

Gelles, R. J., and Straus, M. A. (1988). *Intimate violence: The causes and consequences of abuse in the American family*. New York: Simon and Schuster.

Gelles, R. J., and Straus, M. A. (1985). Is violence toward children increasing? A comparison of 1975 and 1985 national survey rates. Paper presented at the Seventh National Conference on Child Abuse and Neglect, Chicago, IL.

George, W. H., and Martinez, L. J. (2002). Victim blaming in rape: Effects of victim and perpetrator race, type of rape, and participant racism. *Psychology of Women Quarterly, 26*(2), 110–119.

Gerlin, A. (1994, September 1). McDonald's callousness was real issue, jurors say, in case of burned woman. *Wall Street Journal*. Retrieved July 25, 2008, from http://www.vanosteen.com/mcdonalds-coffee-lawsuit.htm.

Gettleman, J. (2009, August 5). Symbol of unhealed Congo. *New York Times*, p. A1.

Gilbert, N. (1991). The phantom epidemic of sexual assault. *Public Interest, 103*, 54–65.

Gilbert, P. R. (2002). Discourses of female violence and societal gender stereotypes. *Violence Against Women, 8*(11), 1271–1300.

Gillespie, C. K. (1989). *Justifiable homicide: Battered women, self-defense, and the law*. Columbus: Ohio State University Press.

Gilligan, C. (1982). *In a different voice*. Cambridge, MA: Harvard University Press.

Giorgio, G. (2002). Speaking silence: Definitional dialogues in abusive lesbian relationships. *Violence Against Women, 8*(10), 1233–1259.

Girshick, L. (2002). *Woman to woman sexual violence: Does she call it rape?* Boston: Northeastern University Press.

Gitlin, T. (1980). *The whole world is watching*. Berkley: University of California Press.

Goldscheid, J. (1999). Gender-motivated violence: Developing a meaningful paradigm for civil rights enforcement. *Harvard Women's Law Journal, 22*, 123–158.

Gondolf, E., and Fisher, E. (1988). *Battered women as survivors: An alternative to treating learned helplessness*. Lexington, MA: Lexington Books.

Gookin, K. (2007, August). *Comparison of state laws authorizing involuntary commitment of sexually violent predators: 2006, Update, revised*. Document No. 07–08–1101. Olympia: Washington State Institute for Public Policy.

Gordon, L. (1988). *Heroes of their own lives: The politics and history of family violence in America*. New York: Viking.

Gordon, M. (2000). Definitional issues in violence against women. Surveillance and research from a violence research perspective. *Violence Against Women, 6*(7), 747–783.

Gover, A. R., MacDonald, J. M., and Alpert, G. (2003). Combating domestic violence in rural America: Findings from an evaluation of a local domestic violence court. *Criminology and Public Policy, 3*, 109–132.

Gover, A. R., Brank, E. M., and MacDonald, J. M. (2007). A specialized domestic violence court in South Carolina: An example of procedural justice for victims and defendants. *Violence Against Women, 13*(6), 603–626.

Gramsci, A. (1971). *Selections from prison notebooks.* London: Lawrence and Wishart.

Gramsci, A. (1983). *The modern prince and other writings.* New York: International.

Greenfeld, L. (1997). *Sex offenses and offenders: An analysis of data on rape and sexual assault.* NCJ-163392. Washington, DC: Bureau of Justice Statistics, Office of Justice Programs, U.S. Department of Justice.

Greenfeld, L. A., Rand, M. R., Craven, D., Klaus, P. A., Perkins, C. A., Ringel, C., Warchol, G., Maston, C., and Fox, J. A. (1998). *Violence by intimates: Analysis of data on crimes by current or former spouses, boyfriends, and girlfriends.* NCJ-167237. Washington, DC: U.S. Department of Justice, Bureau of Justice Statistics.

Griffin, T., Miller, M. K., Hoppe, J., Rebideaux, A., and Hammack, R. (2007). A preliminary examination of AMBER Alert's effects. *Criminal Justice Policy Review, 18*(4), 378–394.

Grover, C. and Soothill, K. (1996). A murderous "underclass"?: The press reporting of sexually motivated murder. *Editorial Board of the Sociological Review, 44,* 398–415.

Hackney, S. (2003). Covering crime and its victims. In Criminal Justice Journalists (Ed.), *Covering crime and justice* (Chapter 5). Retrieved June 25, 2004, from http://www.justicejournalism.org/crimeguide/chapter05/chapter05_pg04.html.

Hagan, J. R. (2001). Can we lose the battle and still win the war? The fight against domestic violence after the death of Title III of the Violence Against Women Act. *DePaul Law Review, 50,* 919–992.

Hall, G. (1995). Sex offender recidivism revisited: A meta-analysis of recent treatment studies. *Journal of Consulting and Clinical Psychology, 63,* 802–809.

Hall, S. (1977). Culture, the media and the ideological effect. In J. Curran, M. Gurevitch, and J. Woollacott (Eds.), *Mass communications and society* (315–348). Beverly Hills, CA: Sage.

Hall, S. (1982). The rediscovery of ideology: Return of the repressed in media studies. In M. Gurevitch, T. Bennett, J. Curran, and J. Woollacott (Eds.), *Culture, society and the media* (56–90). London: Methuen.

Hamberger, L. K., Lohr, J. M., and Bonge, D. (1994). The intended function of domestic violence is different for arrested male and female perpetrators. *Family Violence and Sexual Assault Bulletin, 10,* 40–44.

Hamberger, L. K., and Potente, T. (1994). Counseling heterosexual women arrested for domestic violence: Implications for theory and practice. *Violence and Victims, 9*(2), 125–137.

Hamptom, R. L., and Gelles, R. J. (1994). Violence toward black women in a nationally representative sample of black families. *Journal of Comparative Family Studies, 25*(1), 105–119.

Han, E. L. (2003). Mandatory arrest and no-drop policies: Victim empowerment in domestic violence cases. *Boston College Third World Law Journal, 23,* 159–192.

Hanmer, J., and Maynard, M. (1987). Introduction: Violence and gender stratification. In J. Hanmer and and M. Maynard (Eds.), *Women, violence and social control* (1–12). Atlantic Highlands, NJ: Humanities Press International.

Hanmer, J., and Saunders, S. (1984). *Well-founded fear: A community study of violence to women*. London: Hutchinson.

Hanson, R. K., and Bussiere, M. T. (1998). Predicting relapse: A meta-analysis of sexual offender recidivism studies. *Journal of Consulting and Clinical Psychology, 66*(2), 348–362.

Hanson, R., and Harris, A. (1998). *Dynamic predictors of sexual recidivism*. Ottawa, Canada: Department of the Solicitor General of Canada.

Hanson, R. K., Gordon, A., Harris, A. J. R., Marques, J. K., Murphy, W., Quinsey, V. L., and Seto, M. C. (2002). First report of the collaborative outcome data project on the effectiveness of psychological treatments for sex offenders. *Sexual Abuse: A Journal of Research and Treatment, 14*(2), 169–194.

Harrell, A., and Smith, B. E. (1996). Effects of restraining orders on domestic violence victims. In E. S. Buzawa and C. G. Buzawa (Eds.), *Do arrest and restraining orders work?* (214–242). Thousand Oaks, CA: Sage.

Hartley, J. (1982). *Understanding news*. London: Methuen.

Healey, K., and Smith, C. (1998). *Batterer intervention: Program approaches and criminal justice strategies*. NCJ-168638. Washington, DC: U.S. Department of Justice.

Healey, K., Smith, C., and O'Sullivan, C. (1998). *Batterer intervention: Program approaches and criminal justice strategies*. NCJ-168638. Washington DC: US Department of Justice, Office of Justice Programs, National Institute of Justice.

Henderson, L. N. (1985). The wrongs of victim's rights. *Stanford Law Review, 37*, 937–1021.

Henley, N. M., Miller, M., and Beazley, J. (1995). Syntax, semantics, and sexual violence: Agency and the passive voice. *Journal of Language and Social Psychology, 14*(1–2), 60–84.

Herron, W. G., Javier, R. A., McDonald-Gomez, M., and Adlerstein, L. K. (1994). Sources of family violence. *Journal of Social Distress and the Homeless, 3*, 213–228.

Hirst, E. (2003). The housing crisis for victims of domestic violence: Disparate impact claims and other housing protection for victims of domestic violence. *Georgetown Journal on Poverty Law and Policy, 10*(1), 131–155.

Hoff, L. (1990). *Battered women as survivors*. London: Routledge.

Hoff Sommers, C. (1994). *Who stole feminism? How women have betrayed women*. New York: Touchstone.

Holleran, D., and Spohn, C. (2004). On the use of the total incarceration variable in sentencing research. *Criminology, 42*(1), 211–240.

Holt, V. L., Kernic, M. A., Lumley, T., Wolf, M. E., and Rivara, F. P. (2002). Civil protection orders and risk of subsequent police-reported violence. *Journal of the American Medical Association, 288*(5), 589–594.

hooks, b. (1984). *Feminist theory from margin to center*. Cambridge, MA: South End Press.

hooks, b. (1989). *Talking back: Thinking feminist, thinking black*. Cambridge, MA: South End Press.

Hooper, M. (1996, February). When domestic violence diversion is no longer an option: What to do with the female offender. *Berkeley's Women Law Journal*, 11, 168–181.

Hopkins, C. Q., and Koss, M. P. (2005). Incorporating feminist theory and insights into a restorative justice response to sex offenses. *Violence Against Women*, 11(5), 693–723.

Horney, J., and Spohn, C. (1991). Rape law reform and instrumental change in six urban jurisdictions. *Law and Society Review*, 25(1), 117–153.

Hornstein, R., Atkins, D.G., and Kaye, T.A. (2002). The politics of equal justice. *American University Journal of Gender, Social Policy & Law*, 11, 1089–1105.

Hornstein, R., Kaye, T., and Atkins, D. (2002, March 18). Pearlie Rucker's eviction from HUD housing in 1997: One strike for the poor and how many of the rest of us? *Legal Times*. Retrieved March 24, 2002, from http://www.mapinc.org/newscsdp/v02/n568/a03.html.

Hotaling, G. T., and Sugarman, D. B. (1986). An analysis of risk markers in husband to wife violence. *Violence and Victims*, 1, 101–124.

Howitt, D. (1998). Crime, the media and the law. NCJ-177545. New York: John Wiley and Sons.

Hoyle, C., and Sanders, A. (2000). Police response to domestic violence: From victim choice to victim empowerment? *British Journal of Criminology*, 40, 14–36.

Hudson, B. (1998). Restorative justice: The challenge of sexual and racial violence. *Journal of Law and Society*, 25(2), 237–256.

Hughes, R. (1993). *Culture of complaint: The fraying of America*. New York: Oxford University Press.

Interstate Commission for Adult Offender Supervision (2007). GPS Supervision Update Survey. Retrieved February 6, 2008, from http://www.interstatecompact.org/Documents/Surveys/tabid/105/Default.aspx.

Iovanni, L., and Miller, S. L. (2001). Criminal justice responses to domestic violence: Law enforcement and the courts. In C. M. Renzetti, J. L. Edleson, and R. K. Bergen (Eds.), *Sourcebook on violence against women* (303–327). Thousand Oaks, CA: Sage.

Jacobson, N. S., Gottman, J. M., Waltz, J., Rushe, R., Babcock, J., and Holtzworth-Munroe, A. (1994). Affect, verbal content and psycho-physiology in the arguments of couples with a violent husband. *Journal of Consulting and Clinical Psychology*, 62, 982–988.

Janoff-Bulman, R. (1992). *Shattered assumptions: Towards a new psychology of trauma*. New York: Free Press.

Janus, E. S. (2000). Sexual predator commitment laws: Lessons for law and the behavioral sciences. *Behavioral Science and the Law*, 18(1), 5–21.

Janus, E. S. (2003). Examining our approaches to sex offenders and the law, Minnesota's sex offender commitment program: Would an empirically-based prevention policy be more effective? *William Mitchell Law Review*, 29, 1–37.

Jasinski, J. L. (2001). Theoretical explanations of violence against women. In C. M. Renzetti, J. L. Edleson, and R. K. Bergen (Eds.), *Sourcebook on violence against women* (5–21). Thousand Oaks, CA: Sage.

Jewkes, Y. (2004). *Media and crime.* Thousand Oaks, CA: Sage.

Johnson, H. (1998). Rethinking survey research on violence against women. In R. E. Dobash and R. P. Dobash (Eds.), *Rethinking violence against women* (23–51). Thousand Oaks, CA: Sage.

Johnson, M. P. (1995). Patriarchal terrorism and common couple violence: Two forms of violence against women. *Journal of Marriage and the Family, 57*(2), 283–294.

Johnson, M. P. (2006). Conflict and control: Gender symmetry, and asymmetry in domestic violence. *Violence Against Women, 12*(11), 1003–1018.

Johnson, M. P., and Ferraro, K. J. (2000). Research on domestic violence in the 1990s: Making distinctions. *Journal of Marriage and the Family, 62*(4), 948–963.

Johnson, S. (1989). *Wildfire: Igniting the she/volution.* Albuquerque, NM: Wildfire Books.

Johnstone, J., Hawkins, D., and Michener, A. (1994). Homicide reporting in Chicago dailies. *Journalism Quarterly, 71*(4), 860–872.

Jones, D. (1996). Tough on crime and nasty to children. *Prison Report, 36,* 4–5.

Jones, D. A., and Belknap, J. (1999). Police responses to battering in a progressive pro-arrest jurisdiction. *Justice Quarterly, 16*(2), 249–273.

Justice Research and Statistics Association (JRSA) (n.d.). Status of NIBRS in the states. IBR Resource Center, Washington, DC. Retrieved August 13, 2009, from http://www.jrsa.org/ibrrc/background-status/nibrs_states.shtml.

Kaminer, W. (1992). *I'm dysfunctional, you're dysfunctional.* Reading, MA: Addison-Wesley.

Kaminer, W. (1993). Feminism's identity crisis. *Atlantic Monthly, 272*(4), 51–68.

Kantrowitz, B., Starr, M., and Friday, C. (1991, April 29). *Newsweek,* pp. 27–32.

Kappeler, V. E., Sluder, R. D., and Alpert, G. P. (1998). *Forces of deviance: Understanding the dark side of policing.* (2nd ed.). NCJ-184041. Prospect Heights, IL: Waveland Press.

Karmen, A. (1984). *Crime victims: An introduction to victimology.* Monterey, CA: Brooks/Cole.

Karmen, A. (1990). *Crime victims: An introduction to victimology* (2nd ed.). Pacific Grove, CA: Brooks/Cole.

Karmen, A. (2001). *Crime victims: An introduction to victimology* (4th ed.). Belmont, CA: Wadsworth.

Karmen, A. (2007). *Crime victims: An introduction to victimology* (6th ed.). Belmont, CA: Wadsworth.

Kaufman, J., and Ziegler, E. (1987). Do abused children become abusive parents? *American Journal of Orthopsychiatry, 57,* 186–192.

Kawamoto, K. (2005, January 1). Best practices in trauma reporting: Ideas and insights from award-winning newspaper articles. Dart Center for Journalism and Trauma, Columbia University Graduate School of Journalism. Retrieved December 12, 2006, from http://dartcenter.org/files/da_best_practices_0_1.pdf.

Keilitz, S. (2001, February). *Specialization of domestic violence case management in the courts: A national survey.* NCJ-186192. Washington, DC: U.S. Department of Justice.

Kelley, R. (2009, March 3). Domestic abuse myths: Five mistakes we make when we talk about Rihanna and Chris Brown's relationship. *Newsweek.* Retrieved June 15, 2009, from http://www.newsweek.com/2009/03/08/domestic-abuse-myths.html.

Kelly, L. (1996). Tensions and possibilities: Enhancing information responses to domestic violence. In J. Edleson and Z. Eisikovitz (Eds.), *Future interventions with battered women and their families* (67–86). Thousand Oaks, CA: Sage.

Kelly, M. (n.d.). "Columnist Writes of Daughter's Rape." In Chapter Six of Covering Crime and Justice: A Guide for Journalists. Retrieved June 5, 2008, from http://www.justicejournalism.org/crimeguide/chapter06/sidebars/chap06_xside1.html.

Kilpatrick, D. G., Edmunds, C. N., and Seymour, A. K. (1992). *Rape in America: A report to the nation.* Arlington, VA: National Victim Center and Medical University of South Carolina.

Kimmel, M. S. (2002). Gender symmetry in domestic violence: A substantive and methodological research review. *Violence Against Women, 8,* 1336–1367.

Kitzinger, J. (2004). *Framing abuse: Media influence and public understanding of sexual violence against children.* Ann Arbor, MI: Pluto Press.

Koch, W. (2006, June 6). More sex offenders tracked by satellite. *USA TODAY,* p. A3. Retrieved on March 15, 2007, from http://www.usatoday.com/tech/news/techinnovations/2006-06-06-gps-tracking_x.htm.

Koss, M. P., and Cook, S. L. (1993). Facing the facts: Date and acquaintance rape are significant problems for women. In R. J. Gelles and D. R. Loseke (Eds.), *Current controversies on family violence* (104–119). Thousand Oaks, CA: Sage.

Koss, M. P., Gidycz, C. A., and Wisniewski, N. (1987). The scope of rape: Incidence and prevalence of sexual aggression and victimization in a national sample of higher education students. *Journal of Consulting and Clinical Psychology, 55*(2), 162–170.

Koss, M. P., and Cleveland, H. H. (1997). Stepping on toes: Social roots of date rape lead to intractability and politicization. In M. D. Schwartz (Ed.), *Researching sexual violence against women: Methodological and personal perspectives* (4–21). Thousand Oaks, CA: Sage.

Krajicek, D. (2003). The crime beat. In Criminal Justice Journalists (Ed.), *Covering crime and justice* (Chapter 1). Retrieved June 24, 2004, from justicejournalism.org/crimeguide/chapter01/chapter01_pg06.html.

Krosnick, J. A. (1999). Survey research. *Annual Review of Psychology, 50,* 537–567.

Kruttschnitt, C., Uggen, C., and Shelton, K. (2000). Predictors of desistance among sex offenders: The interaction of formal and informal social controls. *Justice Quarterly, 17,* 62–87.

La Fond, J. (2000). The future of involuntary civil commitment in the U.S.A. after *Kansas v. Hendricks. Behavioral Sciences and the Law, 18,* 153–167.

LaFree, G. D. (1980). The effect of sexual stratification by race on official reactions to rape. *American Sociological Review, 45*(5), 842–854.

Lamb, S. (1991). Acts without agents: An analysis of linguistic avoidance in journal articles on men who batter women. *American Journal of Orthopsychiatry, 61,* 250–257.

Lamb, S. (1996). *The trouble with blame: Victims, perpetrators, and responsibility.* Cambridge, MA: Harvard University Press.

Lamb, S. (1999). *New versions of victims: Feminist struggle with the concept.* New York: New York University Press.

Lamb, S., and Keon, S. (1995). Blaming the perpetrator: Language that distorts reality in newspaper articles on men battering women. *Psychology of Women Quarterly, 19*, 209–220.

Langan, P. A., and Levin, D. J. (2002). *Recidivism of prisoners released in 1994.* NCJ-193427. Washington, DC: U.S. Department of Justice.

Langhinrichsen-Rohling, J., Neidig, P., and Thorn, G. (1995). Violent marriages: Gender differences in levels of current violence and past abuse. *Journal of Family Violence, 10*(2), 159–176.

Laub, J., Nagin, D., and Sampson, R. (1998). Trajectories of change in criminal offending: Good marriages and the desistance process. *American Sociological Review, 63*, 225–238.

Laub, J., and Sampson, R. (2001). Understanding desistance from crime. In M. Tonry (Ed.), *Crime and justice: A review of research*, Vol. 28 (1–69). Chicago: University of Chicago Press.

Laurence, L., and Spalter-Roth, R. (1996). *Measuring the cost of domestic violence against women and the cost-effectiveness of interventions: An initial assessment and proposals for future research.* Washington, DC: Institute for Women's Policy Research.

Lauritsen, R. (2003). Newspaper transforms after tragedy. Dart Center for Journalism and Trauma, Columbia University Graduate School of Journalism. Retrieved June 24, 2004, from www.dartcenter.org/articles/special_features/everett_herald.htm.

Lautenberg Amendment to the Gun Control Act of 1968 (1996). 18 U.S. C.§922. (Domestic Violence Gun Ban). Retrieved August 12, 2009, from http://www.law.cornell.edu/uscode/18/922.html.

Lee, D. (2002). Hegemonic masculinity and male feminisation: The sexual harassment of men at work. *Journal of Gender Studies,*(9)2, 141–155.

Lehmann, P. (2000). Abused men: The hidden side of domestic violence. *Families in Society: The Journal of Contemporary Human Services, 81*, 443–444.

Lemon, N. K. D. (1994, December). Domestic violence and stalking: A comment on the model anti-stalking code proposed by the National Institute of Justice. Battered Women's Justice Project, Minnesota Center Against Violence and Abuse, Duluth. Retrieved January 5, 2004, from http://www.vaw.umn.edu/documents/bwjp/stalking/stalking.doc.

Leonard, E. D. (2003). Stages of gendered disadvantage in the lives of convicted battered women. In B. Bloom (Ed.), *Gendered justice: Addressing the female offender* (97–139). Durham, NC: North Carolina Academic Press.

Lerner, M. J. (1965). Evolution of performance as a function of performer's reward and attractiveness. *Journal of Personality and Social Psychology, 1*(4), 355–360.

Lerner, M. J., and Miller, D. T. (1978). Just world research and the attribution process: Looking back and ahead. *Psychological Bulletin, 85*(5), 1030–1051.

Levenson, J. S. (2004a). Reliability of sexually violent predator civil commitment criteria in Florida. *Law and Human Behavior, 28*(4), 357–368.

Levenson, J. S. (2004b). Sexual predator civil commitment: A comparison of selected and released offenders. *International Journal of Offender Therapy and Comparative Criminology, 48*(6), 638–648.

Levenson, J. (2006). Sex offender residence restrictions. *Sex Offender Law Report, 7,* 46–47.

Levenson, J., and Cotter, L. (2005). The impact of sex offender residence restrictions: 1,000 feet from danger or one step from absurd? *International Journal of Offender Therapy and Comparative Criminology, 49,* 168–178.

Levenson, J., and Hern, A. (2007). Sex offender residence restrictions: Unintended consequences and community reentry. *Justice Research and Policy, 9,* 59–73.

Levy, B. (1998). *Dating violence: Young women in danger.* Seattle, WA: Seal Press.

Lewin, T. (1992, May 10). Feminists wonder if it was progress to become "victims." *New York Times,* p. E6.

Lewis, R. (1988). *Effectiveness of statutory requirements for the registration of sex offenders: A report to the California State legislature.* Sacramento: California Department of Justice.

Lieb, R., and Matson, S. (1998). Sexual predator commitment laws in the United States: 1998 Update. Washington State Institute for Public Policy. Retrieved May 20, 2009, from http://www.wsipp.wa.gov/pub.asp?docid=98-09-1101.

Lieb, R., Quinsey, V., and Berliner, L. (1998). Sexual predators and social policy. In M. Tonry (Ed.), *Crime and justice: A review of research,* Vol. 23 (43–114). Chicago: University of Chicago Press.

Lindhorst, T., and Padgett, J. D. (2005). Disjunctures for women and frontline workers: Implementation of the Family Violence Option. *Social Service Review, 79*(3), 405–429.

Lipschultz, J. H., and Hilt, M. L. (2002). *Crime and local television: Dramatic, breaking, and live from the scene.* Mahwah, NJ: Lawrence Erlbaum Associates.

Lloyd, S. (1997). The effects of domestic violence on women's employment. *Law and Policy, 19,* 139–167.

Logan, T. K., Shannon, L., Walker, R., and Faragher, R. M. (2006). Protective orders: Questions and conundrums. *Trauma, Violence, and Abuse, 7*(3), 175.

Logan, T. K., and Walker, R. (2009). Civil protective order outcomes: Violations and perceptions of effectiveness. *Journal of Interpersonal Violence, 24*(4), 675–692.

Lösel, F., and Schmucker, M. (2005). The effectiveness of treatment for sexual offenders: A comprehensive meta-analysis. *Journal of Experimental Criminology, 1,* 117–146.

Lule, J. (2001). *Daily news, eternal stories: The mythological role of journalism.* New York: Guilford Press.

Lyon, A. D. (1999). Be careful for what you wish for: An examination of arrest and prosecution patterns of domestic violence in two cities in Michigan. *Michigan Journal of Gender and Law, 5,* 253–298.

MacKinnon, C. A. (1993). *Only words.* Cambridge, MA: Harvard University Press.

Maguigan, H. (1991). Battered women and self-defense: Myths and misconceptions in current reform proposals. *University of Pennsylvania Law Review, 140*(2), 379–486.

Maguigan, H. (2003). Wading into Professor Schneider's "murky middle ground" between acceptance and rejection of criminal justice responses to domestic violence. *American University Journal of Gender, Social Policy and the Law, 11,* 427–445.

Mahoney, M. R. (1991). Legal images of battered women: Redefining the issue of separation. *Michigan Law Review, 90*(1), 1–94.

Mahoney, M. R. (1992). Exit: Power and the idea of leaving in love, work, and the confirmation hearings. *Southern California Law Review, 65,* 1283–1319.

Mahoney, M. R. (1994). Victimization or oppression? Women's lives, violence, and agency. In M. A. Fineman and R. Mykitiuk (Eds.), *The public nature of private violence: The discovery of domestic abuse* (59–92). New York: Routledge.

Mahoney, P., Williams, L. M., and West, C. M. (2001). Violence against women by intimate relationship partners. In C. M. Renzetti, J. L. Edleson, and R. K. Bergen (Eds.), *Sourcebook on violence against women* (143–178). Thousand Oaks, CA: Sage.

Malamuth, N. M. (1986). Predicators of naturalistic sexual aggression. *Journal of Personality and Social Psychology, 50*(5), 953–962.

Malamuth, N. M., Sockloscki, R. J., Koss, M. P., and Tanaka, J. S. (1991). Characteristics of aggressors against women: Testing a model using a national sample of college students. *Journal of Consulting and Clinical Psychology, 59*(5), 670–681.

Mansnerus, L. (2003, November 17). Questions rise over imprisoning sex offenders past their terms. *New York Times.* Retrieved January 5, 2004, from http:///www. nytimes.com/2003/11/17/nyregion/17COMM.html?th.

Margolies, L., and Leeder, E. (1995). Violence at the door: Treatment of lesbian batterers. *Violence Against Women, 1*(2), 103–121.

Marques, J., Day, D. M., Nelson, C., and West, M. A. (1994). Effects of cognitive-behavioral treatment on sex offender recidivism: Preliminary results of a longitudinal study. *Criminal Justice and Behavior, 21,* 28–54.

Marques, J., Nelson, C., West, M. A., and Day, D. M. (1994). The relationship between treatment goals and recidivism among child molesters. *Behaviour Research and Therapy, 32*(5), 577–588.

Marshall, L. L. (1992). Development of the Severity of Violence Against Women Scales. *Journal of Family Violence, 7,* 103–121.

Marshall, L. L., and Honeycutt, T. C. (1999). Women, domestic abuse and public assistance. Unpublished manuscript, University of North Texas, Denton.

Marshall, W. L., and Pithers, W. D. (1994). A reconsideration of treatment outcome with sex offenders. *Criminal Justice Behavior, 21*(1), 10–27.

Martin, D. (1976). *Battered wives.* San Francisco: Glide Publications.

Martin, M. E. (1997). Double your trouble: Dual arrest in family violence. *Journal of Family Violence, 12*(2), 139–157.

Martin, P. Y. (2005). *Rape work: Victims, gender, and emotions in organization and community context.* New York: Routledge.

Marshall, L. L., and Rose, P. (1990). Premarital violence: The impact of family of origin violence, stress, and reciprocity. *Violence and Victims, 5*(1), 51–64.

Marshall, W. L., and Pithers, W. D. (1994). A reconsideration of treatment outcome with sex offenders. *Criminal Justice Behavior, 21*(1), 10–27.

Massey, J., Miller, S. L., and Wilhelmi, A. (1998). Civil forfeiture of property: The victimization of women as innocent owners and third parties. In S. L. Miller (Ed.), *Crime control and women: Feminist implications of criminal justice policy* (15–31). Thousand Oaks, CA: Sage.

Matthews, N. A. (1994). *Confronting rape: The feminist anti-rape movement and the state.* New York: Routledge.

Mawby, R. I., and Walklate, S. (1994). *Critical victimology.* London: Sage.

Maxwell, C. D., Garner, J. H., and Fagan, J. A. (2001, July). *The effects of arrest on intimate partner violence: New evidence from the spouse assault replication program* (Research in brief).Washington, DC: U.S. Department of Justice, Office of Justice Programs, National Institute of Justice.

McKnight, J. (1989). Do no harm: Policy options that meet human needs. *Social Policy, 20*(1), 5–15.

McLaughlin, E. (2009, September 2). Monitoring tools failed to unearth Garrido's secret. CNN.com. Retrieved September 6, 2009, from http://www.cnn.com/2009/CRIME/09/01/california.garrido.monitoring/index.html.

McMahon, M., and Pence, E. (2003). Making social change: Reflections on individual and institutional advocacy with women arrested for domestic violence. *Violence Against Women, 9*, 47–74.

Meadows, R. J. (2001). *Understanding violence and victimization* (2nd ed.). Upper Saddle River, NJ: Prentice Hall.

Meili, T. (2003). *I am the Central Park Jogger.* New York: Scribner.

Meloy, M. L. (2006). *Sex offenses and the men who commit them.* Boston: Northeastern University Press.

Meloy, M. L., and Miller, S. L. (2002). Focus group findings of women mandated to domestic violence treatment groups. Unpublished manuscript.

Meloy, M. L., and Coleman, S. (2009). GPS supervision of sex offenders. In R. G. Wright (Ed.), *Sex offender laws: Failed policies, new directions* (243–266). New York: Springer.

Meloy, M. L., and Miller, S. L. (2009). Words that wound: Print media's presentation of gendered violence. In D. Humphries (Ed.), *Women, violence, and the media: Readings in feminist criminology* (29–56). Boston: Northeastern University Press.

Meloy, M. L., Miller, S. L., and Curtis, K. M. (2008). Making sense out of nonsense: The deconstruction of state-level sex offender residence restrictions. *American Journal of Criminal Justice, 33*(2), 209–222.

Meloy, M. L., Saleh, Y., and Wolff, N. (2007). Sex offender laws in America: Can panic driven legislation ever create safer societies? *Criminal Justice Studies, 20*, 423–443.

Mendelsohn, B. (1940). Rape in criminology. Translated and cited in S. Schafer (1968), *The victim and his criminal.* New York: Random House.

Messner, M. A., and Solomon, W. S. (1993). Outside the frame: Newspaper coverage of the Sugar Ray Leonard wife abuse story. *Sociology of Sport Journal, 10,* 119–134.

Meyer, S. L., Vivian, D., and O'Leary, K. D. (1998). Men's sexual aggression in marriage. *Violence Against Women, 4*(4), 415–435.

Meyer, W. J., Molett, M., Richards, C. D., Arnold, L., and Latham, J. (2003). Outpatient civil commitment in Texas for management and treatment of sexually violent predators. *International Journal of Offender Therapy and Comparative Criminology, 47*(4), 396–406.

Meyers, M. (1997). *News coverage of violence against women: Engendering blame.* Thousand Oaks, CA: Sage.

Meyers, M. (2004). African American women and violence: Gender, race, and class in the news. *Critical Studies in Media Communication, 21*(2), 95–118.

Miedzian, M. (1993). How rape is encouraged in American boys and what we can do to stop it. In E. Buchwald, P. R. Fletcher, and M. Roth (Eds.), *Transforming a rape culture* (153–163). Minneapolis: Milkweed.

Miller, N. (2001, October). *Stalking laws and implementation practices: A national review for policymakers and practitioners.* Washington, DC: U.S. Department of Justice, Institute for Law and Justice.

Miller, S. L. (1989). Unintended side effects of pro-arrest policies and their race and class implications for battered women: A cautionary note. *Criminal Justice Policy Review, 3*(3), 299–316.

Miller, S. L. (2000). Mandatory arrest and domestic violence: Continuing questions. In R. Muraskin and T. Alleman (Eds.), *It's a crime: Women and justice* (283–310). New York: McGraw-Hill.

Miller, S. L. (2001). The paradox of women arrested for domestic violence. *Violence Against Women, 7,* 1339–1376.

Miller, S. L. (2005). *Victims as offenders: The paradox of women's violence in relationships.* Piscataway, NJ: Rutgers University Press.

Miller, S. L., and Barberet, R. (1994). A cross-cultural comparison of social reform: The growing pains of the battered women's movements in Washington, DC and Madrid, Spain. *Law and Social Inquiry, 19*(4), 923–966.

Miller, S. L., and Meloy, M. L. (2006). Women's use of force: Voices of women arrested for domestic violence. *Violence Against Women, 12*(1), 89–115.

Miller, S. L. (Forthcoming, 2011). *After the Crime: The Power of Restorative Justice Dialogues between victims and violent offenders.* New York: NYU Press.

Milloy, C. D. (2003). *Six-year follow-up of released sex offenders recommended for commitment under Washington's Sexually Violent Predator law, where no petition was filed* (Document No. 03-12-1101). Olympia, WA: Washington State Institute for Public Policy.

Milloy, C. D. (2007). *Six-year follow-up of 135 released sex offenders recommended for commitment under Washington's Sexually Violent Predator law, where no petition was filed* (Document No. 07-06-1101). Olympia, WA: Washington State Institute for Public Policy.

Mills, L. G. (1999). Killing her softly: Intimate abuse and the violence of state intervention. *Harvard Law Review, 2*, 550–613.

Minnesota Department of Corrections (2003). *Level three sex offenders residential placement issues.* St. Paul.

Minnesota Department of Corrections (2007). *Residential proximity and sex offense recidivism in Minnesota.* St. Paul.

Mirchandani, R. (2006). "Hitting is not manly": Domestic violence court and the re-imagination of the patriarchal state. *Gender and Society, 20*(6), 781–804.

Mirchandani, R. (2008). Beyond therapy: Problem-solving courts and the deliberative democratic state. *Law and Social Inquiry, 33*(4), 853–893.

Moorti, S. (2002). *Color of rape: Gender and race in television's public spheres.* Albany: State University of New York Press.

Moreno, J. A. (1997). Whoever fights monsters should see to it that in the process he does not become a monster: Hunting the sexual predator with silver bullets—Federal Rules of Evidence 413–415—and a stake through the heart—*Kansas v. Hendricks. Florida Law Review, 49*(4), 505–562.

Moutrie, D. (2001, March 8). Jury urges death for man who killed wife. *Los Angeles Times*, p. B3.

Mullender, A. (1996). *Rethinking domestic violence: The social work and probation response.* New York: Routledge.

National Center for Victims of Crime & Crime Victims Research and Treatment Center. (1992). *Rape in America: A report to the nation.* Arlington, VA: National Center for Victims of Crime.

National Domestic Violence Hotline (n.d.). Get educated: Violence Against Women Act. Retrieved August 31, 2009, from http://www.ndvh.org/get-educated/violence-against-women-act-vawa/.

National Institute of Justice (1996). *Critical criminal justice issues: ASC-Reno Task Force.* NCJ-158837. Washington, DC: U.S. Department of Justice.

Nelson, M. B. (1991). *Are we winning yet? How women are changing sports and sports are changing women.* New York: Random House.

Nelson, M. B. (1995). *The stronger women get, the more they love football.* New York: HarperCollins.

New Jersey State Parole Board (2007). Report on New Jersey's GPS monitoring of sex offenders. Retrieved March 1, 2007, from www.state.nj.us/parole/docs/reports/gps.pdf.

Nourjah, P. (1999). *National Hospital Ambulatory Medical Care Survey: 1997 Emergency Department summary. Advance data from vital and health statistics.* No. 304. Hyattsville, MD: National Center for Health Statistics.

NOW Legal Defense and Education Fund (2003). Why NOW Legal Defense opposes federal marriage promotion in TANF reauthorization. Issue Backgrounder. NOW Legal Defense and Education Fund, New York.

Office for Victims of Crime (1998). *New directions from the field: Victims' rights and services for the 21st century.* Washington, DC: U.S. Department of Justice.

Office for Victims of Crime. (2001). *Victim empowerment: Bridging the systems, mental health and victim services providers*. Grant No. 95-MU-GX-k003. Washington, DC: U.S. Department of Justice.

Office for Victims of Crime. (2002). *Enforcement of protective orders*. Legal Series Bulletin No. 4. Washington, DC: U.S. Department of Justice. Retrieved July 30, 2009, from http://www.ojp.usdoj.gov/ovc/publications/bulletins/legalseries/bulletin4/ncj189190.pdf.

Office of Management and Budget. (2004). *Performance and management assessments: Budget of the United States Government*. Washington, DC: Government Printing Office.

Office of Management and Budget. (2007). Expectmore.gov Web site. Retrieved August 5, 2009, from http://www.whitehouse.gov/omb/expectmore.

O'Leary, K. D. (1993). Through a psychological lens: Personality traits, personality disorders, and levels of violence. In R. Gelles and D. R. Loseke (Eds.), *Current controversies on family violence* (7–30). Newbury Park, CA: Sage.

Osthoff, S. (2002). But, Gertrude, I beg to differ, a hit is not a hit is not a hit. *Violence Against Women, 8*(12), 1521–1544.

O'Toole, L., and Schiffman, J. R. (Eds.). (1997). *Gender violence: Interdisciplinary perspectives*. New York: New York University Press.

Oukrop, C. E. (1982). *Views of Newspaper Gatekeepers on Rape and Rape Coverage*, Manhattan, KS: Kansas City University.

Pagelow, M. D. (1981). *Woman battering: Victims and their experiences*. Beverly Hills, CA: Sage.

Pagelow, M. D. (1984). *Family violence*. New York: Praeger.

Pagelow, M. D. (1992). Adult victims of domestic violence: Battered women. *Journal of Interpersonal Violence, 7*(1), 87–120.

Paglia, C. (1990). *Sexual personae: Art and decadence from Nefertiti to Emily Dickinson*. New Haven, CT: Yale University Press.

Parade Magazine. (1997). "Do You Believe What Newspeople Tell You?" Arlington, VA: Newseum and The Roper Group.

Pearson, P. (1997). *When she was bad: Violent women and the myth of innocence*. New York: Viking.

Pearson, J., Thoennes, N., and Griswold, E. A. (1999). Child support and domestic violence: The victims speak out. *Violence Against Women, 5*(4), 427–448.

Pearson, J., Griswold, E. A., and Thoennes, N. (2001). Balancing safety and self-sufficiency: Lessons on serving victims of domestic violence for child support and public assistance agencies. *Violence Against Women, 7*(2), 176–192.

Pence, E. and Paymar, M. (1993). *Education groups for men who batter: The Duluth model*. New York: Springer.

Penelope, J. (1990). *Speaking freely: Unlearning the lies of the fathers' tongues*. New York: Teachers College Press.

Perilla, J. L., Frndak, K., Lillard, D., and East, C. (2003). A working analysis of women's use of violence in the context of learning, opportunity, and choice. *Violence Against Women, 9*(1), 10–46.

Petersilia, J. (2003). *When prisoners come home: Parole and prisoner reentry.* New York: Oxford University Press.

Petrosino, A. J., and Petrosino, C. (1999). The public safety potential of Megan's Law in Massachusetts: An assessment from a sample of criminal sexual psychopaths. *Crime and Delinquency, 45,* 140–158.

Phillips, L. M. (1997). *Unequal partners: Exploring power and consent in adult-teen relationships.* Hackensack: Planned Parenthood of Greater Northern New Jersey.

Phillips, L. M. (1999). Recasting consent: Agency and victimization in adult-teen relationships. In S. Lamb (Ed.), *New versions of victims: Feminist struggle with the concept* (57–81). New York: New York University Press.

Phipps, A. (1988). Ideologies, political parties and victims of crime. In M. Maguire and J. Pointing (Eds.), *Victims of crime: A new deal?* Milton Keynes, UK: Open University Press.

Pleck, E. (1989). Criminal approaches to family violence, 1640–1980. In L. Ohlin and M. Tonry (Eds.), *Crime and justice: An annual review of research,* vol. 11 (19–57). Chicago: University of Chicago Press.

Pollack, M.A. (1996). The new institutionalism and EC governance: The promise and limits of institutionalist analysis. *Governance, 9*(4), 429–458.

Pollitt, K. (1994). *Reasonable creatures: Essays on women and feminism.* New York: Alfred A. Knopf.

Prentky, R. A., Lee, A. F., Knight, R. A., and Cerce, D. (1997). Recidivism rates among child molesters and rapists: A methodological analysis. *Law and Human Behavior, 21,* 635–659.

Prescott, J. J., and Rockoff, J. (2008). *Do sex offender registration and notification laws affect criminal behavior?* Cambridge, MA: National Bureau of Economic Research. Retrieved October 17, 2008, from http://www.nber.org/papers/w13803.

President's Task Force on Victims of Crime (1982). *Final report.* Washington, DC: U.S. Government Printing Office.

Presser, L., and Gaarder, E. (2004). Can restorative justice reduce battering? In B. Raffel Price and N. J. Sokoloff (Eds.), *The criminal justice system and women: Offenders, prisoners, victims, and workers* (3rd ed.) (403–419). Boston: McGraw-Hill.

Quinsey, V. L. (1998). Treatment of sex offenders. In M. Tonry (Ed.), *Oxford criminology handbook* (403–425). New York: Oxford University Press.

Raj, A., and Silverman, J. (2002). Violence against immigrant women: The roles of culture, context and legal immigrant status on intimate partner violence. *Violence Against Women, 8*(3), 367–398.

Rantala, R. R., and Edwards, T. J. (2000). *Effects of NIBRS on crime statistics.* NCJ-178890. Washington, DC: Office of Justice Programs, U.S. Department of Justice. Retrieved March 4, 2005, from http://www.ojp.usdoj.gov/bjs/pub/pdf/encs.pdf.

Raphael, J. (1995). *Domestic violence: Telling the untold welfare-to-work story.* Available from Taylor Institute, 915 N. Walcott, Chicago, IL 60222.

Raphael, J. (1996). *Prisoners of abuse: Domestic violence and welfare receipt.* Available from Taylor Institute, 915 N. Wolcott, Chicago, IL 60222.

Raphael, J. (2000). *Saving Bernice: Battered women, welfare, and poverty*. Boston: Northeastern University Press.

Rasche, C. P. E. (1995). Minority women and domestic violence: The unique dilemmas of battered women of color. In B. Raffel Price and N. J. Sokoloff (Eds.), *The criminal justice system and women: Offenders, victims, and workers* (246–261). New York: McGraw-Hill.

Rennison, C. M., and Welchans, S. (2000). *Intimate partner violence*. NCJ-178247. Washington, DC: U.S. Department of Justice.

Renzema, M., and Mayo-Wilson, E. (2005). Can electronic monitoring reduce crime for moderate to high-risk offenders? *Journal of Experimental Criminology, 1*, 215–237.

Renzetti, C. (1992). *Violent betrayal: Partner abuse in lesbian relationships*. Thousand Oaks, CA: Sage.

Renzetti, C. (1997). Violence and abuse among same sex couples. In A. Cardarelli (Ed.), *Violence between intimate partners: Patterns, causes, and effects* (70–89). Needham Heights, MA: Allyn and Bacon.

Renzetti, C. (1999). The challenge to feminism posed by women's use of violence in intimate relationships. In S. Lamb (Ed.), *New versions of victims: Feminists struggle with concept* (42–56). New York: New York University Press.

Rhode, D. (1997). Media images/feminist issues. In M. Fineman and M. McCluskey (Eds.), *Feminism, media and the law* (8–21). New York: Oxford University Press.

Rhode Island Coalition of Domestic Violence. (n.d.). Handbook for Journalists. Retrieved June 15, 2009, from http://www.ricadv.org/handbook-for-journalists. html.

Richie, B. E. (1996). *Compelled to crime: The gender entrapment of battered black women*. New York: Routledge.

Richie, B. E. (2000). A black feminist reflection on the antiviolence movement. *Signs, 25*(4), 1133–1137.

Roberts, J. (2003). Between the heat of passion and cold blood: Battered woman's syndrome as an excuse for self-defense in non-confrontation homicides. *Law & Psychological Review, 27*, 135–136.

Robinson, J., and Godbey, G. (1997). *Time for life: The surprising ways Americans use their time*. State College: Pennsylvania State University Press.

Rodgers, S., and Thorson, E. (2001). The reporting of crime and violence in the *Los Angeles Times*: Is there a public health perspective? *Journal of Health Communication, 6*(2), 169–182.

Roiphe, K. (1991, November 20). Date rape hysteria. *New York Times*, p. A27.

Roiphe, K. (1993). *The morning after: Sex, fear, and feminism on campus*. Boston: Little, Brown.

Rosen, L., Dragiewicz, M., and Gibbs, J. (2009). Fathers' rights groups: Demographic correlates and impact on custody policy. *Violence Against Women, 15*(5), 513–532.

Rosenbaum, A. (1988). Methodological issues in marital violence research. *Journal of Family Violence, 3*, 91–104.

Russell, D. E. H. (1982). *Rape in marriage*. New York: Macmillan.

Russell, D. E. H. (1984). *Sexual exploitation: Rape, child sexual abuse, and workplace harassment.* Beverly Hills, CA: Sage.

Russell, D. E. H. (1990). *Rape in marriage* (Rev. ed.). Indianapolis: Indiana University Press.

Russo, A. (1997). Lesbians, prostitutes, and murder. In M. Fineman and M. McCluskey (Eds.), *Feminism, media and the law* (249–266). New York: Oxford University Press.

Ryan, J., and Wentworth, W. (1999). *Media and society: The production of culture in the mass media.* Boston: Allyn and Bacon.

Ryan, W. (1971). *Blaming the victim.* New York: Vintage.

Saunders, D. G. (2002). Are physical assaults by wives and girlfriends a major social problem? A review of the literature. *Violence Against Women, 8,* 1424–1448.

Salter, A. (2003). *Predators: Pedophiles, rapists, and other sex offenders.* New York: Basic Books.

Saltzman, L. E., Fanslow J. L., McMahon, P. M., and Shelley, G. A. (1999). *Intimate partner violence surveillance: Uniform definitions and recommended data elements* (version 1.0). Atlanta, GA: Centers for Disease Control and Prevention, National Center for Injury Prevention and Control.

Sample, L., and Streveler, A. (2003). Latent consequences of community notification laws. In S. H. Decker, L. F. Alaird, and C. M. Katz (Eds.), *Controversies in criminal justice* (353–362). Los Angeles: Roxbury.

Schafer, S. (1968). *The victim and his criminal.* New York: Random House.

Schechter, S. (1982). *Women and male violence: The visions and struggles of the battered women's movement.* Boston: South End Press.

Scheppele, K. L., and Bart, P. B. (1983). Through women's eyes: Defining danger in the wake of sexual assault. *Journal of Social Issues, 39*(2), 63–80.

Scherer, M. (2003, July 28). Naming the victims of rape: Why it hurts, what can help. Dart Center for Journalism and Trauma, Columbia University Graduate School of Journalism. Retrieved August 11, 2009, from http://dartcenter.org/content/naming-victims-rape.

Schlattner, C., and Linehan, M. (n.d.). Personal safety and online resources—check the source. Santa Cruz, CA, Kidpower. Retrieved August 12, 2009, from http://www.kidpower.org/ARTICLES/email-myths.html.

Schmidt, J. D., and Steury, E. H. (1989). Prosecutorial discretion in filing charges in domestic violence cases. *Criminology, 27*(3), 589–610.

Schneider, E. M. (1986). Describing and changing: Women's self-defense work and the problem of expert testimony on battering. *Women's Rights Law Reporter, 9,* 195–222.

Schneider, E. M. (1992). Particularity and generality: Challenges of feminist theory and practice in work on woman abuse. *New York University Law Review, 67,* 520–568.

Schneider, E. M. (2000). *Battered women and feminist lawmaking.* New Haven, CT: Yale University Press.

Schram, D., and Milloy, C. (1995). *Community notification: A study of offender characteristics and recidivism.* Olympia: Washington State Institute for Public Policy. Retrieved May 23, 2006, from http://www.wsipp.wa.gov/rptfiles/chrrec.pdf.

Schram, D. and Milloy, C. (1998). Sexually violent predators and civil commitment: A study of the characteristics and recidivism of sex offenders considered for civil commitment but for whom proceedings were declined. Washington State Institute for Public Policy. Retrieved May 15, 2009, from http://www.wsipp.wa.gov/pub.asp?docid=98-02-1101.

Schram, S. F. (2000). *After welfare: The culture of postindustrial social policy.* New York: New York University Press.

Schram, T. (2002). Ruling on housing law a blow to battered women. Women's E-news website. Retrieved April 19, 2002, from http://www.womensenews.org/article.cfm/dyn/aid/863/context/cover.

Schwartz, M. D., and Pitts, V. L. (1995). Exploring a feminist routines activities approach to explain sexual assault. *Justice Quarterly, 12,* 9–31.

Schwartz, M. D., and DeKeseredy, W. S. (1997). *Sexual assault on the college campus: The role of male peer support.* Thousand Oaks, CA: Sage.

Scott, C., and Gerbasi, J. (2003). Sex offender registration and community notification challenges: The Supreme Court continues its trend. *Journal of the American Academy of Psychiatry and the Law, 31,* 494–501.

Scully, D. (1994). *Understanding sexual violence: A study of convicted rapists.* (2nd ed.). New York: Routledge.

Scully, D. (1995). Rape is the problem. In B. Raffel Price and N. J. Sokoloff (Eds.), *The criminal justice system and women: Offenders, victims, and workers* (197–215). New York: McGraw-Hill.

Seattle Times. (2003, 8 May), Editorial. Many eyes, long arms: AMBER Alert pays off. B6.

Sellin, T., and Wolfgang, M. E. (1964). *The measurement of delinquency.* New York: Wiley.

Sexual Assault Services Program (2008, November). U.S. Department of Justice, Office on Violence Against Women. Retrieved April 10, 2009, from http://www.ovw.usdoj.gov/sasp.htm.

Sheffield, C. J. (1987). Sexual terrorism: The social control of women. In B. Hess and M. Ferree (Eds.), *Analyzing gender: A handbook of social science research* (171–189). Beverly Hills: Sage.

Sheley, J. F., and Ashkins, C. D. (1981). Crime, crime news, and crime views. *Public Opinion Quarterly, 45,* 492–506.

Sherman, L. W., and Berk, R. A. (1984). The Minneapolis domestic violence experiment. *Police Foundation Reports, 1,* 1–8.

Shields, N. M., and Hanneke, C. R. (1983). Battered wives' reactions to marital rape. In D. Finkelor, R. J. Gelles, G. T. Hotaling, and M. A. Straus (Eds.), *The dark side of families: Current family violence research* (132–148). Beverly Hills: Sage.

Shichor, D., and Tibbetts, S. (2002). *Victims and victimization.* Prospect Heights, IL: Waveland Press.

Sinwelski, S. A., and Vinton, L. (2001). Stalking: The constant threat of violence. *Affilia, 16*(1), 46–65.

Skinner, B. F. (1953). *Science and human behavior.* New York: Macmillan.

Skipp, C., and Campo-Flores, A. (2009). A bridge too far: The lobbyist who put sex offenders under a bridge. Retrieved August 10, 2009, from http://www.newsweek.com/id/208518/output.

Small, M. A., and Tetreault, P. A. (1990). Social psychology, "marital rape exemptions," and privacy. *Behavioral Sciences and the Law, 8*, 141–149.

Smallbone, S., Marshall, W. L., and Wortley, R. (2008). *Preventing child sexual abuse: Evidence, policy, and practice.* Cullompton, Devon, UK: Willan Publishing.

Smith, M. D. (1994). Enhancing the quality of survey data on violence against women. *Gender and Society, 8*(1), 109–127.

Smith, S. R., and Freinkel, S. (1988). *Adjusting the balance: Federal policy and victim services.* Westport, CT: Greenwood.

Snyder, H. (2000). Sexual assault of young children as reported to law enforcement: Victim, incident, and offender characteristics. Washington, DC: U.S. Department of Justice.

Sonkin, D. J., and Durphy, M. (1997). *Learning to love without violence: A handbook for men* (5th ed.). Volcano, CA: Volcano Press.

Sorenson, S. B., Peterson Manz, P. G., and Berk, R. A. (1998). News media coverage and the epidemiology of homicide. *American Journal of Public Health, 88*(10), 1510–1514.

Spears, G., and Seydegart, K. (1993). *Gender and violence in the mass media.* Ottawa, Canada: Family Violence Prevention Division, National Clearinghouse on Family Violence.

Spender, D. (1980). *Man made language.* London: Routledge and Kegan Paul.

Spohn, C. (1999). The rape reform movement: The traditional common law and rape law reforms. *Jurimetrics, 39*, 119–130.

Spohn, C., and Holleran, D. (2001). Prosecuting sexual assault: A comparison of charging decisions in sexual assault cases involving strangers, acquaintances, and intimate partners. *Justice Quarterly, 18*(3), 651–688.

Spohn, C., and Horney, J. (1992). *Rape law reform: A grassroots revolution and its impact.* New York: Plenum Press.

Spohn, C., and Horney, J. (1996). The impact of rape law reform in the processing of simple and aggravated cases. *Journal of Criminal Law and Criminology, 86*(3), 861–886.

Staggenborg, S. (1988). The consequences of professionalization and the formalization in the pro-choice movement. *American Sociological Review, 53*, 585–605.

Stalans, L. J. (2004). Adult sex offenders on community supervision: A review of recent assessment strategies and treatment. *Criminal Justice and Behavior, 31*(5), 564–608.

Stanko, E. A. (1989). Missing the mark? Police battering. In J. Hanmer, J. Radford, and B. Stanko (Eds.), *Women, policing, and male violence* (46–69). London: Routledge & Kegan Paul.

Stanko, E. A. (1992). The case of fearful women: Gender, personal safety and fear of crime. *Women and Criminal Justice, 4*, 117–135.

Stanko, E. A. (1998). Making the invisible visible in criminology: A personal journey. In S. Holdaway and P. Rock (Eds.), *Thinking about criminology* (35–54). Toronto: University of Toronto Press.

Steele, S. (1990). *The content of our character: A new vision of race in America*. New York: HarperCollins.

Stephenson, J. (1995). *Men are not cost effective: Male crime in America*. New York: HarperCollins.

Stets, J. E., and Straus, M. A. (1990). Gender differences in reporting marital violence and its medical and psychological consequences. In M. A. Straus and R. J. Gelles (Eds.), *Physical violence in American families: Risk factors and adaptations to violence in 8,145 families* (151–165). New Brunswick, NJ: Transaction.

Stop Family Violence (2009, August 15). CA governor eliminates state funding to domestic violence programs. Retrieved September 4, 2009, from http://www.stopfamilyviolence.org/pages/441.

Straus, M. A. (1979). Measuring intrafamily conflict and violence: The Conflict Tactics (CT) Scales. *Journal of Marriage and the Family, 41*, 75–88.

Straus, M. A. (1990). Social stress and marital violence in a national sample of American families. In M. A. Straus and R. J. Gelles (Eds.), *Physical violence in American families: Risk factors and adaptations to violence in 8,145 families* (181–201). New Brunswick, NJ: Transaction.

Straus, M. A. (1993). Physical assaults by wives: A major social problem. In R. J. Gelles and D. R. Loseke (Eds.), *Current controversies on family violence* (67–80). Newbury Park, CA: Sage.

Straus, M. A., and Gelles, R. J. (1986). Societal change and change in family violence from 1975 to 1985 as revealed by two national surveys. *Journal of Marriage and Family, 48*(3), 465–479.

Straus, M. A., and Gelles, R. J. (1990). *Physical violence in American families: Risk factors and adaptations to violence in 8,145 families*. New Brunswick, New Jersey: Transaction Books.

Straus, M. A., Gelles, R. J., and Steinmetz, S. K. (1980). *Behind closed doors: Violence in the American family*. Garden City, NY: Anchor Press.

Straus, M. A., Hamby, S. L., Boney-McCoy, S., and Sugarman, D. B. (1996). The revised Conflict Tactics Scales (CTS2). *Journal of Family Issues, 17*, 283–316.

Strube, M. J., and Barbour, L. S. (1984). Factors related to the decision to leave an abusive relationship. *Journal of Marriage and Family, 46*(4), 837–844.

Stubbs, J. (2002). Domestic violence and women's safety: Feminist challenges to restorative justice. In H. Strang and J. Braithwaite (Eds.), *Restorative justice and family violence* (42–61). Cambridge: Cambridge University Press.

Sutherland, E. H. (1950). The diffusion of sexual psychopath laws. *The American Journal of Sociology, 56*(2), 142–148.

Sykes, C. J. (1992). *A nation of victims: The decay of the American character*. New York: St. Martin's Press.

Talbot, M. (2002, October 13). Men behaving badly. *New York Times Magazine*, 52–57, 82, 84, 95.

Taslitz, A. E. (1999). *Rape and the culture of the courtroom.* New York: New York University Press.

Telljohann, S. K., Price, J., Summers, J., Everett, S., and Casler, S. (1995). High school students' perceptions of nonconsensual sexual activity. *Journal of School Health* 65, 107–112.

Tennessee Board of Probation and Parole, with Middle Tennessee State University (2007). Monitoring Tennessee's sex offenders using global positioning systems: A project evaluation. Retrieved February 8, 2008, from http://www2.state. tn.us/bopp/Press%20Releases/BOPP%20GPS%20Program%20Evaluation,%20 April%202007.pdf.

Tewksbury, R., and Lees, M. (2006). Consequences of sex offender registration: Collateral consequences and community experiences. *Sociological Spectrum, 26,* 309–334.

Tewksbury, R. and Mustaine, E. E. (2006). Where to find sex offenders: An examination of residential locations and neighborhood conditions. *Criminal Justice Studies: A Critical Journal of Crime, Law and Society, 19*(1), 61–75.

Tiegreen, S., and Newman, E. (2009, February 18). Violence: Comparing reporting and reality. Dart Center for Journalism and Trauma, Columbia University Graduate School of Journalism. Retrieved August 5, 2009, from http://dartcenter.org/ content/violence-comparing-reporting-and-reality.

Tiegreen, S., and Newman, E. (2008, January 1). The effect of news "frames." Dart Center for Journalism and Trauma, Columbia University Graduate School of Journalism. Retrieved August 5, 2009, from http://dartcenter.org/content/ effect-news-frames.

Tjaden, P. (1997). *The crime of stalking: How big is the problem?* FS-000186. Washington, DC: National Institute of Justice.

Tjaden, P., and Thoennes, N. (1998a, November). *Prevalence, incidence and consequences of violence against women: Findings from the National Violence Against Women Survey.* Research in Brief, NCJ-172837. Washington, DC: Office of Justice Programs, National Institute of Justice, U.S. Department of Justice.

Tjaden, P., and Thoennes, N. (1998b, April). *Stalking in America: Findings from the National Violence Against Women Survey.* Research in Brief, NCJ-169592. Washington, DC: Office of Justice Programs, National Institute of Justice, U.S. Department of Justice.

Tjaden, P., and Thoennes, N. (2000). Extent, nature and consequences of intimate partner violence: Findings from the National Violence Against Women Survey. Washington, DC: National Institute of Justice and the Centers for Disease Control and Prevention.

Tjaden, P., and Thoennes, N. (2006). *Extent, nature, and consequences of rape victimization: Findings from the National Violence Against Women Survey.* Retrieved January 7, 2008, from http://www.ncjrs.gov/pdffiles1/nij/210346.pdf.

Tobolowsky, P. M. (1999). Victim participation in the criminal justice process: Fifteen years after the President's Task Force on Victims of Crime. *New England Journal on Criminal and Civil Confinement, 25,* 21–106.

Tolman, R. M., and Raphael, J. (2002). A review of research on welfare and domestic violence. *Journal of Social Issues, 56(4)*, 655–682.

Turner, S., Jannetta, J., Hess, J., Myers, R., Shah, R., Werth, R., and Whiltby, A. (2007). Implementation and early outcomes for the San Diego High Risk Sex Offender (HRSO) GPS Pilot Program. University of California, Irvine. Center for Evidence-Based Corrections (Irvine, Ca). Retrieved February 6, 2008, from http://ucicorrections.seweb.uci.edu/pubs.

Turrell, S. C. (2000). A descriptive analysis of same-sex relationship violence for a diverse sample. *Journal of Family Violence, 15*(3), 281–293.

Umbreit, M. S. (2000). *The restorative justice and mediation collection: Executive summary.* NCJ-180301. Office for Victims of Crime Bulletin. Washington, DC: U.S. Department of Justice.

Umbreit, M. S., Vos, B., Coates, R. B., and Brown, K. A. (2003). *Facing violence: The path of restorative justice and dialogue.* Monsey, NY: Criminal Justice Press.

U.S. Conference of Mayors (2006, December). A status report on hunger and homelessness in America's cities: A 23-city survey. Retrieved August 12, 2008, from http://usmayors.org/hungersurvey/2006/report06.pdf.

U.S. Conference of Mayors (2007, December). Hunger and homeless survey: A status report on hunger and homelessness in America's cities: A 23-city survey. Retrieved August 12, 2008, from http://usmayors.org/HHSurvey2007/hh survey07.pdf.

U.S. Department of Labor (2000). *Employment and earnings.* Washington, DC: U.S. Department of Labor.

U.S. Department of Labor (2004). *Bureau of labor statistic, women in the labor force: A databook* Washington, DC: U.S. Department of Labor.

Valente, R. L., Hart, B. J., Zeya, S., and Malefyt, M. (2001). The Violence Against Women Act of 1994: The federal commitment to ending domestic violence, sexual assault, stalking and gender-based crimes of violence. In C. M. Renzetti, J. L. Edleson, and R. K. Bergen (Eds.), *Sourcebook on violence against women* (279–301). Thousand Oaks, CA: Sage.

Van Ness, D., and Strong, K. H. (1997). *Restoring justice.* NCJ-165803. Cincinnati, OH: Anderson Publishing Company.

Viano, E. (1997). Victim's rights and the Constitution. *Crime and Delinquency, 33*, 438–451.

Violence Against Women Act (VAWA). (1994). 42 U.S.C. 13981.

Violence Against Women Office (1996). The Violence Against Women Act fact sheet 1998. Retrieved from http://www.usdoj.gov/vawo/vawafct.html.

Von Hentig, H. (1948). *The criminal and his victim: Studies in the sociobiology of crime.* New Haven, CT: Yale University Press.

Von Hentig, H. (1941). Remarks of the interaction of perpetrator and victim. *Journal of Criminal Law, Criminology, and Police Science, 31*, 303–309.

Waldner-Haugrud, L.K. (1999). Sexual coercion in lesbian and gay relationships: A review and critique. *Aggression and Violent Behavior, 4*(2), 139–149.

Waldner-Haugrud, L., Gratch, L., & Magruder, B. (1997). Victimization and perpetration rates of violence in gay and lesbian relationships: Gender issues explored *Violence and Victims, 12*, 173–184.

Walker, G. (1990). The conceptual politics of struggle: Wife battering, the women's movement, and the state. *Studies of Political Economy, 33*, 63–90.

Walker, J. T., Madden, S., Vásquez, B. E., VanHouten, A. C., and Ervin-McLarty, G. (2006). *The influence of sex offender registration and notification laws in the United States.* Unpublished manuscript sponsored by the Arkansas Crime Information Center. Retrieved May 12, 2006 from http://www.acic.org/statistics/Research/SO_Report_Final.pdf.

Walker, J. T., and Ervin-McLarty, G. (2000). *Sex offenders in Arkansas.* Little Rock: Arkansas Crime Information Center.

Walker, L. E. (1984). *The battered woman syndrome.* New York: Springer.

Walker, L. E. A. (1984). Battered women, psychology, and public policy. *American Psychologist, 39*(10), 1178–1182.

Walsh, A. (1986). Placebo justice: Victim recommendations and offender sentences in sexual assault cases. *Journal of Criminal Law and Criminology, 77*(4), 1126–1141.

Walsh, A. (1987). The sexual stratification hypothesis and sexual assault in light of the changing conceptions of race. *Criminology, 25*, 153–173.

Weed, F. J. (1995). *Certainty of justice: Reform in the crime victim movement.* New York: Aldine de Gruyter.

Weisburg, D. K. (1984). The discovery of sexual abuse: Experts' role in legal policy formulation. *U.C. Davis Law Review, 18*(1), 1–57.

West, R. (1988). Jurisprudence and gender. *University of Chicago Law Review, 55*, 1–72.

Westervelt, S. D. (1998). *Shifting the blame: How victimization became a criminal defense.* Piscataway, NJ: Rutgers University Press.

Williams, B. (1999). *Working with victims: Policies, politics, and practice.* Philadelphia: Jessica Kingsley.

Wilson, M., and Daly, M. (1993). Spousal homicide risk and estrangement. *Violence and Victims, 8*(1), 3–15.

Wolf, N. (1993). *Fire with fire: The new female power and how it will change the twenty-first century.* New York: Random House.

Wolff, N., Meloy, M., Saleh, Y., & Shi, J. (2005). *Legislatively mandated study of the five-year recidivism rates and behavior of sex offenders released from New Jersey prisons* (Report submitted to the NJDOC). New Brunswick, NJ: Rutgers University, Center for Mental Health Services & Criminal Justice Research.

Wolfgang, M. (1958). *Patterns in criminal homicide.* Philadelphia: University of Pennsylvania Press.

Wolfgang, M. E., and Ferracuti, F. (1982). *The subculture of violence* (2nd ed.). London: Tavistock.

Wood, J. T. (2004). *Gendered lives: Communication, gender, and culture* (5th ed.). Belmont, CA: Wadsworth.

Woodwell, D. A. (1999). *National Hospital Ambulatory Medical Care Survey: 1997 Emergency Department Summary. Advance data from vital and health statistics.* No. 305. Hyattsville, MD: National Center for Health Statistics.

Worchester, N. (2002). Women's use of force: Complexities and challenges of taking the issue seriously. *Violence Against Women, 8,* 1390–1415.

Worden, A. P. (2000). *The changing boundaries of the criminal justice system: Redefining the problem and the response in domestic violence.* NCJ-185525. Washington, DC: National Institute of Justice.

Wriggins, J. (1983). Rape, racism, and the law. *Harvard Women's Law Journal, 6,* 103–142.

Yoshihama, M. (1999). Domestic violence against women of Japanese descent in Los Angeles. *Violence Against Women, 5*(8), 869–897.

Young, I. M. (1994). Gender as seriality: Thinking about women as a social collective. *Signs, 19*(3), 713–738.

Young, K. (1998). Against the odds: How women survive domestic violence. *Partnerships Against Domestic Violence,* Commonwealth Government of Australia, Canberra.

Zalin, L. (2001, March). Not much help: Stress on the press: Reporters alone in dealing with trauma. *Columns Magazine.* Seattle Washington: University of Washington and UW Alumni Association. Retrieved August 11, 2009, from http://www.washington.edu/alumni/columns/march01/press2.html.

Zanbergen, P., and Hart, T. (2006). Reducing housing options for convicted sex offenders: Investigating the impact of residency restriction laws using GIS. *Justice Research and Policy, 8,* 1–24.

Zatz, M. S. (2000). The convergence of race, ethnicity, gender and class on court decision making: Looking toward the 21st century. In J. Horney (Ed.), *Policies, processes, and decisions of the criminal justice system* (503–552). Washington, DC.

Zilbergeld, B. (1983). *The shrinking of America: Myths of psychological change.* Boston: Little, Brown.

Zorza, J. (1992). The criminal law of misdemeanor of domestic violence, 1970–1990. *The Journal of Criminal Law and Criminology, 83,* 46–72.

Zorza, J., and Woods, L. (1994). *Mandatory arrest: Problems and possibilities.* NCJ-153684. New York: National Center on Women and Family.

Index

Accused, The, 22

Acquaintance rape, 10, 27, 46–49, 57–58, 66, 78, 114–115, 168, 195n54
  See also rape

Alvera, Tiffanie, 124

AMBER (America's Missing: Broadcast Emergency Response) Alert, 84, 88, 91, 97–98

American Society of Criminology, 198n28

Amir, Menachem, 6

Anti-Drug Abuse Act of 1988, 123

Anti-stalking laws, 161

Association for Treatment of Sexual Abusers (ATSA), 99

Attorney generals, 135

Bachman, Ronet, 48

Bart, Pauline, 72

Battered woman, 30
  See also battering

Battering, 198n28, 200n90
  alternative interventions, 168–169
  battered husbands, 34–35
  civil forfeiture, 125–126
  constructions of attributions, 21–22
  court processing of women arrested, 134–137

difficulties in leaving relationship, 128–129

domestic violence, 81

elder battering, 171–172

female "offender" treatment findings, 137–144

gender differences in use of violence, 132–134

lesbian battering, 178n30

media, 71

politics of battering, 150–152

public housing, 122–125

reporting in the news, 78–79

research studies, 60–66

STOP grants to fight battering, 163

STOP programs targeting battering, 160–161

surveys, 53–59

VAWA, 127–128

victim blaming, 8–13

victim empowerment, 28–31

welfare reform, 118–122

women arrested for domestic violence, 130–132

women battering, 180n56

Battered men, 34
  See also gender symmetry

Battered Women's Syndrome (BWS),
  10, 29–30
  See also learned helplessness
Behavioral self-blame, 7
Benedict, Helen, 21, 70
Berg, Barbara, 63
Berliner, Lucy, 87
Best, Joel, 17
Bobbitt, Lorena, 10
Bonge, Dennis, 133
Brown v. State, 47
Brown, Chris, 75
Brown, Tracy, 100
Brown-McBride, Susan, 100
Brown Simpson, Nicole, 10, 75, 187n36
Browne, Angela, 60
Brzonkala, Christy, 127
Brzonkala v. Virginia Polytechnic, 127
Brush, Lisa, 119
Bryant, Kobe, 73, 82
Bullock, Cathy, 74
Bundy, Ted, 22
Bush, George, 18
Byerly, Carolyn, 76, 78

Caringella, Susan, 48, 115
Cascardi, Michele, 132
Central Park jogger, 17, 72, 178n4
  See also gang rape
  See also Meili, Trisha
Chambers, Robert, 21
Characterological self-blame, 7
Child-safety or child protection zones,
  92, 100
  See also exclusionary zones
Civil commitment, 88, 91, 114
  efficacy of civil commitment, 96
  fiscal impact of civil commitment,
    97, 101
  legal background, 190n19, 191n20,
    193n99
  See also sex offender laws;
  See also Sexually Violent Predator
    Law

Civil litigation, 26
Civil protection order, 44, 139, 148, 158
Cole, Alyson, 10
Community notification, 87, 90–91
  perspectives of sex offenders,
    112–114
  research studies and effectiveness,
    93–95
  unintended consequences, 100
  See also Megan's Law;
  See also sex offender laws
Conflict Tactic Scale (CTS), 34, 54, 61
Context of battering, 12, 35
Consequences of sexual victimization,
  88
Cook, Phillip, 26, 34–35
Cook, Sarah, 57
Commodification of victimhood, 23
Criminal justice system:
  role as victim blamers, 8
  system's contemporary reforms to
    male battering, 41–45
  system's historical views to male
    battering, 38–40
  system's contemporary reforms to
    rape, 47–49
  system's historical response to rape,
    45–47
  system's response to sexual offenders,
    89–93
  system's response to stalking, 49–51
  victim's feelings towards the system,
    14–17
  victim oriented reforms, 156–159
Cycle of violence, 129

Dahmer, Jeffrey, 8
Dasgupta, Shamita Das, 137
Date rape:
  college campuses, 57–58
  contrasting perspectives, 32–34
  comparisons to "real" rape, 195n54
  media coverage, 81
  media presentation, 78

misperceptions and fears about, 20
rape hype, 27
victim blaming, 10
rejecting label of date rape 153–154
See also rape
"Defensive behavior", 140–142
Dershowitz, Alan, 10
*Department of Housing and Urban
    Development (HUD) v. Rucker,*
    123
Diversionary programs, 167–169
Domestic violence:
    battered husbands, 34–35
    contemporary legal response, 41–45
    difficulties in leaving a violent
        relationship 128–129
    definition 197n107, 200n93
    effects on welfare reform 118–122
    effects on public housing 122–125
    gender differences in use of violence
        132–134
    gender motivated federal crimes
        126–128
    historical legal response, 38–41
    interface with civil forfeiture laws
        125–126
    lesbians, 178n30
    media, 71, 74–78,
    Simpson, Nicole Brown,
        187–188n36
    survey data, 53–62
    restorative justice, 167–169
    STOP grants, 163–167
    treatment programs for women
        arrested for domestic violence
        137–144
    VAWA related research, 159–163
    women arrested for domestic
        violence 129–132
    women's court experiences with
        domestic violence arrests 134–137
    See also battering;
    See also intimate-partner violence
Dobash, Rebecca Emerson, 59

Dobash, Russell, 59
Dugard, Jaycee Lee, 87, 93

Elias, Robert, 150
Elliott, Pam, 12
Exclusionary zones, 92, 100
    See also sex offender laws

Family violence, 187–188n36
    alternative sanctions, 168–169
    community surveys, 59–62
    elder abuse, 171–172
    historical definitions of family
        violence, 39–40
    research issues, 62–66
    survey research, 53–59
    welfare reform, 118–122
    UCR data, 51–52
Family Violence Option (FVO), 120–121
Feminists:
    backlash to, 10
    bring awareness to women's
        violence, 16
    definition of feminism, 179n21
    interface with victim culturalists,
        24–28
    interactions with victim supporters,
        29–31
    perceptions on date rape, 32–34
    perceptions on battered husbands,
        33–36
Feeney Amendment, 91–92
Finkelhor, David, 61
First Offenders Program, 135–137
Follingstad, Diane, 63
Foster, Jodie, 22
Fraser, Nancy, 151
"Frustration response behavior",
    142–144

Gang rape, 17, 72, 178n4
    See also Central Park jogger
    See *Brzonkala v. Virginia Polytechnic*
    See also *The Accused*

Gavey, Nicola, 153–154
Gay marriage, 18–19
    See also same-sex marriage
Gelles, Richard, 34–35, 53
Gender harassment, 154–156
Gender neutrality, 133
Gender symmetry, 35
    See also sexual symmetry
Girshick, Lori, 65
Global positioning system
    legislation, 92
Global positioning monitoring, 88,
    92–93, 101, 165
    See also GPS surveillance
Global Positioning Surveillance (GPS),
    13, 93
    See also sex offender laws;
    See also GPS Monitoring
Global positioning tracking, 93, 100–101,
    115
    See also GPS Monitoring
Goldman, Ronald, 75
Grassroots activists, 9, 16, 129

Hagerman, Amber, 87, 91
Hamberger, Kevin L., 133
Hanneke, Christine, 61
Hause, Elizabeth, 63
Hendricks, Leroy, 91, 190n19, 193n99
Hernandez, Evelyn, 77
Hoff Sommers, Christina, 10, 26,
    32–33, 35
hooks, bell, 31
Hughes, Robert, 10

Intergenerational transmission of
    violence, 39
Interpersonal violence, 13, 175
Intimate-partner violence:
    alternative sanctions, 168–169
    barriers to women leaving violent
        relationships, 128–129
    battered husbands, 34–35
    civil forfeiture, 125–126

contemporary responses to IPV,
    41–44
elder abuse, 171–172
gender differences in use of violence,
    132–134
historical response to IPV, 38–40
media coverage, 74
Mike Tyson case, 76–77
O.J. Simpson case, 75–76
public housing, 122–125
Rihanna-Chris Brown case, 75
stalking, 49–51
STOP programs targeting battering,
    160–161
treatment findings for female
    offenders, 137–144
unintended consequences of policies,
    144–148
welfare reform, 118–122
women arrested for domestic
    violence, 129–132

Jacob Wetterling Crimes Against
    Children and Sexually Violent
    Offender Registration Act, 90, 92
Janoff-Bulman, Ronnie, 7
Jessica's Law, 92–93
Just world hypothesis, 7

Kanka, Megan, 87, 90, 115, 189n1,
    193n99
    See also Megan's Law
Karmen, Andrew, 5
Kelley, Raina, 75
Klass, Polly, 87
Koss, Mary, 57, 168

Lamb, Sharon, 33, 71, 152
Langhinrichsen-Rohling, Jennifer, 132
Lautenberg Amendment (Domestic
    Violence Gun Ban), 200n73
Law and order movement, 40
Learned helplessness, 29–30
Lee, Deborah, 155

Lehmann, Peter, 34
Lieb, Roxanne, 87
Leonard, Juanita, 79
Leonard, Sugar Ray, 78
Lesbian, 12, 65
Lesbian battering, 35, 178n30
Levin, Jennifer, 21
Levenson, Jill, 96
Lohr, Jeffrey, 133
Lunde, Sarah, 87, 92
Lunsford, Jessica, 87, 92
Lyon, Andrea, 119, 132

McDonald's "burning coffee" case, 26
"Madonna vs. whore" duality, 70
Mandatory arrest:
    contemporary system change to
        domestic violence, 41
    effects on public housing
        eligibility, 124
    effects on women's arrests, 130–134
    effects on "offender" treatment for
        women, 137–144
    unintended consequences for
        victims, 146–148
Marital rape, 11, 16, 45, 48–49, 60–62
    See also rape
Married Women's Property Act, 45
Marital rape exemption, 45
    See also marital rape
Matza, David, 105
McCabe, Steven, 100
Maximalist perspective, 23
McLaughlin, Elliot, 93
Media:
    crime victims, 80–84, 86–87
    gender influence, 78–80
    influential storytellers, 69
    presentation of events, 70–72
    public interest in crime, 18
    raises public awareness about
        violence against women, 37
    selection of cases, 74–78
    sensationalized cases, 28, 73–77, 82

use of language, 71–72
violent crime coverage, 72–74
Mediation programs, 167–169
    See also restorative justice;
    See also victim offender mediation;
    See also diversionary programs
Megan's Law, 91, 94
    See also Kanka, Megan
Meili, Trisha, 17
    See also Central Park jogger
Men Can Stop Rape, 173
Mendelsohn, Benjamin, 6
Menendez brothers, 21
Meyer, Shannon-Lee, 132
Miller, Susan, 133–135, 168
Milloy, Cheryl, 96
Minimalist perspective, 23
    See also battered men
Minneapolis Domestic Violence
        Experiment (MDVE), 41
    replication findings, 182n31
Mustaine, Elizabeth, 99
Mutual combat hypothesis, 35
    See also battering;
    See also Conflict Tactic Scale (CTS)

National Center for Victims of Crime
        (NCVC), 49
National College Women Sexual
        Victimization Survey (NCWSV),
        52, 58
National Crime Victimization
        Survey (NCVS), 54–55, 57, 64,
        132
National Incident Based Reporting
        System (NIBRS), 52, 95
National Stalker and Domestic Violence
        Reductions Act, 158–159
National Violence Against Women
        Survey (NVAW), 56–59, 66–67, 132,
        185n153
Neidig, Peter, 133
No-drop policy/prosecution, 43, 130,
        147, 156

Office of Child Support Enforcement
(OCSE), 121
Office on Violence Against Women, 17,
160
Osthoff, Sue, 137

Pagelow, Mildred, 61
Paglia, Camille, 25, 27, 32
Paternoster, Raymond, 48
Patriarchy, 38–39, 81, 180n47
Pearson, Patricia, 35
Pearson, Paula, 10, 26, 35
People v. Murphy, 47
People v. Poynton, 37
Personal Responsibility and Work
Opportunity Reconciliation Act
(PROWORA), 118
Peterson, Laci, 77
Peterson, Scott, 77
Petrosino, Anthony, 94
Petrosino, Carolyn, 94
Phillips, Lynn M., 152–154
Polek, Darlene, 63
Politics of victimization:
victim's rights movement, 150–151
violence against women, 150–152
war on drugs and crime, 150
Police discretion, 42
Pollitt, Katha, 27
Probation:
augmented with GPS, 101, 115
containment approach, 103, 107
lifetime terms for sex offenders,
92–93
with convicted sex offenders, 102–103,
107–108, 114, 192n66
with convicted domestic batterers,
131, 135–137
Public defender, 135
"Pure" victim, 138
Puritan laws, 39
"Preppie murder", 21
See also Chambers, Robert and
Levin, Jennifer

Presidential Task Force on Victims of
Crime, 15, 17
Presumptive arrest policy, 41, 130
Pro-arrest policy:
contemporary system reform to
domestic violence, 41–42
criminal justice system changes to
victims, 156, 161
effectiveness questioned, 131–132
unintended consequences for
battered women, 130, 134–144
Proximity laws, 88
See also proximity restrictions
Proximity restrictions, 13, 92, 98
See also sex offender laws
Postpartum depression, 18
Postpartum psychosis, 18

Quinsey, Vernon, 87

Rape:
contrasting perspectives, 32–34
contemporary reforms, 47–49
consequences, 88
gang, 21–22
historical overview, 45–47
intimate relationships, 60–62
rape reform legislation, 89
media, 71–73,80–83
research issues, 62–66
survey data, 54–57
victim precipitation, 6
victim blaming, 7–11
victim prominence, 15–17
victim culture perspectives, 23–28
See also acquaintance rape
See also date rape
See also marital rape
See also statutory rape
See also stranger rape
Rape "hype", 27
Rape law reform, 47–49, 89, 115
Rape myths, 46, 71, 73, 80
Rape shield legislation; 48, 115, 159, 162

Raphael, Jody, 119
"Real" rape, 45–46, 49, 195n54
Rennison, Callie Marie, 55
Residence restrictions, 92, 99–100,
    192n66 See also sex offender
    laws
Restorative justice, 14, 149, 167–169
Restraining order:
    denial to unmarried couples, 19
    stalking victims, 51
    when women invoke while in public
        housing 122, 124, 128
    research findings, 160, 162
    Violence Against Women Act,
        199n56
Rihanna, 75
Roiphe, Katie, 10, 24–27, 32–33
Ross, Karen, 76, 78
Russell, Diana, 61
Rutledge, Larry, 63
Ryan, William, 9

Same-sex marriage, 18–19
Saunders, Daniel, 132
Schaffer, Rebecca, 49
Scheppele, Kim, 72
Scherer, Migael, 82
Schneider, Elizabeth, 30
Schram, Donna, 96
Schwarzenegger, Arnold, 28, 117
"Second victimization":
    blaming victims, 6
    criminal justice treatment, 128
    effects on crime reporting, 112
    media, 73, 83
    rape victims, 46, 164
    victim protections, 16,
"Second wound", 82, 112
    See also second victimization
Sensationalized news cases, 28
Sellin, Thorsten, 6
Serial killer, 22
Serial murder, 8
Sexual abuse child, 8

Sex crime, 70, 80, 126, 191n24
    effectiveness of sex offender laws,
        93–101
    policy recommendations, 113–115
    sex crimes are different, 88–89
    sex offender laws, 89–93
    sex offender perceptions, 102–113
Sex offender:
    efficacy of sex offender laws, 93–101
    high-profile stranger victimizations,
        190–191n19, 191n20, 192n66
    profile of sex offender profiles, 88–89
    sex offender perceptions, 102–113
    See also sex offender laws
Sex offender laws:
    AMBER Alerts, 97–98
    civil commitment, 96–97
    effectiveness of sex offender laws,
        93–101
    evolution of sex offender laws,
        88–93
    GPS monitoring, 100–101
    proximity/residence restrictions,
        98–100
    sex offender registration and
        community notification, 93–96
    sex-offender perspectives on
        registration and community
        notification, 112–113
    unintended consequences, 100
    See also AMBER Alerts
    See also child-safety or child
        protection zones
    See also civil commitment
    See also community notification
    See also exclusionary zones
    See also GPS surveillance
    See also Jessica's Law
    See also Megan's Law
    See also proximity restrictions
    See also sex offender legislation
    See also sex offense policies
    See also sexual psychopath law
    See also sex offender registration law

Sex offender laws (*continued*)
  See also sex offender statutes
  See also sex offender supervision
    legislation
  See also residence restrictions
Sex offender legislation, 89–90, 93, 96
Sex offense policies 89
  See also sex offender laws
Sex offender registration:
  child victim related cases, 90–91
  efficacy, 93–96, 100
  Megan Kanka case, 193n99,
  sex offender perceptions, 112–114
Sex offender registration law, 92
  See also sex offender laws
  See also sex offender registration
Sex offender supervision legislation, 93
  See also sex offender laws
Sex offender statutes, 94
  See also sex offender laws
Sex offender supervision, 93, 97, 101,
  103
Sex offender treatment:
  civil commitment, 96–97, 99
  probation, 102, 107–108
  treatment and the law, 89–91
  victim empathy, 110–113
Sexual assault:
  Chambers, Robert rape case, 21
  contemporary reforms, 47–49
  historical overview, 45–47
  victim culturalists, 26–28
  victim empowerment views, 30–34
  victim identities, 153–154
  See also rape
  See also sexual violence
Sexual harassment, 24, 27–28, 32, 78,
  152, 155–156
Sexual psychopath law, 89, 90, 94,
  191n21
Sexual symmetry, 35
  See also gender symmetry
Sexual violence:
  See also rape

See also sex crime
See also sex offender
See also sex offender laws
See also sexual assault
Sexually Violent Predator (SVP), 91, 97
Shelter workers, 136
Shields, Nancy, 61
Simpson, O. J., 10, 75, 187n36
Smart, Elizabeth, 87
Social capital, 7–8, 78
Stalking:
  anti-stalking laws, 161
  contemporary responses to stalking,
    50–51
  characteristics of stalking, 185n153
  consequences of stalking, 185n155
  definition of stalking; incidence
    figures, 49–50
  ethical issues, 66
  methodological constraints for
    research, 62
  NVAW prevalence rates, 56–59
  recommendations for future
    research, 66–67
  reporting problems, 63–64
  See also intimate-partner violence
Statutory rape:
  labeling, 154–155
  victim paradoxes, 152–153, 156–161
  sex offender crimes, 102–103
  sex offenders speak out, 104–105, 113
  See also rape
Steele, Shelby, 10
STOP (Services/Training/Officers/
  Prosecutors) grants, 160, 161, 162,
  163, 166
Stranger rape, 9–10, 11, 45, 48, 57, 62, 78,
  80, 87, 115, 128
  See also rape
Straus, Murray, 34–35, 53, 132
Subculture of violence, 39
System blaming, 9–10
Sykes, Charles, 10, 25–27, 32
Sykes, Gresham, 105

Temporary Assistance for Needy
    Families (TANF), 118
Tewksbury, Richard, 99
Thorn, George, 133
Thurman v. City of Torrington, Conn, 41
Thurman, Tracey, 41
Tolman, Richard, 119
Treatment providers, 136
"Truly violent behavior", 138–140
Tyson, Mike, 76

Umbreit, Mark, 168
Uniform Crime Report (UCR), 51–52
United States Supreme Court, 15
U.S. v 107.9 Acre Parcel of Land, 125
U.S. v. Sixty Acres, 125

van Dam, Danielle 87
Victim advocate, 16, 43, 83, 115, 129,
    136, 159
Victim blaming, 3–7, 9–10
Victim culture perspective, 23–27
Victim empathy:
    Offenders accept responsibility,
        107–108, 110–113
    Sex offender perspectives, 103
Victim empowerment perspective,
    28–31
Victim, "false", 26
Victim labeling, 9
Victims movement, 3, 5, 40
Victim-offender duet, 6
    See victim-offender relationship
Victim-offender dyad, 6, 38
    See victim-offender relationship
Victim-offender relationship, 6, 29, 38,
    49, 52, 63, 73, 103
Victim-Offender Mediation (VOM),
    167
Victim rights movement, 5, 9–10, 16
    See victim movement
Victimologists, 5, 6, 31, 51
Victim politics, 25
Victim puritanical, 21

Victim precipitation, 6
Victim precipitation theory, 6
Victim provocation, 6
Victim resiliency, 22
Victim sympathy, 7, 8
Violence Against Women:
    challenges for research, 62–68
    commodification of female
        victims, 23
    diversionary programs, 167–169
    media, 70–72, 74–83
    National Stalker and Domestic
        Violence Reductions Act, 158–159
    politics, 150–152
    Presidential Task Force Report,
        157–158
    School based programs, 169–171
    social recognition, 16
    research findings, 51–61
    victim culturalists views, 23–28
    victim empowerment perspectives,
        28–32
Violence Against Women Act
    Legislation, 158–167
    See also battering
    See also domestic violence
    See also intimate-partner violence
    See also family violence
    See also rape
    See also sexual assault
    See also stalking
    See also Violence Against Women Act
Violence Against Women Act (VAWA):
    ARREST programs, 160
    civil redress for domestic violence,
        126–128
    civil rights protection, 145–148
    economic analysis, 159–160
    elder victims, 171–172
    funding/programs, 159–167
    influence, 85
    passage, 16
    Urban Institute Report, 160–162
    SANE programs, 164

Violence Against Women Act (*continued*)
STOP programs, 160–163, 164
See also *Brzonkala v.VA Polytechnic*
ruling;
See also STOP grants
Vivian, Dina, 132
Von Hentig, Hans, 6

Walker, Gillian, 151
Walker, Jeffrey, 95, 99
Walker, Lenore, 31, 129
Washington, Desiree, 76
War on crime, 122
Weed, Frank, 151
Welfare reform, 118

Welchans, Sarah, 55
Wellford, Charles, 100
Wolfgang, Marvin, 6
Wife beating, 39, 40, 181n19
See also battering
See also domestic violence
See also intimate-partner violence
Wolf, Naomi, 24
Women who kill, 22
Women's use of force, 132
See also battering
See also mutual battering

Yates, Andrea, 18
Yllo, Kersti, 61

CPSIA information can be obtained at www.ICGtesting.com
Printed in the USA
BVOW02*0932290713

327140BV00003B/77/P